TEACHING AND LEARNING IN A NETWORK WORLD

Frontiers in Artificial Intelligence and Applications

Series Editors: J. Breuker, R. López de Mántaras, S. Ohsuga and W. Swartout

Volume 60

Previously published in this series:

Vol. 59, In production
Vol. 58, In production
Vol. 57, M. Mohammadian (Ed.), New Frontiers in Computational Intelligence and its Applications
Vol. 56, In production
Vol. 55, G. Cumming et al. (Eds.), Advanced Research in Computers and Communications in Education
Vol. 54, In production
Vol. 53, E. Motta, Reusable Components for Knowledge Modelling
Vol. 52, In production
Vol. 51, H. Jaakkola et al. (Eds.), Information Modelling and Knowledge Bases X
Vol. 50, S.P. Lajoie and M. Vivet (Eds.), Artificial Intelligence in Education
Vol. 49, P. McNamara and H. Prakken (Eds.), Norms, Logics and Information Systems
Vol. 48, P. Návrat and H. Ueno (Eds.), Knowledge-Based Software Engineering
Vol. 47, M.T. Escrig and F. Toledo, Qualitative Spatial Reasoning: Theory and Practice
Vol. 46, N. Guarino (Ed.), Formal Ontology in Information Systems
Vol. 45, P.-J. Charrel et al. (Eds.), Information Modelling and Knowledge Bases IX
Vol. 44, K. de Koning, Model-Based Reasoning about Learner Behaviour
Vol. 43, M. Gams et al. (Eds.), Mind Versus Computer
Vol. 42, In production
Vol. 41, F.C. Morabito (Ed.), Advances in Intelligent Systems
Vol. 40, G. Grahne (Ed.), Sixth Scandinavian Conference on Artificial Intelligence
Vol. 39, B. du Boulay and R. Mizoguchi (Eds.), Artificial Intelligence in Education
Vol. 38, H. Kangassalo et al. (Eds.), Information Modelling and Knowledge Bases VIII
Vol. 37, F.L. Silva et al. (Eds.), Spatiotemporal Models in Biological and Artificial Systems
Vol. 36, S. Albayrak (Ed.), Intelligent Agents for Telecommunications Applications
Vol. 35, A.M. Ramsay (Ed.), Artificial Intelligence: Methodology, Systems, Applications
Vol. 34, Y. Tanaka et al. (Eds.), Information Modelling and Knowledge Bases VII
Vol. 33, P. Pylkkänen et al. (Eds.), Brain, Mind and Physics
Vol. 32, L. de Raedt (Ed.), Advances in Inductive Logic Programming
Vol. 31, M. Ghallab and A. Milani (Eds.), New Directions in AI Planning
Vol. 30, A. Valente, Legal Knowledge Engineering
Vol. 29, A. Albert (Ed.), Chaos and Society
Vol. 28, A. Aamodt and J. Komorowski (Eds.), Fifth Scandinavian Conference on Artificial Intelligence
Vol. 27, J. Hallam (Ed.), Hybrid Problems, Hybrid Solutions
Vol. 26, H. Kangassalo et al. (Eds.), Information Modelling and Knowledge Bases VI
Vol. 25, E. Hillebrand and J. Stender (Eds.), Many-Agent Simulation and Artificial Life

ISSN: 0922-6389

Teaching and Learning in a Network World

TechEd 2000 Proceedings

Edited by

P. Hoffman
Community College Foundation, Sacramento, CA, USA

D. Lemke
Community College Foundation, Sacramento, CA, USA

IOS Press
Ohmsha

Amsterdam • Berlin • Oxford • Tokyo • Washington, DC

ISBN 1 58603 052 3 (IOS Press)
ISBN 4 274 90348 6 C3000 (Ohmsha)
Library of Congress Catalog Card Number: 00-100424

Publisher
IOS Press
Van Diemenstraat 94
1013 CN Amsterdam
The Netherlands
fax: +31 20 620 3419
e-mail: order@iospress.nl

Distributor in the UK and Ireland
IOS Press/Lavis Marketing
73 Lime Walk
Headington
Oxford OX3 7AD
England
fax: +44 1865 75 0079

Distributor in the USA and Canada
IOS Press, Inc.
5795-G Burke Centre Parkway
Burke, VA 22015
USA
fax: +1 703 323 3668
e-mail: iosbooks@iospress.com

Distributor in Germany
IOS Press
Spandauer Strasse 2
D-10178 Berlin
Germany
fax: +49 30 242 3113

Distributor in Japan
Ohmsha, Ltd.
3-1 Kanda Nishiki-cho
Chiyoda-ku, Tokyo 101
Japan
fax: +81 3 3233 2426

PRINTED IN THE NETHERLANDS

Preface

The Technology in Education International Conference and Exposition (TechEd) is an annual four-day conference, organized under the auspices of the Sacramento-based Community College Foundation. TechEd2000 was held March 6–9, 2000 at the Palm Springs Convention Center in Palm Springs, California.

This year's theme was *TechEd2000, Teaching and Learning in a Network World.* Just saying it conjures up a vision of the future. And that's what this conference is about. The conference brings together thousands of professionals, from all sectors and levels of education, and provides a vision of the exciting, interactive, technology-rich future of education. And this vision is already coming true today!

TechEd2000 plays a vital role in equipping universities, colleges, and schools with a strong base technology awareness and the knowledge needed to tackle the increasing challenges of teaching and learning.

We are pleased to report that TechEd2000 attracted more than 400 presentation submissions. The presentations accepted for TechEd2000 demonstrate innovative solutions for key technology issues faced by educational institutions from throughout the world.

For more information about future TechEd conferences, please visit our Website at www.TechEdEvents.org.

The Editors

Tech ed 2000

A Hands-On Conference

Contents

Teaching and Learning in a Network World
P. Hoffman and D. Lemke (Eds.)
IOS Press, 2000

Getting On Board with Multimedia and Internet Training

Patricia Ryaby Backer, *Department of Technology*
Miriam Saltmarch, *Department of Nutrition and Food Science*
San Jose State University, 1 Washington Square, San Jose, CA 95192

Abstract. This paper describes the results of three summers of teacher training initiatives in multimedia and the Web for the classroom as well as a trainer of trainers model currently being undertaken for faculty at San Jose State University based upon the results of the summer workshops. An original objective of the summer workshops was directed at providing faculty who could function as trainers of other faculty. Moving from the year one model (training faculty to utilize a wide range of multimedia equipment and tools to build complete projects) to the year three model (training faculty in specific applications) changed the extent to which faculty could act as trainers of other faculty at their school sites. The current model focuses on empowering faculty to complete technology-based projects for their university classrooms and become trainers of other faculty in their academic units, within the realistic constraints imposed in a teaching-centered university.

1. Introduction

The constant theme of the past five years has been increasing the use of technology, particularly computer-based ones, in education. Many articles and white papers accumulate to create this message with "a new insistence that teachers must become technologically literate" [1]

> "Information technologies can so enhance classroom communications and resources that, when properly applied, they can transform conventional pedagogical paradigms and create new and powerful contexts for learning and teaching. Connected classrooms potentially offer open-ended, dynamic, discovery-oriented learning experiences. The more advanced the classroom use of telecommunications is, the greater the potential to change the learning environment, the teacher's role in the classroom, the flow of information to students and overall classroom dynamics; each can evolve to form more natural and much richer learning processes." [2]

In concert with this call for technological literacy is the increased use of multimedia and the WWW in everyday society. These two forces serve to create an overpowering impetus for instructors to utilize technology in their classrooms.

However, along with this call to arms is the reality that, in general, college instructors are generally unprepared to integrate technology into their classrooms. There is a small (but growing) cohort of early adopters of technology in universities but the majority of professors are either non-users or just beginning to explore multimedia and the World Wide Web in the classrooms. One of the major reasons for this dichotomy is that technical support for university instructors is inadequate.

In 1995, the National Academy of Sciences and National Academy of Engineering completed a report on the use of technology in education entitled: Re-Inventing Schools: the Technology is Now [3].

Statistics shown in this report contain indicate the trend in technology training for teachers. When teachers were asked what the source of their training was (for those familiar with computers) 96% of the teachers surveyed indicated that they had been self taught; 72% indicated that conferences or workshops were sources of training, while only 45% indicated that they received much of their training from their school district and even less (40%) suggested that their training came from courses within the school.

Although the report, Re-Inventing Schools: the Technology is Now, focused on K-12 faculty, the situation is no different among faculty from institutions of higher education. Over the past few years, the number of university-level courses with components utilizing multimedia and the WWW has exploded. However, a persistent problem still remains: how do you transfer the use of these technologies to "mainstream" faculty?

Much of the existing training that has been developed is focused on the "innovators or early adopters" of technology. A standard strategy of presenting the technology itself and teaching people how to use the technology is most appealing and appropriate to faculty interested in technology, the "innovators." However, mainstream faculty have different motivations and reasons for adopting technology as compared to "early adopters." "Early adopters" and innovators are "techies" who are willing to explore and play with new technologies [4]. According to Freeman, Brimley, and Rosen [5], mainstream faculty are more likely "to show interest in a new technology if it is easy to use and does not require a major change in the skills they already possess."

Most universities have established teaching and/or training initiatives related to multimedia and the WWW. Many of these initiatives have evolved from training center models—where faculty sign up for pre-established "workshops" to learn a new skill. The most successful attempts to equip faculty with the skills and knowledge, as well as equipment to create multimedia based learning materials, have occurred where there is a institution-wide effort; as demonstrated at Pennsylvania State University with Project Empower [6], with the STARS program at Wake Forest [7] and outlined in the TESSI Project adopted by the Ministry of Education in British Columbia [8]. Unfortunately, not all higher education institutions or educational agencies have arrived at this juncture.

2. Description of MASTEP Workshops

This paper builds upon previous work by Backer and Saltmarch [9] and describes the results of three consecutive summers of teacher training initiatives in multimedia and the Web for the classroom. Sponsored by MASTEP, an NSF funded collaborative to improve mathematics and science teacher education in the greater San Francisco Bay Area.

2.1. Summary of First year workshop

The structure for the first-year training consisted of two one-week "basic" workshops and two three-week "advanced" workshops. Workshop participation in the "basic" workshop ranged from 15 to 25 attendees. Attendance in the "advanced" workshops was much lower and ranged from 4 to 10 daily. The "basic" workshops were very structured and introductory in nature while the "advanced" workshops were project-oriented and open-ended in format. The participants who entered the advanced workshops with a clear project idea were most able to take advantage of the instructional materials presented during the advanced workshops and were also closest in their performance and outcome expectations to those of the workshop instructors. Approximately one-third of the faculty attending the "basic" workshops were mainstream faculty while, in the "advanced" workshops, all attendees were "early adopters."

Many participants in the "basic" workshops were not aware of the state of multimedia technology prior to the workshops. They would have benefited by having more time to be "brought into the technology" using an approach similar to that developed at Pennsylvania State University through the Project Empower program [6]. In our training sessions, as was noted by Oliver and Lake [10], using technology seemed to hinder learning when technical problems arose.

Many of the participants in the "advanced" workshops also had trouble devoting enough time and energy to the workshops since they were not compensated in monetary terms nor were they assigned college or continuing education credit for attending the workshops except for the K-12 teachers. The higher education instructors from the state and community colleges were taking time from personal projects and other work projects in order to attend the workshops at cost to them. Because of these factors, attendance and attrition during the advanced workshops was a problem during the latter part of the workshop where participants did not receive formal instruction but were expected to work on individual projects. Some higher education instructors looked forward to release time during the next academic year to continue the multimedia projects developed during the summer workshops and these participants were more motivated to complete their projects.

2.2. Summary of second year workshop

2.2.1. June Higher Education Workshop

In all, fourteen faculty (from local Community Colleges and San Jose State) participated in the June 1998 workshop. Based upon feedback from the first year, we changed the workshop structure to four one-week sessions rather than the one-week "basic", three-week "advanced" model of Year 1. The topics for the one-week sessions were: Week 1 Pedagogy, Week 2 Desktop Multimedia, Week 3 Using the WWW, and Week 4 Special projects. Workshop participation in the one-week workshops ranged from 4-10 attendees. Most of the workshop attendees in the June Workshop were again "early adopters."

The attendees of this workshop differed in many respects from the workshops of the previous year. Most of the faculty entered this session with highly defined, preconceived ideas of what they wanted to do. Sometimes, this led to a conflict between teacher and student expectations; incidentally, *this situation was not reflected in the teaching evaluations that were excellent.* In many ways, students were resistant to any suggestion or teaching that did not fit into their paradigm regardless of the need of their design. For example, two engineering faculty members attended the June workshop with a Web-page design goal. These faculty members refused to participate in any tutorials or class discussions, or learn any software, that was not directly related to their task at hand. Although this goal seems acceptable, this resistance precipitated the re-teaching of many concepts and software throughout the four weeks.

2.2.2. July K-12 Workshop

The July workshop session was structured differently than the June workshop in some respects. This session was again divided into four weeks. However, the fourth week had a different focus (the first three weeks of this workshop paralleled the content of the same weeks in the June workshop). The attendees of this workshop were all K - 12 teachers who had been selected to receive equipment and software through a proposal competition run by MASTEP. All of the workshop attendees in the July Workshop were again "early adopters."

The teachers, by their own admission, expected that the workshops would follow a "chalk and talk" format. At first, the teachers were dismayed that they had to actively learn and produce tangible products. However, compliance to teacher expectations and motivation was high. Also, the students in this section were graded on the quality and appropriateness of their outcomes.

2.3. Summary of third year workshops

After reviewing participant feedback from both years, a consistent thread emerged. The workshop time commitment was too great for most faculty. In addition, the researchers were concerned about extending this training to mainstream faculty rather than just serving the pool of "early adopters." It was decided to move to a topic-specific training model with short one to four day training sessions. Additionally, over the three year period, specific workshop instruction had been transformed from an open-ended, project focus emphasis into a specific topic tutorial-based, structured environment. The attendees and other faculty drove this transformation, which began in year 2 and was fully evident in year 3, interested in the workshops. To meet a trainer of trainer's objective, each topic specific workshops required that a mini project be completed after initial tutorials. Participants, who were predominantly mainstream faculty, were very satisfied with this format.

3. Current Training Model for MASTEP

An original objective of these workshops within the MASTEP Collaborative was directed at providing faculty who could function as trainers of other faculty. Moving from the year one model (training faculty to utilize a wide range of multimedia equipment and tools to build complete projects) to the year three model (training faculty in specific applications) changed the extent to which faculty could act as trainers of other faculty at their home school sites. Since complete multimedia or WWW projects normally require the use of various applications and equipment, faculty would have to attend a series of topic specific workshops and then attend a separate series of project based workshops to assemble a complete desktop or WWW project. The intention of this model is to meet the time constraints of mainstream faculty and yet provide the necessary training and project management skills necessary to develop a fully realized desktop or WWW project.

4. *Development of a Training Model for SJSU Faculty Through ITL*

4.1 Fall 1999 ITL Workshops

During Fall 1999, based upon the three years of MASTEP workshops, a workshop model was developed for faculty at San Jose State University (SJSU) who were interested in creating technology-based instruction. The workshop model was funded through SJSU's Institute for Teaching and Learning (ITL) that is designed to support the University's mission of enriching the lives of students through their contact with faculty members who effectively combine teaching, scholarship and service. The long-term goal of the Institute is to help create a culture that values and supports excellence in instruction. To meet this goal, ITL serves as a campus clearinghouse of ideas related to the enhancement of students learning through the improvement of teaching practices. To this end ITL sponsors a variety of faculty programs designed to facilitate scholarly conversations about teaching and learning.

The workshop model included a series of two to three hour workshops held at ITL addressing various aspects of technology-mediated instruction. In addition to the formal workshops, we offered two activities to help faculty develop materials for their classrooms. The Portfolio Series, offered weekly, was an open lab in the instructional development center (Alquist Center) where faculty could receive individual guidance and help while developing multimedia or web projects. The last aspect of this training model was the offering of specially designed workshops based upon departmental needs that were held on-site in individual departments.

There was a wide range of attendee disciplines at the workshops that indicated that the university faculty community at large were aware of the workshop offerings. The best attended were workshops offered at the beginning of the semester when teaching pressures are traditionally lower or those that were introductory or narrowly focused on a particular software application. However, a number of the formal workshops were under-enrolled, especially during the latter part of the semester. The Portfolio Series overall was underutilized in spite of extensive publicity and vigorous instructor efforts to recruit attendees at the "formal" workshops to initiate projects beyond the scope of the two to three hour workshop period. The most common reason given by faculty for not attending the Portfolio Series was "lack of time to devote to a technology-based project." The faculty correctly perceived that the time required to complete a project was far beyond the Portfolio Series time commitment. *It is important to note that regular SJSU faculty teach an average class load of three to four courses per semester with minimal teaching assistance.*

In marked contrast to faculty involvement in formal workshops and the Portfolio Series held at ITL, the departmental on-site workshops were popular and well attended. Even though the on-site workshops did not begin until the last month of the semester, five were held with departments from across the university. One of the main reasons contributing to the good attendance was the departmental commitment of time normally devoted to faculty meetings being used for the workshops. Also, since the departments played an active role in the workshop content selection, the faculty were more motivated to attend.

4.2. Spring 2000 ITL Workshops

The experience of Fall 1999 led to a commitment of SJSU through ITL to provide support to faculty in the form of release time for the Spring 2000 semester to attend a series of workshops and to commit to developing a technology-based project for the classroom. Response to the RFP was enthusiastic with enrollments quickly filled. This response bears out our conclusions that lack of faculty participation is directly related to teacher workloads. As noted above, the most successful attempts to create multimedia based learning materials have occurred where there is an institution-wide effort [6] [7] [8].

References

[1] D. Ely *et al.*, Trends in Educational Technology 1995. ED 396 717. ERIC Clearinghouse on Information and Technology, Syracuse, NY, 1996, p. 3.

[2] B. Berenfeld, Telecommunications in Our Classroom: Boondoggle or a Powerful Teaching Tool? Available: http://www.isoc.org.ar/inet96/proc/c1/c1_2.htm. *Proceedings of INET'96.*

[3] National Academy of Sciences and National Academy of Engineering, Reinventing Schools: The Technology is Now. Available: http://www.nap.edu/readingroom/books/techgap/index.html, 1995.

[4] W. H. Geoghagen, What ever happened to instructional technology? Paper presented at the 22nd Annual Conference of the International Business Schools Computing Association, Baltimore, Maryland, July 17-20, 1994.

[5] W. Freeman *et al.*, Early Experiences in Broadening the Use of Web-Based Learning to Mainstream Faculty. In: B. Collis and R. Oliver (eds.), Proceedings of Ed-Media 99, AACE, Charlottesville, VA, 1999, pp. 1364-1365.

[6] J. S. Noel *et al.*, Implementing Collaborative Learning Through Mainstreaming Faculty Use of Technology. In: T. Muldner and T. Reeves (eds.), Proceedings of Ed-TELECOM 97. AACE, Charlottesville, VA, 1997.

[7] D. G. Brown, Faculty Development Strategies. In: B. Collis and R. Oliver (eds.), Proceedings of Ed-Media 99. AACE, Charlottesville, VA, 1999, pp. 1229-1230.

[8] J. E. J Woodrow *et al.*, Technology Enhanced Instruction: A Successful Model for Improving Science Teaching and Learning. In: T. Muldner and T. Reeves (eds.), Proceedings of Ed-TELECOM 97. AACE, Charlottesville, VA, 1997.

[9] P. R., Backer and M. Saltmarch, Evaluation of a Multimedia Workshop Model: Training Iinstructors to use Technology in the Classroom. In: B. Collis and R. Oliver (eds.), Proceedings of Ed-Media 99, AACE, Charlottesville, VA, 1999, pp. 516-521.

[10] R. Oliver and M. Lake Training Teachers for World and Distant Education: Using Authentic and Meaningful Context. In: T. Muldner and T. Reeves (eds.), Proceedings of Ed-TELECOM 97. AACE, Charlottesville, VA, 1997.

Teaching and Learning in a Network World
P. Hoffman and D. Lemke (Eds.)
IOS Press, 2000

ADAPTABILITY OF MULTIMEDIA COURSES USING INTELLIGENT HYPERTEXTS

Pr. M.Amine BENKIRAN
Ecole Mohammadia d'Ingénieurs, B.P. 765 RABAT, MOROCCO
Rachida AJHOUN
Institute for Study and Research on Arabic, B.P. 6261 Rabat, MOROCCO
Y. BELQASMI
ENSET, Mohammadia, MOROCCO

Abstract.
We are mainly interested, in this paper, to present a system based on powerful techniques that allow a reliable adaptability of the courses to learners, and based on tools that are largely available and easy to use. Our objective is to produce a generic course, which will be used for the generation, at learning phase of the specific courses according to the learner profiles.

1. Introduction

These last years, the field of telecommunication and multimedia data processing knew a visible progress. The exploitation of those new technologies by researchers in the field of telelearning makes it possible to improve the teaching methods in order to satisfy the users of this kind of application.

This study is part of a SMART-Learning (System for Multimedia Adaptative and coopeRative TeleLearning) project [13] [14] at the RIM research unit (Réseaux Informatiques et Multimédia) at EMI. The goal of this project is to provide courses to distant learners without any space or time constraint, including the possibility of having synchronous sessions (real time) for the conversation between the various actors intervening in the process of learning (learners, trainers,...). In addition, the fundamental goal is the adaptability of the courses to the learner according to teaching requirements and learner capabilities.

This system is currently under development. We are trying to achieve the maximum benefit through new learning and teaching methods and tools, and simplicity of use, for both the learners and trainers.

Our approach makes a significant advance compared to the used approach, which provides courses as hypertext documents (WebCT, MANIC, Virtual-U,...) [10][11][12]. The permissive structure of the hypertext and the reading modes it leads to, are opposed to some educational principles. A learner can access any part of a course without order constraints on these parts and without having the necessary knowledge. Consequently, the teaching objectives (specialty, type of formation...) aimed by the access to the course will not be reached. In our view and to ensure a pedagogical learning, the course must take account of the learner profile (capacities of training, previous knowledge, language, desired formation...) and the learners evolution (prerequisite, speed...).

To avoid this problem and with the aim of respecting the educational principles for telelearning [1][2][3] and particularly the active learning [4], each learner must have his own course which is adapted to his aptitudes and his objectives. The most current methods is to produce several versions of a course according to various profiles and objectives and a learner can have access to one of these versions. We think that such a solution is rigid. In fact, adding a new type of profile requires a new version of the course.

To avoid the multiplicity of the same course, we propose an approach based on the production of a *generic course*. This approach makes it possible to generate an individual course for each learner based on his profile by using a system of generation (figure-1-). If the profile of a learner is modified as a result of an evaluation, for example, this course will be automatically regenerated in order to take account of the new knowledge acquired by the learner.

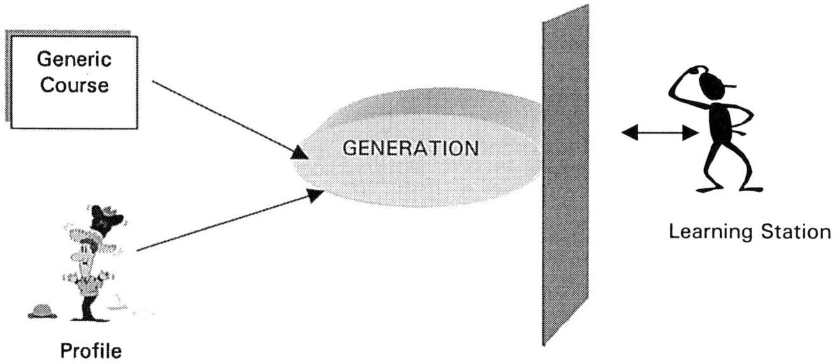

Figure 1: Functional Diagram of the Learning Process

Before starting a course, the system must have enough knowledge about the learner in order to construct his profile. This knowledge are then used to select the contents and the organization of future information. However, this means that the author of the generic course must parameterize the various parts of his course according to the objectives pursued and the prerequisites necessary for reaching a specific part [5][6][7].

Two key elements must be taken into account: the *modeling of the generic courses* according to the educational objectives and the *learner profile* which will help to validate the choice of a course or parts of a course for the learner.

2. Learner profile

The learner profile is the key element in the SMART Learning education process. It is a set of information that characterizes a learner and during all the steps of the learning process. It consists of the main information: capabilities, learning Objectives, psychological factors and others.

With the same capabilities, each learner will have his own course according to his psychological factors and learning objectives. This makes it possible to have a targeted and better adapted learning, thus more interesting than the traditional teaching and more educational than the rough hypertext.

Further, we can say that at every moment, the profile reflects a reliable and complete intellectual image of the learner. It keeps tracks of the progress of a learner in the course so that the next accesses will take account of the real profile and provide adequate knowledge of the learner.

3. Generic course modeling

A generic course is a document which contains the learning material to give to learners and the access conditions to each part of the course according to the various objectives pursued by the course and the various types of profiles of the learners who will have access to the course.

We think that it is necessary to model the generic courses, a double interest results from this:

- To help the author to easily conceive his course based on this model;
- To take account of the various educational constraints which are defined in the model.

Our modeling is done in two phases:

a- General structure: The generic course must be sufficiently flexible to fit to a large variety of learners in order to adequately meet the needs for training according to educational objectives. Any production of a course is based on an educational design which is used to structure the contents in order to facilitate the learning. The principal criteria to be respected are the following [1]:

- To stratify information in order to take account of the complexity levels and to adjust it with the preliminary knowledge of the learner
- To structure the presentation in learning units in order to facilitate the selection, the organization and the integration of information
- To produce the course in several languages in order to improve its deployment for the larger number of possible learners
- To consider the use of various media (text, audio, video...) which encourages the learner to carry out a telelearning course
- To consider the presence of optional activities (illustrations, reminders,...)
- To provide indications and means of self-evaluation allowing the learner to know the progress state of his understanding.

b- Educational graph: we now wish to generate an individual course for a given learner. Once the course generated, the learner starts the first part, at the end of this part, an evaluation is carried out to test his understanding and according to the result, he will have access to a specific part of the course or to redo the same part if necessary [figure 2]. Thus the passage from a part to another is not made in a random or automatic manner but according to an educational approach. This approach is based on the relations between the parts, and it is the author of course who clearly defines these relations in the form of an the graph of the educational network or *the educational graph*. Finally, the course consists of a multitude of passages between the various parts in a positive and progressive way.

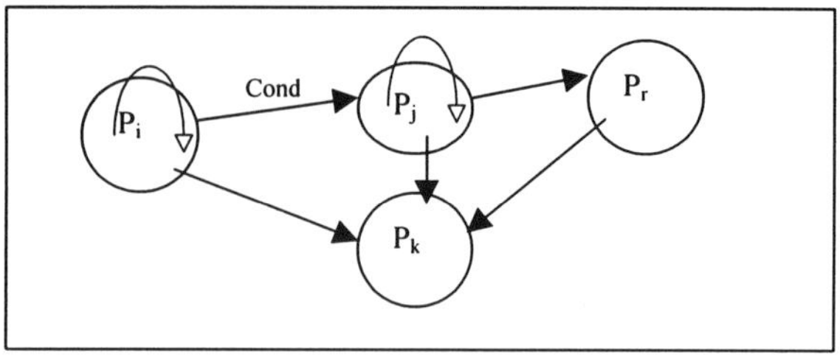

Figure 2: An Educational Graph

4. Course production

After the definition of the courses model, the remainder of this article presents the methods which we conceived in order to produce a course that respects the model and the techniques used to make a learner follow a course on the Internet according to his individual profile.

The author of a course must, of course, respect our model. He will be able to produce a well structured course based on this model and the learning material to be given to learners according to their profiles [figure 3].

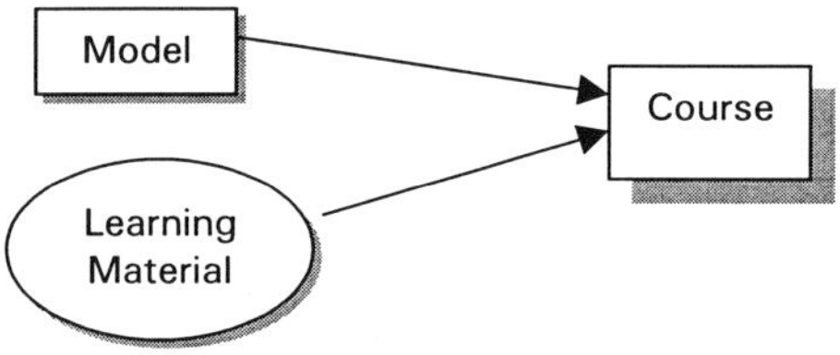

Figure 3: Production Process

The XML (eXtended Markup Language) language [8][9], reputed by its facility to exchange complex document on the Internet, have been selected to be able to structure the course. To solve the problem of adaptability in its practical phase, we have defined an approach based on some XML specific tools.

As the course is produced only once and the system generates specific versions, our functional model is constituted by two components, one for the production of the courses and the other for the learning process [figure 4].

The courses modeling is easily made by DTD (Document Type Definition) document. To structure the course, the DTD imposes the various constituting elements and the different links between them. The use of the DTD, ensures the coherence of the courses structure.

An XML document makes it possible to describe the contents of the course without being concerned with its appearance. It is the style sheet which is changed to describe the way in which the XML document is displayed. Thus, we separate the core information material and the form into two distinct documents. This permits to modify easily the way in which is displayed a course and to add simply information. We choose to adapt the course by the use of the style sheet [8]. The style sheet language we choose is XSL (eXtensible Stylesheet Language) due to its strong capabilities compared to other languages such as CCS [8].

In order to use all the facilities provided by XML or the tools which are based on XML and with the aim of optimizing the processing to provide to a learner the specific course according to his profile, we distinguished four different documents which the author of the course produces [figure 4]:

- learning units (LUs), they represent the atomic elements of the course material which form the basis for the curriculum. They are the learning material: at present, the whole set of the learning units are composed from simple media: text, audio and images.;

- a generic XML document based on the DTD, that corresponds to the description of the course integrating all the specialties treated by the course, all the versions in the provided languages as well as the different levels treated by the course. It is composed of a set of Learning Units (Lus)
- a generic XSL document that describe, for a presentation, all the elements of the generic XML document. It also defines the Uls that will be presented according to profile characteristics ;
- an educational graph: for the first version of our application, this network is translated by scripts which permit to carry out the processing leading to choose the part of the course to be followed.

This separation of the course in several parts makes it possible to improve the extensibility of the course and to facilitate the improvement of the learning units. Furthermore, generic XML documents and generic XSL documents can be useful for the production of several courses by modifying the learning units.

5. Learning process

After the production of the various elements of the course, these documents are stored in an external peripheral that the learners can access through the Network according to their profiles. At the learning process [figure 4], our system generates an individual XSL document for the learner using the generic XSL document and the learner profile. The combination of generic XML document and individual XSL document will, of course, constitute the individual course.

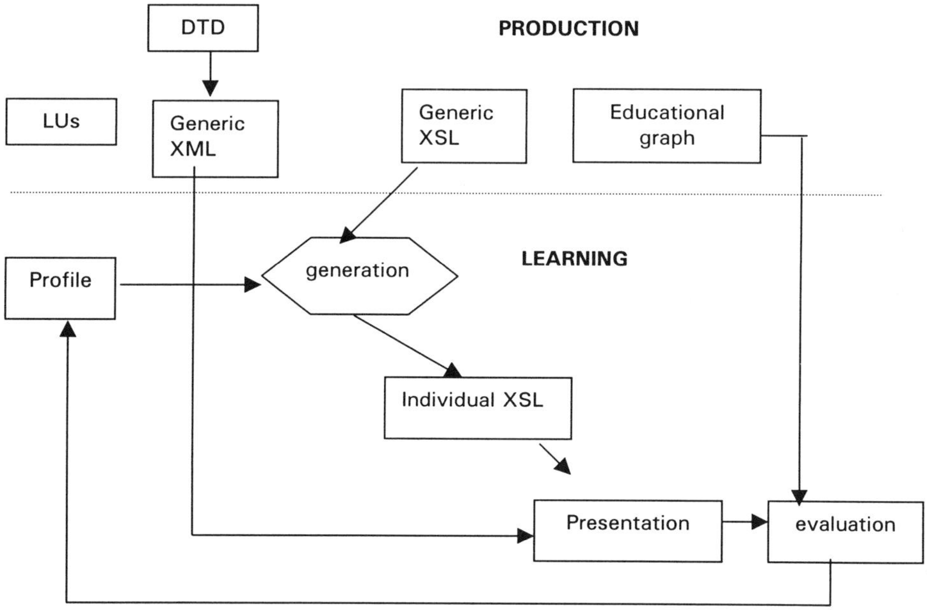

Figure 4: Functional Model

At the end of each part and if necessary, the learner make a self-evaluation test to control the knowledge obtained during this part. According to the result, and other parameters (e.g.: speed) and based on the educational graph, the system chooses the next part to present to the learner. The educational graph represents the whole of the learning rules, which control the succession of the different course parts in order to achieve a teaching goal (succession, choice...). The modification of the profile, following an evaluation, automatically regenerates a new individual XSL document.

6. Prototype

To test our design, we produced a prototype to evaluate our model. The general architecture is described in the figure 5. All the communications between the learner and the server is based on HTTP protocol. Our implementation is made in the Java environment for the high level of portability that provides and the set of tools available (e.g.: security manager, network package,...)[9].

To access a course, the learner sends a request which contains his personal information and his curriculum vitae. This registration will be valid if the learner has all necessary knowledge to start this course. The system generates the learner profile based on this information. This profile is updated by the application as the learner progresses in the course.

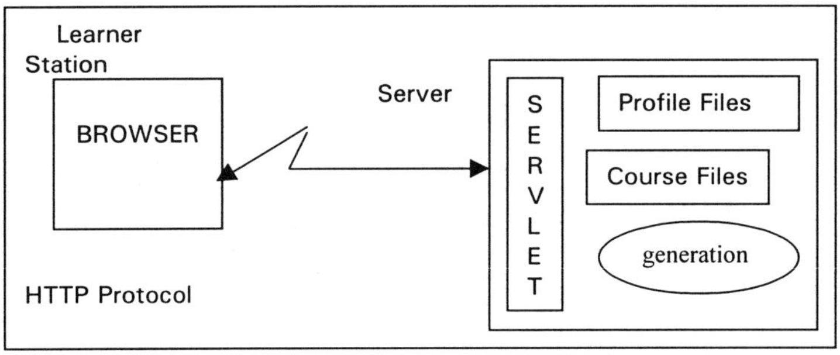

Figure 5: Prototype Architecture

The course document is constituted with an XML and XSL document. The XML document is generated from a prototype DTD document which we had realized, and the XML entities are composed from text, images and audio files.

The system is constituted of two main components

1. the generation module takes as input the generic XML document, the generic XSL document and the profile to generate the individual XSL;
2. the Servlet manage the communication with the learner and generate the profile according the previous one and the result of evaluation.

7. Conclusion

The realization of this prototype was carried out and tested at our research unit with a great success and satisfaction. we had carried out the techniques of adaptability which we had been tested on a demo course. Furthermore, we underline the simplicity of our system, the transfer of the structure of the individual course from the course server to the learners, allows to upload only the elements of the learner is in need, also one can anticipate the transfer of the course elements which will be used later. Another advantage lies in the fact that our application requires only one light processing to adapt the course to one learner.

After the realization of this prototype, we started the second phase of this project characterized by:

- Improvement of the prototype by the implementing the various tasks of our architecture components;
- Improvement of architecture by the integration of the intelligent agents technology in the process of learning;
- Our educational graph is based on a kind of simple relations between the course parts. It is intended to improve these relations to take account of several factors and to approach much more reality as complex as it is. The relation between the parts depends on the profile elements (objective, capacity, psychological factors...);

REFERENCES

[1] Fleury M. Implications de certains principes de design pour le concepteur des systèmes multimédias interactifs Faculté des sciences de l'éducation, Université Laval.

[2] Martin P. La conception pédagogique de systèmes d'apprentissage multimédia interactif : fondements, méthodologie et problématique Directeur du groupe de recherche GRAIM, Faculté des sciences de l'éducation, Université Laval

[3] Bloom B.S, Krathwohl D.R,.Masia B.B(1970). Taxonomie des objectifs pédagogiques. Tome 2. domaine affectif Education nouvelle, Inc. 1970

[4] Kannat S.E., Conil D., Sicard P. Une expérience de télé-enseignement pour autoroute de l'information LSR-IMAG.

[5] Khalifa M. (1998) Effects of Hypertext on Knowledge Construction Department of Information Systems. City University of Hong Kong, IEEE 1998

[6] Abunawass A., Neumann K., Maskarinec M. (1998) heuristics for the design of an effective distance learning curriculum proceeding of the IASTED International Conference, Mexico,1998

[7] Jonas A. Montilvac C. (1998) Designing Web based study guides for distance education courses proceeding of the IASTED International Conference, Mexico,1998

[8] Michard A. (1999) XML langage et applications 1999 Editions Eyrolles

[9] Bosak J. (1997) XML, Java, and the future of the Web Sun Microsystems, 1997

[10] Dietinger T. , H. Maurer, M. Pivec. Multimedia Learning Environment : Combining easier courseware production and new learning methods.

[11] Harasim L. (1999) A framework for online Learning: the Virtual-U IEEE Computer September 1999

[12] Padhye J., Kurose J. (1999) Continuous-Media Courseware Server: A Study of Client Interactions IEEE Internet Computing, Vol. 3, No. 2, March/April 1999

[13] Ajhoun R., Benkiran A., Belqasmi Y. (2000) A Methodology for Adaptative Courses on the Web, proceedings of DEC'2000 the 7th Distance Education Conference, Austin, Texas, January 2000.

[14] Ajhoun R., Benkiran A., Belqasmi Y. (2000), SMART Learning : How to build Adaptatives Courses on the Web, Stop Surfing and Start Teaching 2000 Conference, Charleston, South Carolina, February 2000.

Teaching and Learning in a Network World
P. Hoffman and D. Lemke (Eds.)
IOS Press, 2000

Quenching the Thirst of Technology Through Joint Use Facilities

Stephanie Benoit,CCSN, *6375 West Charleston Blvd, Las Vegas Nevada*

ABSTRACT

Educators in the new millennium will continue to struggle with the implementation of technology. In one of the fastest growing cities in the nation providing technology is a constant challenge. The University System (UCCSN) is faced with double digit enrollment growth in FTE. The eighth largest school district in the nation, the Clark County School District, (CCSD) undoubtably suffers from growing pains. The growth of the community in general increases by over 3000 people per month with no end in sight. It is this growth, the need for a higher skilled work force and a lack of resources to educate the population that creates the ultimate challenge. We as educators must rise to the opportunity to meet this challenge. In order to fully utilize resources, with limited funding, creativity and partnerships are the vehicle to move education into a more pro-active approach for meeting the needs of a variety of students. The implementation of joint use facilities is just one way to quench the thirst of technology for a variety of educational institutions and school districts. CCSD and CCSN have created such a partnership and the benefits and results far outweigh the issues. This partnership has provided a way for education to touch more people in the Las Vegas community than ever before.

WHAT IS A JOINT USE FACILITY?

In traditional educational institutions, college campus sites have their own locations. With the explosion of growth in the area, UCCSN struggles for funding of new buildings, and the new building construction time lines constantly seem to be chasing the need. CCSN and CCSD have some similar issues. Not enough classroom space and not enough technology in the classrooms. It was this issue that brought together secondary and post education in an attempt to better accommodate the needs of students in Clark County. The careful dance steps of the area superintendent, Dr. Brian Cram, and the President of CCSN, Dr. Richard Moore created the choreography for a tango that now dances on three sites. The three sites are located near or on a high school campus and service both college and high school students simultaneously.

Due to the increasing number of students that require technology as part of their education to be competitive in today's job market, CCSN determined that additional sites with high technology computer facilities were essential to accommodate this growing need. Furthermore, CCSN desired to create a facility that was located directly on a high school campus to attract a growing number of students to further their education after high school.

Additional benefits were realized in share facilities with the ability to have the high school use the center during the daytime while the college uses the same facility in the evening. This shared use of systems throughout the day, provided substantial cost benefits to both learning institutions and the taxpayers of Nevada. Creative teaching and learning will flourish in interactive classes, fostering critical thinking. To guarantee an enriching experience, faculty will use team teaching, group discussions and projects, multimedia presentations, computer software and the Internet on over 230 computer systems in each of the over 33,000 square foot facilities.

TECHNOLOGY USED

These centers incorporate some of the latest in computer learning equipment as well as offering access to various learning technologies including the Internet. The requirements for the system are as follows:

User login and authentication system
Security Subsystem
Internet Subsystem
Desktop Environment Subsystem
Printing Subsystem
Administrative Application Subsystem
Desktop Software Control and Management System
Software Application Delivery System
Imaging System
Training/Staff Development

Hardware and Network

The hardware configurations were adjusted to accommodate the requirements of CCSN as well as CCSD. The network design follows the existing guidelines for the following types of hardware including, switches, routers, hubs, network interface cards, firewalls, CD-ROM towers, servers, disk subsystems, tape backup devices, network management tools and network security devices. All devices have been integrated and provide a high availability, high bandwidth solution for the centers. All network devices are SNMP compliant and able to be monitored from an SNMP management station

The centers all utilize efficient floor cable ducting system to distribute data communication cabling throughout the center. All data information outlets run to a central "head end" room where centralized computing and network resources will be housed. The facility utilize high performance, Category 5, unshielded twisted pair cabling for its data transmission needs. This cabling has been certified by the installing contractor to be Category 5 compliant. All non-computer classrooms are wired with at least one data information outlet to facilitate interactive computer instruction. Additional jacks are wired into faculty workroom areas for connection to permanent and user provided laptop computer systems.

In addition, multimode fiber optic cabling was placed between the high tech center building and the existing CCSD high school buildings in order to provide connectivity between the high school and college resources. Other network infrastructure components include provisions for video distribution into each classroom and telephone/intercom communication cabling throughout the center.

Infrastructure

The center's data transmission infrastructure incorporates a high bandwidth, high availability gigabit rated switching framework to provide a minimum of 10 megabits per second dedicated connection to each workstation and 100 megabits per second or greater connections to the network file servers. The network infrastructure provided unique and isolated bandwidth to each workstation offering the needed performance to support network intensive applications such as multimedia, Internet access and centralized software management and distribution.

Network Software

This concept of joint use facilities was the first high technology learning center of its kind using the latest available hardware and software. It was also the first computer lab to utilize Novell's Netware 5 (sm) pure TCP/IP product.

The High Tech Center at Summerlin was originally slated to use Novell's Intranetware (sm) product, which is a proven technology but didn't fit the need of the new center. After conversations with Novell, it was suggested that we become part of there Live with Five program which gave us the ability and resources to implement Novell's Netware 5, Z.E.N. Works, Border Manager, ManageWise and GroupWise in a production environment. CCSN's High Tech Center was the first production installation of Netware 5 in the United States prior to its general release in September 1998.

The combination of products allows CCSD and CCSN students to login to the network and receive a variety of services with a single login. These products also allow both networks to be accessed from any of the facilities.

ISSUES

The concept of joint use facilities raise some interesting concerns to all the entities involved. These concerns range from the diversity of needs based on the user, to facility issues of which students will occupy the site at any given time during the day or night. The rooms at these sites are occupied by high school faculty from the hours of 6:30am to 2:00pm and then taken over by college instructors who will then use the exact same room, machines and technology in their implementation of curriculum. The technology is also an on going concern. The High Tech Centers need to provide a high availability computer learning environment for its faculty, staff and students. In addition, security is a major concern that has to be addressed between all organizations who to use the centers. Some of the technical problems in providing these types of services included connectivity between multiple networks, providing filtered and non-filtered Internet access, providing resource management, and operational issues associated with a joint use faculty.

Sometimes these types of challenges force technical implementation to the cutting edge. The Computing Services Department at CCSN is constantly required to think of new strategies and techniques to provide successful solutions, while utilizing a limited amount of technical resources and staff. Based on the college's current technology staffing level of one technician to 743 users, it was imperative to implement a technology strategy, that could be managed remotely with minimum intervention.

In the first year of operation the High Tech Center network had a potential 57,000 users that could walk through the door, sit down at a computer and experience the technology, surf the web, or work on a project.

BENEFITS

The High Tech Center concept provides the opportunity for students to receive an education using state of the art technology by making available all resources regardless of the media or location. By consolidating the resources of the high school and the college, a more efficient and robust facility has been developed.

Students and faculty within the center have an increased level of access to global information resources from a single computer workstation. This technology has nurtured new creativity in the educational learning experience and has fostered new methods for instruction.

The advantage of the center is its location within the community. By placing high tech education centers directly within the communities they serve, increased access to educational and student services for area residents has been accomplished.

RELATIONSHIPS

This type of facility does not exist or succeed without relationships. The relationships range from technical coordination from multiple IT staffs to the collaboration of faculty from the neighboring high schools and CCSN faculty. The most important relationship is the Tango that is danced at the administrative levels. It was a vision establish at this level and a commitment to making the partnership work that laid the foundation for success.

The second set of relationships that aid in the implementation of technology of this type is partnerships and relationships with manufacturers. This type of environment is very unique. It was the close relationships with the innovator of technology that assisted the vision. Not only did manufactures step on to the road with us, but then based on our findings made modifications to code for better stability in our environment. It is also the same relationships that now help us define to the technology community how we as an educational community need to conduct business.

RESULTS

The impact from the relationships that have been created are felt by faculty and staff. Yet the true results unmeasurable due to the fact that the implementation of the concept is only a little over one year old. The collaborative efforts between faculty have fostered new ways to deliver instruction. This ranges from general studies classes such as psychology, math and English to CADD, programing, graphic animation and GIS. Instructors at these centers express the success in there classroom. “We’ve had a wonderful opportunity to enhance the educational experience of Palo Verde students. The additional computer lab space due the shared facility of the Summerlin campus allows many more Palo Verde students access to course offerings. Students are exploring cutting edge technology making Palo Verde students truly ready for careers of the future.” Karen Kegley, Palo Verde High School.

The technology has fostered a new level of communication between faculty and students. Instructors can now have virtual office hours while students can submit homework and get information anytime of the day. This type of technology allows us to transform instruction beyond the traditional classroom experience.

The task of educating students has dramatically changed from the traditional classroom environment to one that utilizes the electronic media resources available to faculty and staff. Class syllabi, assignments and projects are now presented electronically via the World Wide Web, electronic mail and online discussion groups.

OPPORTUNITY AND FUTURE

As we look forward to the next decade of education it comes with a breath taking challenge. The history of teaching with the continued growth in enrollment, the lack of substantial dollars to fund technology, buildings and infrastructure the educational community is dependant on the creativity and vision of the organizations. The dynamics of what technology can bring to our classrooms and schools moves us as a society closer to the true vision of "who do you want to be today, and who will you be tomorrow." Technology is like the yellow brick road. None of us are sure how far the Emerald City is, or even if we know what it looks like. The road is not very smooth, and the vehicles we choose at times to travel are unconventional, slow and sometimes not exactly reliable. In the pursuit of the vision we can not afford to get lost or misdirected in the complication of the process. Although we are not sure how far the vision is away. The pursuit of this vision is building our present, and our future. In order to succeed in our environment we must push the edge of technology and relationships to provide cutting edge solutions, so that we as educational organizations can complete our mission of, Creating Opportunities and Changing Lives, by quenching the thirst of technology through the creation of joint use facilities.

REFERENCES

[1] Beering, Steven C. "Technology benefits but costs education." Indianapolis Business Journal. 06/28/99: p23a.

[2] Bork, Alfred. "The future of computers and learning." The Journal.

[3] UCCSN Board of Regents. "UCCSN Information Bulletin." 7/12/99:p1.

Teaching and Learning in a Network World
P. Hoffman and D. Lemke (Eds.)
IOS Press, 2000

Putting Your Best Web-Foot Forward: Adapting Web-Technologies to Fit You, Your Teaching Style, and Your Students

Judith Browning and Janice Carter
Golden Gate University
536 Mission Street
San Francisco, CA 94105

How can faculty create a Web-enhanced environment that works for them? We explore ways faculty can customize readily-available web technologies to meet their teaching styles and their students.

How do you want to use technology or create a web-enhanced environment that works for your teaching and your students? How can you find the technology that fits your objectives and your level of comfort, and that your students can easily access?

As we have struggled with these questions, we have developed a collaborative process of working with faculty that is driven by faculty needs and interests. In our grant project, we helped faculty members find their own best use of web-technologies using enhancement tools such as web searches, word processing, extended use of e-mail, conferencing, library tutorials, and web links.

In the presentation for TechEd 2000, we explore ways faculty can determine objectives and select and customize readily-available web technologies to meet their own particular goals, interests, and level of comfort with technology. We draw upon projects such as those described below.

Designing Web Projects for individual courses to increase student motivation

We wanted to teach a course on research writing that would utilize WEB technology and create a dynamic research process in the classroom. We wanted to teach students to search the web effectively, to articulate their research strategies, and, more importantly, to be able to evaluate their resources during this process.
One of the first assignments helped to personalize the students' first encounter with the web. Students wrote a short vignette of one event from their life experience which was later posted on the class web page in the form of a class profile. Students then documented their research process in the form of progress reports or "Process Papers" and shared the details of their struggles with setting up interviews, researching the electronic databases in the library, or finding good search engines or URLs for their topics on the Internet. In addition to these progress reports, students wrote "Reflection Papers," in which the students reflected upon what they had learned in retrospect from a particular assignment.

For example, students wrote about the importance of making bookmarks during the research process, or the importance of keeping a hard copy of websites, since websites sometimes moved or disappeared and the students had difficulty relocating sources. Others wrote about how to organize notes, or provided tips about what not to do during an interview. Many wrote about the benefits of being able to navigate the electronic databases in the library. These are all points an instructor could make, but it is far more effective when the students share this knowledge with each other. The reflection papers also helped students evaluate the process they were following as well as the resources they were using.

As the students' work became posted on the Web, an unexpected dynamic to the research process took over. Motivated by the initial assignment of the student vignette, students began to see themselves as authors of texts for others to read. By sharing their stories and assignments with others, students understood the need for edited writing and began to overcome their fear of writing. The Web provided an added urgency to the task of writing because the students' texts were leaving the classroom and being published to a virtually unlimited audience. The potential audience added seriousness and commitment to the writing tasks.

Another benefit to the class was that the work never ended in the classroom. Students from the web group met frequently outside of class and e-mailed one another continually. Since the web group was also responsible for posting the page to represent the class for that particular semester, they spent many hours designing and organizing the page.

There were benefits for the instructors as well. As the students posted their work for one another, we, as instructors, were able to more clearly evaluate the nature of their research process. We were therefore able to make adjustments to the course more quickly than we could have done without using this technology. For example, while analyzing the progress reports on the Internet searches, we discovered that students weren't evaluating their sources carefully. We therefore added a resource to the University Library page on Evaluating Sources (http://internet.ggu.edu/university_library/eval.html. We were able to see more clearly how to build bridges from where the students were rather than from where we were.

The reflection papers, showed us how students wrestled with and interpreted what we tried to teach. We learned what to clarify, what to emphasize, and what to augment, based on students' descriptions of their research process. Some reflection papers are posted on the English IB website (http://www.ggu.edu/schools/ls&pa/english/j_browning/eng1B/reflect.html).

Every semester we improve upon our work from the previous semester. For example, we developed a template for the English 1B page that students could use to create websites. This template provided an easy way for them to create their initial web page. (http://internet.ggu.edu/university_library/eng1btem.html). We also created an English 1B Research Strategy guide (http://internet.ggu.edu/university_library/eng1bstr.html).

While teaching the students to create web pages, we tried to link what they were doing with strategies they could use in their research. We hoped they would draw on the process they had used in creating web sites to search the Internet more effectively and to evaluate other sources. For example, when they created their web sites, we explained that the title field <title> would become the label for bookmarks, so people tend to give websites titles that are descriptive. Once the students created the titles for their own pages, they could understand better why searching Altavista and other search engines by title field might be an effective way to focus their searches.

We encouraged the students to look for the kinds of information they had included on their sites when evaluating other sites. We wanted them to discover the purpose of each site, determine who created it, and identify when it was last updated.

Incorporating WEB technology into the class enabled us to create research assignments that were meaningful and fun. The use of web technology helps us begin where the students are, fascinated with technology.

Working with Other Faculty

We were eager to share what we had gained with other faculty. As we worked with other faculty, we learned to begin where *they* were. We developed a list of ways faculty could incorporate ideas from the English 1B web project depending upon their own objectives and their own comfort level with technology. Faculty who wanted nothing to do with technology might still consider having students write papers reflecting on the research process, or they might put sample student papers on reserve in the Library. A next easy step, for faculty feeling more adventurous, would be to put sample student papers on electronic reserve, or to post them on a class electronic bulletin board or e mail conferencing system. Some faculty might want to have research strategy guides, or other websites, developed for their classes. Others might want to develop their own websites, or locate web resources to enhance their classes.

Locating Web Resources to Enhance Classes

There may be web resources that could enhance classes--but how can faculty find them without wasting hours sifting through irrelevant sites? We have developed a research strategy guide faculty can use to identify relevant web resources for their courses. We can easily tailor the guide to meet needs of faculty in specific disciplines. The guide, a webpage faculty can bookmark to refer to when needed, links faculty easily to 1) clearinghouses of teaching resources, 2) guides by subject specialists, such as the Virtual Library, 3) other guides organized by subject such as the Scout Report and BUBL, 4) strategies for locating information from organizations and governmental agencies on the web, and 5) tips for using search engines effectively. (See Attachment 1.) For on-line guide, see http://internet.ggu.edu/university_library/findweb.html.

Providing Resources for On-Line Writing Center and Humanities Courses

In addition, we worked with faculty to develop an On-Line Writing Center, to use primary sources available on the Net to enhance history courses, and to bring science resources to students via the Net.

This, of course, is just the beginning. As we continue to work with students and faculty we learn new ways of using the web to make classes more effective -- and more fun.

Attachment 1

Research Strategy for Faculty to Use in Locating Websites for Course Enrichment -- via GGU University Library

Please remember that library staff will be glad to help you

- work out a specific research strategy for finding resources for your subject
- locate web resources--and other resources, including books and journal articles for your subject
- develop a research strategy summary guide and/or pathfinders so your students can make most efficient and best use of all resources available

Please see *Internet Resources for Web Enhanced Classes*, and *Research Services and Support for Faculty* via GGU University Library.

Check Clearinghouses of Teaching Resources often designed by University or College networks to bring together online resources other faculty have found effective. See for example:

- *Academic Info* "An independent directory compiled and maintained by Mike Madin." "of Internet resources tailored to a college or advanced high school audience. Each subject guide is an annotated listing of the best general Internet sites in the field, as well as a gateway to more advanced research tools. On each page you may find links to online publications, language and study aids, reference materials, databases, archives, virtual libraries, tutorials, as well as other educational materials." (Quotes from website, April 1, 1999)
- *Merlot* Multimedia Repository for Learning and Online Teaching California State University. Includes links to online learning tools for various disciplines, technical tools, such as course templates, papers, news, and other resources for integrating technology into the curriculum.
- *Online Educational Resources* Discipline Specific Teaching Resources via the Centre for Curriculum Transfer Technology, Association of Canadian Community Colleges. Focuses on Business, English as a Second Language, Culinary Arts, and Geography.

  These are often organized as listings of sites. If you find them difficult to scan, check, guides by subject specialists, listed below.

Check Guides by Subject Specialists, such as:

- *Virtual Library* Each site is created and maintained by specialists in and devoted to that particular topic. Virtual Library developed originally through the Institute for Particle Physics in Geneva Switzerland, so at least in the beginning, websites in the Virtual Library tended to emphasize research oriented and scholarly links. We benefit from the experts' ever increasing knowledge of relevant links and their skill in organizing the links for their topic. See, for example:

    - *History* Virtual Library, with links to Index of Resources for United States History
    - *Virtual Library for Finance* from Ohio State University.
- *Argus Clearinghouse of Subject-Oriented Internet Research Guides* "The Argus Clearinghouse provides a central access point for value-added topical guides which identify, describe, and evaluate Internet-based information resources." (Quote from website, March 18, 1999)
- Sometimes you can locate guides by subject specialists through specialized museums, such as: *Exploratorium,* which has links to *Cool Sites of the Month*, which are then organized into an archive by subject. See *Museums* via GGU University Library to locate museums of interest, or as librarians for assistance.
- Associations are often a good source of links for a particular field. To locate associations for your topic, see *Associations* links via GGU University Library, or check *Subjects* via GGU University Library website.
- Governmental or intergovernmental organizations may also provide useful links. See for example: Library of Congress for sites such as:
    - American Memory for primary source collections such as *California As I Saw It First* Person Narratives of California's Early Years, 1849-1900
    - *BEOnline* Country Information via Library of Congress

  To identify government agencies and international organizations, see Political Science and Government or your topic on *Subject* websites from GGU University Library
- We have tried to provide key research starting points for subjects on the GGU University Library Subject webpages. Many times our pages develop through our work with you, so we are always delighted to work with you on projects, and as you see other key resources, please send them to us.
- You may wish to join *E-Mail Conferences* in your subject area, to gain ongoing information on new resources as they develop.

Check Other Guides Organized by Subject

Because these are not organized by subject specialists, they may not provide the same depth or coherent structure as sites done by subject specialists, but they can be useful, as a next step, in identifying resources of value. Examples include:

- *Scout Report Signpost* Internet resources are chosen by Scout editorial staff, cataloged and organized by Library of Congress Classification System. You can search, browse by subject headings, or browse by Library of Congress Classification System. The Internet Scout Project, located in the Computer Science Department of the University of Wisconsin-Madison, is funded by the National Science Foundation. Its mission is to assist in the advancement of resource discover on the Internet." (From website February 4, 1998).

- *BUBL*"Libraries of Networked Knowledge covering all main subject areas"; with arrangement by Dewey Decimal System. From Andersonian Library, Strathclyde University, Glasgow, Scotland. See *Bubl* 5:15 for subject-based interface to Internet resources.
- *AlphaSearch* via Calvin Theological Seminary. Purpose is to "link to the finest Internet 'gateway' sites." Quote from web site, February 10, 1998.)
- *Infomine* from the University of California at Riverside Library
- *Where the Wild Things* Are Librarians' Guide to the Best Information on the Net. Index is maintained by Marylaine Block for St. Ambrose University, Davenport, Iowa.
- *Michigan Electronic Library*
- *Searching by Subject* via University of Texas
- *Academic Resources on the World Wide Web* Capital-Community Technical College. Resource guide developed and maintained by Dr. Charles Darling.
- *Direct Search* by Gary Price, MLIS, George Washington University Washington D.C. and Ashburn VA. "This page is a growing compilation of DIRECT LINKS to the search interfaces of resources that are not easily searchable from general search tool such as Alta Vista, Hotbot, and Infoseek. While general search tools tools are essential for information retrieval of Internet materials[,] many users do not realize that large amounts of information are not searchable via these tools." (Quote from website, April 9, 1998)
- *Cyberstacks* CyberStacks(sm) is a centralized, integrated, and unified collection of significant World Wide Web (WWW) and other Internet resources categorized using the Library of Congress classification scheme. Resources are organized under one or more relevant Library of Congress class numbers and an associated publication format and subject description. The majority of resources incorporated within its collection are monographic or serial works, files, databases or search services. All of the selected resources in CyberStacks(sm) are full-text, hypertext, or, hypermedia, and of a research or scholarly nature." (Quote from website 7/15/97.)
- *Librarians' Index to the Internet* Document maintained on http://sunsite.berkeley.edu by Carole Leita. Formerly Berkeley Public Library Index to the Internet.
- *Internet Resources Meta-Index*
- *Searchcom* C/Net compilation of directories, can select directory, then use search engine.
- *Yahoo!* Go beyond the search engine to use the powerful subject listings.

Use Search Engines After using resources organized by subject specialists, and Yahoo! we can enter another realm of searching, using search engines. Search engines use robots or spiders to locate resources. There are new search engines every day. Over time, we have learned that it is better to know how to use a few of the best search engines well, rather than try to search using all of them.

- Different search engines serve different purposes. A useful tool for identifying search engines or other Internet resource guides suited to your needs is: *Choose the Best Search Engine for Your Purpose* by Debbie Abilock, Librarian at Nueva, a private school, kindergarden through 12th grade, in Hillsborough, California.
- For insight into what search engines cover and how to use them most effectively, consult Internet Tutorials, such as *Finding Information on the Internet: A TUTORIAL* by the U.C.Berkeley Teaching Library. This is a superb guide you can return to at any time, and read as little or as much as you want each time. When people ask me what books I recommend they read on Internet Searching, I refer them to this site.

Scan down and click on the Table of Features of the Boolean Logic-Based Search Tools. (Don't let the title scare you away.) You will see a handy chart with hot links to and descriptions of search engines, what they cover, and how they can be searched most effectively.

Using Altavista Advanced Search

Scan down the column under Altavista, and note some of the ways you can make your search on Altavista more precise. Altavista indexes full text of over 100 million web sites. Since no one is organizing the sites by topic, if we do a simple search on Altavista, we may get thousands of hits and have trouble sorting through them to find the ones which will be most useful for our research. Using "Altavista Advanced Search" however, we can create a more specific search query, that can cut down on false drops, or irrelevant resources. Here are some tips:

Put Phrases in Quotation Marks

If I do a simple search for South East Asia I may get some links that deal with South, some that deal with East, some that deal with Asia. By doing an Advanced Search in Altavista, however, I can put a phrase such as South East Asia in quotation marks "South East Asia" thus signaling to Alta Vista Advanced that I want it to treat the phrase as one entity, not separate words. As a result, I do not have to wade through search results on the South Pole, South Carolina, etc.

Use NEAR to Signal that Search Elements Need to Be Within 10 Words of Each Other, e.g., "South East Asia" NEAR environment*

Use * to Pull Up Variant Forms of Root Word Use * at the end of a word to pick up all forms of that root word, e.g., environment* picks up environment, environmental

Search by Title of Website to Create a More Focused Search One of the most useful ways to limit a search is often by title, since the title field of a web site becomes the bookmark. Therefore most sites will have a title field that describes the site as a whole. If, for example, you want to find the home page for Kellogg's Cereals, you could search for cereal* AND title:"Kellogg*"

- Using Other Search Engines

The tutorial guide from UC Berkeley can help you identify how to use other search engines most effectively. See also: *Searching by Keywords* on GGU University Library website for additional guides and links to other search engines.

To keep up with the ever-changing world of search engines, see *Search Engine Watch*

What would make this site more useful?

Send your suggestions to the Eclectic Strategist jcarter@ggu.edu

Teaching and Learning in a Network World
P. Hoffman and D. Lemke (Eds.)
IOS Press, 2000

Smart Ways to Manage Technology

Rich Chapin*
SmartStuff Software, PO Box 82284, Portland, OR 97282, USA

Successful management of technology not only lowers the total cost of ownership, but makes life considerably easier for technology coordinators. As Tim Landeck recently wrote in the Jan./Feb issue of the C.U.E. Newsletter, "No K-12 school should be without a desktop security system on every student computer. Desktop security will restrict student access to such things as the control panes and prevent students (and teachers, if you set it up this way) from installing, moving, or deleting programs and files....We use FoolProof because it is cross-platform and easy to install and manage...". It is a given that desktop security software is a requirement in todays schools. Technology management problems multiply when schools allow student access to the Internet.

Let's face it.

Pornography is almost impossible to avoid on the Internet. Referring to obscenity, Supreme Court Justice Potter Stewart said in the landmark 1973 Supreme Court case, " I know it when I see it." And it is virtually impossible not to see it on the net.

The net's openness, its anonymity, its ability to deliver high quality graphic images make it a perfect home for "adult" content. It is impossible to quantify the amount of "adult content" on the net, but there should be no question that there is lots of it, all over the place, in places you might least expect to find it.

The flip side, and the dilemma for educators, is that the Web's worldwide reach opens doors to a vast warehouse of information for students. With the openness of the Web come both danger and opportunity, and the need for increased understanding and responsible use of browsing tools and technologies. We must learn to manage the Web's openness to protect our students, while taking advantage of its vast information resources to improve their education.

Pornography: Ubiquitous and Unavoidable

Zona Research has estimated that "60-70% of all Web traffic is adult in nature" and more that $560 million dollars will be spent on access to "adult" sites. Searchterms.com has compiled a list of the one hundred most frequently searched for words. Number one is "sex," and 37% of the top one hundred are related to adult content. While counts of frequently used search terms do not translate into a direct measure of Web pornography, they do suggest that search engines are a primary on-ramp to it.

---

* Rich Chapin is co-founder of SmartStuff Software (http://www.smartstuff.com). SmartStuff's software products include FoolProof Security and FoolProof Internet. Before founding SmartStuff, Rich taught for twenty years in kindergarten through college. (Published in part in the September 1999 edition on THE Journal)

The most obvious way to understand how prevalent and unavoidable pornography is on the Web is to go to popular search engines and search for "sex" or related words. If you haven't done this, be prepared for a shock. While each of the search engines returns different material, most of them prominently feature banner ads for "adult" sites. All of them will return hundreds, if not thousands of sites and pages containing adult content. The search engine results themselves often contain adult language (obscenities, words depicting sexual acts, etc.). Worse yet, in an effort to be "helpful," some search engines will provide search tips that are downright obscene.

Even an innocent search for terms such as "girls" or "pics" will return pornographic content. Adult sites want to be found and they do everything possible to make it happen. They create decoy sites such as http://www.whitehouse.com. They cram search engines with data that increase their relevance. They employ technology that makes it difficult to leave once you have wandered in.

Kids Will Find It

Students at school will not be able to escape "adult content" on the net – even if they want to. Data released by the Utah Public Education (http://www.helpdesk.k12.ut.us/filter.htm) indicates that student attempts to access "adult content" is a relatively small percentage of overall Internet use (April 1999: less than 1% - 265,833 pages out of 55,045,096) But the data also reveals it growing by a factor of 10 (July 38,493 pages out of 4,159,410) and will continue to grow as Internet usage grows. (The Utah data may significantly understate student attempts to access "adult content" as student awareness of the state's use of filtering software arguably reduces their attempts to access "adult content".)

Filtering is Not Censorship

The fact that pornography on the Internet is both ubiquitous and unavoidable and that students will almost certainly access it – from school, at home, from the library, with friends, etc. – suggests only that we as parents, teachers and community members must be aware of the risks and consequences. Most importantly we should understand the difference between censorship and filtering.

The Merriam Webster Dictionary (http://www.m-w.com/netdict.htm) defines "censor" as "an official who examines materials for objectionable matter; an official (as in time of war) who reads and deletes material considered sensitive or harmful." Censorship is an act of government that, by definition, precludes free choice. The US constitution guarantees free speech, and thus restricts government censorship dramatically – mainly to times of war. Censorship at other times is a violation of our civil rights.

Parents and teachers filter students and children's' exposure to all sorts of things all the time. We keep our kids home when they are sick. We monitor whom they play with and don't let them talk to strangers. We are encouraged to monitor and control what shows they watch on TV, the songs they listen to on the radio and the books they read. This is to a very great degree what good parenting is all about. By extension it is arguably what good teaching is all about.

Schools act in "loco parentis" when teaching children and so standards of health and safety that apply to parents apply generally to teachers. Just as importantly, teachers teach by providing students with information and accompanying analysis. The whole notion of a scope and sequence suggests that as teachers we take responsibility for determining the information content of a child's education. By teaching them arithmetic before we teach them calculus we filter their exposure to mathematical information.

Understand the Problem - Surf and Search with Students

How comfortable and knowledgeable are we about the Internet? Do we understand the problem? The "problem" is larger than pornography and extends from free speech to include health and safety, and basic privacy protections.

What are our concerns? Pornography? Sex? Violence? Illegal Activity? Hate Speech? Do we have different concerns for younger students than for older students? Are we concerned about words or pictures? Do we want our students to use search engines? Email? Chat? Discussions? How much of the Internet do we want to restrict our students to or from? Are we willing to restrict some students to a relatively "safe" portion of the Internet? Are we worried about what our students say and to whom they say it? How much do we want to monitor how our students use of the Internet? If the Internet is a teaching tool, how do we assess their interests and skills in using the new medium? How much time do we have to spend while "paying attention"? Are we more concerned with transmitting inappropriate material than we are with viewing it? What are the consequences for breaking the rules? What tools are available to help enforce the rules?

In approaching the new realities the Internet is creating, we must stay involved and become informed. In short, we need to talk with our kids about the Internet. We need to surf and search with them. We need to create rules that we feel comfortable with at home and policies that are responsive at school. The new technology of the Internet may have changed the pace of the problem, but it has not created the problem. Just as technology didn't create the problem we must not rely solely on technology to "fix" the problem.

Acceptable Use Policies

Many schools are adopting "Acceptable Use Policies" – documents which describe how the Internet is to be used in school and the consequences for its misuse.

To be most effective, acceptable use policies should be based on a thorough analysis of student needs for information and protection. Schools should post their policies on their Web sites, send them home to parents and teach them to students. Some schools require students to sign the Acceptable Use Policy, often before granting free Internet access. Schools should consider linking their Acceptable Use Policies to any filtering technology they employ. Fortunately, there are multiple technologies available to help monitor and enforce acceptable use policies, so policies can be enforced in a flexible way that accommodates the needs of different schools and different students.

Monitoring Web Usage

Standard browser and server technology can help guide our students to appropriate content while helping us to stay involved and aware of what they are doing. All browsers include a 'history' file that lists the time and date of every Web site accessed. Web proxy servers also provide a history or audit of sites accessed for all of the machines served. Some proxy servers include powerful reporting tools as well. These tools are basic to school use of the Web, however , monitoring alone can only be reactive, identifying problems after they happen. For proactive control, additional content filtering technology is necessary.

Filtering Technology

Filtering Technologies fall into three general types – list-based URL filtering, text filtering, and content recognition technology.

List-Based Filtering

URL filtering, the most commonly used technology, is a database of 'unacceptable' Web sites and domains. These lists are frequently categorized by type of content. Categories include obscenity, sexual content, alternative lifestyles, illegal activity, drugs, violence, hate speech and crimes, sports and various forms of leisure.

List-based filtering has two weaknesses. It is costly. The lists must be updated frequently, and users must pay on-going subscription fees. Second, and more important, vendors' ability to maintain their lists is being out-stripped by the current growth of the Web. Some analysts estimate that a new Web site is added an average of every 18 seconds. List-based technology cannot possible keep up.

A more restrictive alternative to "prohibited site" lists is to only allow student browsers to go to certain Web sites - "virtual playgrounds" that are trusted to provide content appropriate to students and children. There are a variety of tools available that can "tune" the browser to a trusted site or virtual playground. This kind of filtering has the advantage of restricting students to appropriate content while providing the safest access, and may be entirely appropriate for very young students.

Text Filters

Web content can also be managed through the use of "text filters." Text filtering technology limits the words that can be displayed in the browser and can be used to block pages containing inappropriate content. Unfortunately, simple text filters have trouble distinguishing appropriate uses of the same word from inappropriate uses. Thus filtering solutions relying on text filters often block pages that students and teachers want to access.

Content Recognition

Recently a new class of filtering technology has been developed which employs neural networks and other artificial intelligence to reduce the dependence on human reviewers and to provide more sophisticated content screening than simple text filtering. Content recognition technology uses trained neural networks to identify patterns on incoming Web pages and to permit or block the page. For example, when content recognition tools encounter the word "breast", they will check the context and structure for words such as "mammogram". Students will be allowed to see the medical information, while a pornographic site will be blocked. By dynamically evaluating Web content in real time, content recognition technology is always current and avoids the costs and limitations of list-based filtering.

Filtering designed to give students free access to the entire Web is the least restrictive way to keep students from adult or inappropriate content. But this technology is only as good as the filtering criteria and technology. Filtering solutions should combine the best of the available technologies – real time dynamic content recognition, and "virtual playgrounds" combined with list and text based filtering.

Instructional Management and Content Filtering

Instructional management and filtering is the most proactive approach to creating a positive Web experience for students. Through a combination of teacher direction, browser technology, Web servers and directories, and filtering technologies, teachers can direct the student to subject-specific Web locations. For example, science teachers can direct students to the Eisenhower National Clearinghouse (http://www.enc.org), math teachers can direct students to the Math Forum (http://forum.swarthmore.edu/), and language arts teachers can direct students to the English Server (http://www.eserver.org).

"Safe" Search engines and directories can be employed to avoid inadvertent access to inappropriate material. Teachers can extend and enrich the Web as an educational experience using information sources such as EBSCO and Proquest, or unique Web-based excursions such as ThinkQuest and MayQuest. Web activities and materials such as the Scholastic Network or CCCNet can provide valuable supplements to standard information sources.

Bookmarks and Favorites Help Students Find What They Want

Helping students find what they want – quickly and easily -- may be the most effective form of filtering. The easiest way to find something on the Internet is via a bookmark or favorite file. Search engines are notorious for providing too much information and students may not know how to access the most useful subject directories.

School browsers should be set with well-organized bookmark / favorite files and students should be trained in their use. Like the history file bookmarks can be edited and organized, saved, searched, sorted and cleared.

Because bookmarking is so much a part of effective surfing, schools should consider creating and securing standard bookmark sets for all students or groups of students and "personal" bookmarks for individual students. Science classes need different bookmarks than Language Arts classes. Seniors need different bookmarks than 8th graders. And all students need to be able to edit and save their personal bookmarks.

Privacy Protection

Students in schools share computers. In a given period of time, 25 to 250 students may have access to the same computer, the same browser. As a consequence, students are subject to loss of privacy in a variety of ways. The same tools in the browser (caching, history file, bookmark file) that make filtering and focusing possible also reveal private information. The browser's history file contains all the web sites accessed – regardless of whom accessed them. Thus it is to easy "snoop" to determine where other users are surfing.

Student privacy can be violated through chat rooms or through routine Web site access. Web sites regularly collect data about their users. Standard server technology provides basic information about all Web site visitors: email addresses, the operating system of your computer, and whether you accessed the site from an online service, an Internet access provider, an educational institution or a business. All of this information could be useful to potential abusers or unwanted solicitors. To combat this double threat, schools can use content filtering and cookie management to keep students from intentionally or unwittingly transmitting personal information over the Web.

Cookie Management

Many Web sites maintain user privileges such as email accounts through the use of "cookies," digital markers employed by Web servers to maintain users information as they surf through the site. If a student leaves their computer without quitting the browser, the cookie file will be maintained and the next student to sit down at the computer may have access to whatever private accounts have been opened. Persistent cookies of this type are risks to student privacy on school computers. Browser options and preferences provide some support for "cookie management." Both standard browsers provide the ability to decline cookies and to notify users before accepting cookies. The latest version of Navigator also supports a feature that accepts only cookies that get sent back to the originating server. The best solution is to associate cookies with individual users and browser sessions – thereby supporting site access while avoiding the privacy pitfalls.

Outgoing Content Filtering

Outbound content that users voluntarily submit in e-mail, chat room forums and server based forms may be the most dangerous and difficult risks to manage for students using the web. Text filtering or content recognition technology can be used to block users from sending out personal information such as full name, age or address and chat rooms can be blocked. But these technologies can only be partially effective and in many cases may have the effect of blocking student access to desired sites and information. Ultimately students must be made aware of the inherent danger of revealing personal information on the web – via e-mail, chat and discussion servers and server based forms. They should be taught to follow the same rules of safe conduct on the web as they do at the local park or playground.

Conclusion

As a vast global storehouse of information, the World Wide Web offers a rich learning opportunity to educators and students. To take full advantage of this learning opportunity, we must manage its risks to create a safe yet open learning environment. New technologies and information sources appearing everyday hold the potential to significantly improve how we use the Web to teach and learn.

Acceptable Use Policy Links

TIES Web Acceptable Use Policy Links -- http://www.ties.k12.mn.us/accept/

Safe Surfing Tools -- http://esu15.esu15.k12.ne.us/safesurf.html

NMCTE Selected Acceptable Use Policy Resources -- Web Use Policies http://sde.state.nm.us/nmcte/aup.html

School Librarian Links -- Acceptable Use Resources -- http://www.nyx.net/~rbarry/aup.html

AUP Paper-11-6-97 -- http://www.Websolutionz.com/cimt647/ disc3/0000011d.htm

Acceptable Use Policies - A Handbook Virginia Department of Education -- http://www.pen.k12.va.us/go/VDOE/Technology/AUP/home.shtml

Acceptable Use Policies -- http://athena.wednet.edu/project/teacher/manage/aup.html

Acceptable Use Policies -- http://www.netc.org/tech plans/aup.html

Privacy on the Web

How Information is gathered -- http://www.larrysworld.com/privacy.html

Protecting Privacy Online - The Basics -- http://www.Weballiance.org/project-open/layout.html#info

Quick Tips for Protecting Privacy -- http://www.Weballiance.org/project-open/layout.html#quick

Protecting Your Privacy When You Go Online -- http://www.Weballiance.org/project-open/layout.html#protect

Privacy and E-Mail -- http://www.Weballiance.org/project-open/layout.html#email

Children's Privacy -- http://www.Weballiance.org/project-open/layout.html#child

Web Privacy Protections and Considerations for Students Privacy on the Web -- http://www.4j.lane.edu/4jnet/privacyguide.html

Filtering - Censorship Debate & Issues

FamilyEducation Forums - America Links Up -- http://connect.familyeducation.com/Webx/Webx.dll?230@@.ee6d7e1

The Cyberporn Debate -- http://www2000.ogsm.vanderbilt.edu/cyberporn.debate.cgi

Sex, Censorship, and the Web -- http://www.eff.org/CAF/cafuiuc.html

The New York Times Communications Decency Page -- http://www.nytimes.com/library/cyber/week/cda-index.html

Censorship, Freedom of Speech, and Child Safety on the Web -- http://www.voicenet.com/~cranmer/censorship.html#resources

Web Directories

Web Public Library -- http://www.ipl.org

KidsClick -- http://sunsite.Berkeley.EDU/KidsClick!/

Kathy Schrock's Guide for Educators -- http://www.discoveryschool.com/schrockguide/index.html

Blue Web'N -- http://www.kn.pacbell.com/wired/blueWebn/

Teaching and Learning in a Network World
P. Hoffman and D. Lemke (Eds.)
IOS Press, 2000

CompSpeak 2050: How Talking Computers Will Completely Change Teaching, Learning, and Everything Else in the 21st Century

William Crossman, *Faculty, Vista Community College, Berkeley, CA; Director, CompSpeak 2050 Institute for the Study of Talking Computers and Oral Cultures,* ***<www.compspeak2050.org>*** *P.O. Box 20164, Oakland, CA 94620;* ***willcross@aol.com.*** *This article is a slightly revised version of Chapter 1 of the author's soon-to-be-published book, CompSpeak 2050: How Talking Computers Will Recreate an Oral Culture by Mid-21st Century.*

In the 21st Century, VIVOs (voice-in/voice-out computers using visual displays but no text) will make written language obsolete. Written language is essentially a technology created 6,000 to 10,000 years ago for storing and retrieving information. VIVOs will perform this same function more easily, efficiently, and universally without requiring people to learn to read and write. There will be no compelling reason for schools to teach literacy skills. By 2050, the electronically-developed nations will become oral cultures; by 2150, a worldwide oral culture will be in place. Today's push to develop VIVOs is a further step in the human evolutionary drive to move past written language's limits and return to the biogenetic, oral-aural, pre-alphabetic roots of human communication and information storage. Young people's choosing TV, telephone, stereo, and computer games over books, letter-writing, etc.--and the resulting literacy crisis that engulfs our schools--is not the result of mental laziness or poor schools, but is an irreversible symptom of this deeper evolutionary process. VIVOs will transform every area of human activity in the 21st Century, including education, the arts, human relations, politics, and commerce. Billions of nonliterate people, using VIVOs, will finally be able to access the world's stored information--if they can gain access to VIVOs. Access to VIVO technology looms as a key human rights issue of the 21st Century.

The 20th Century is behind us, the new millennium has arrived, and, in the United States:
*most people would rather talk to someone on the telephone than write to them;
*most people would rather watch TV than read a book;
*most schools and most school children are engulfed in a deep literacy crisis, with little hope for a breakthrough.

Why is all this happening now? Superficial explanations--such as blaming it on TV, on people's mental laziness or backwardness, or on the schools--simply won't do. Something much deeper, and more difficult to see, is going on.

The growing feelings of alienation from writing and reading, which school children and people of all ages are experiencing and expressing through their day-to-day behavior, are signs and symptoms of a profound historical, social, technological, and evolutionary change.

They are symptomatic of a massive shift that is taking place: away from the use of written language and back to the use of spoken language to communicate, store, and retrieve information in our daily lives.

In the United States and other electronically-developed countries, we're witnessing nothing less than the abandonment of reading and writing, of written language itself, and, in its place, the recreation of oral culture. The push to develop voice-recognition technology and VIVOs--Voice-In/Voice-Out computers that we can talk to and that can talk back to us--is part of this evolutionary leap.

It truly is evolutionary. Historically, before our human ancestors developed written language, they accessed stored information orally-aurally, by speaking and listening--as well as by seeing, smelling, tasting, and touching. They relied on their memories to store information that they heard--as well as saw, smelled, tasted, and touched--and they retrieved it for others by speaking and acting.

Six thousand to ten thousand years ago, people's memories were no longer efficient and reliable enough to store and retrieve the influx of new information that arose with the onset of the agricultural revolution. To transcend their memories' limits, our ancestors came up with a remarkable solution: written language.

It was a feat that required great imagination and complexity of thought and, in today's terms, involved the creation of: new software--pictographs and alphabets forming written languages; new hardware or the adaptation of old hardware to new tasks--pens, pencils, brushes, knives, chisels, inks, chalk, pigments, animal skins, paper, leaves, wood, stone; and new operations--writing and reading. Using this new technology, our ancestors freed themselves from the limits of human memory. Written language enabled them to freeze and thaw as much information as their hardware allowed.

Today, we in the electronically-developed countries view writing and reading as one of the necessities of human existence, as something we can't do without, like water, food, and sleep. This may be the view we see through our culturally-biased, pro-text eyeglasses, but it's just plain wrong. Not only is written language not necessary to human existence, but we could have reached today's level of information storage-retrieval without ever having created written language in the first place.

If some early society had found or carved a wooden, bone, or stone cylinder, coated it with beeswax, attached a porcupine quill to a hollow gourd, let the quill rest on the wax-coated cylinder, and spoken into the gourd while rotating the cylinder, written language might never have happened. Humanity might have gone right from storing and retrieving speech-based information by memory to doing it by phonograph without entering the world of print culture at all. Humanity's First Golden Age of oral culture might never have ended.

I'm overdramatizing this point somewhat to help lay the groundwork for a different view of written language. Throughout this article, I characterize written language as a technology, a technological solution to specific information-storage-retrieval problems that people faced at a specific moment in history 6,000 to 10,000 years ago. Like most technologies, written language will serve its function until some better technology comes along to replace it. Written language isn't an eternal verity. We can admire it, but we shouldn't worship it.

With written language about to make its exit, and its replacement already stepping through our front door, it is vital that we see written language clearly for what it is: a transitory technology. This reality-check will help us prepare ourselves to say "goodbye" to it and to welcome back its replacement: our old friend, spoken language.

Unlike written language, spoken language--by which I mean speech itself--wasn't/isn't a technology devised by people to overcome human limitations in the face of social and environmental changes. In this sense, spoken language isn't a technology at all. Though we humans created or devised particular spoken languages, we didn't create or devise spoken language itself any more than we created our circulatory systems.

Our ability to speak language, period, is an inborn characteristic of our species. We carry in our genes and our brains the capacity for spoken language. If the day ever arrives that we wave a final "goodbye" to spoken language--and to the sign languages used by people with hearing and/or speaking disabilities--we'll be waving "goodbye" to the species of human beings that we are.

In contrast to written language, spoken and sign language is "user friendly." As very young children, we just start understanding it and speaking or signing it. We don't have to spend years in school learning to speak. Nor does spoken language drive a wedge into the world's population the way written language does--dividing humanity into those who can read and write and those who can't. Everyone who is mentally and physically able can speak a language.

Historically, spoken language came--and had to come--to humans before written language. Biologically, speech or sign language comes--and has to come--to each child before literacy. This is because written languages are symbolic representations of spoken languages. Had we no spoken language, we could not have created written language. Written language may have emerged as the primary method used to store and retrieve information in certain areas of the world, but it is based on and derived from spoken language.

In the 21st Century, people with access to VIVO-computer technology will once again be able to use spoken language to access all stored information. Talking computers are going to make writing, reading, spelling, alphabets, punctuation, written numerals, music notation, and all other notational systems obsolete.

The obituary for written language won't be written. It will be spoken by someone talking to a VIVO computer in 2050.

Since the mid-19th Century, humanity has been waging a furious assault against written language. This has taken the form of people inventing and developing devices which use spoken language, rather than written language, to communicate, store, and retrieve information. A cornucopia of speech-based devices now exists which has simplified and sped up--and/or completely redefined--the tasks we formerly assigned to text and text-based devices. For the past 125 years, particularly in North America, Europe, and Japan, these speech-based devices have been relentlessly usurping the functions of the text-based devices.

The letter, the magazine, the newspaper, the broadside, the book, the flyer, the written advertisement, the memo or written message, the file, the written record, the official document, the written school exercise--all have come under attack. In some cases, direct or instantaneous oral-aural communication devices (telephone, telegraph, live radio, live television) have been doing the usurping. In other cases, devices which store information in the form of speech (phonograph, audiocassette, compact disc, "talkie" movie film, videocassette) have been responsible.

Since 1990, our minds and resources have turned to the development of talking computers. In our rush to create VIVOs, we're continuing the process Edison, Morse, Tesla, Bell, and their counterparts began.

E-mail appears to be an exception to the above: a form of written message whose popularity is surging in the electronically-developed countries. However, today we are already able to send and receive spoken e-mail, and, given this option, I predict that most of us will soon start speaking our messages instead of typing them. Goodbye e-mail; hello e-talk!

Why have we been so obsessed with researching and developing oral-aural replacements for written language? Because biologically, psychologically, and technologically, we have again hit limits on the efficiency and reliability of our main method for freezing and thawing information.

Formerly, as I mentioned above, it was the limits of human memory to retain the influx of information during the agricultural revolution that led people to create written language. For the last 125 years, it has been the *limits of written language use* that have driven people to seek and develop oral-aural replacements. I'll return to these limits in a moment.

Even though the scientific sector has been working overtime these past 125 years to develop oral-aural and non-text visual technologies, from the wax-cylinder phonograph to the talking computer, the true nature of this process and its goal--to supersede written language's limits by returning to oral-aural methods of information communication and storage--has been largely *undeclared, unacknowledged, and unconscious*, even among the chief developers themselves.

This article has, as one of its main objectives, to acknowledge this process and to raise it to the level of consciousness and awareness. If we understand what is happening and why, we'll be better able to evaluate it and direct its course.

VIVOs will be the last nail in written language's coffin. By making it possible for us to access stored information orally-aurally, talking computers will finally make it possible for us to replace all written language with spoken language. Once again, we'll be able to store and retrieve information simply by talking and listening--and by looking, too, but at graphics, not at text. With this giant step forward into the past, we're about to recreate oral culture on a more efficient and reliable technological foundation.

From a Darwinian perspective, written language is a 6,000-to-10,000-year-old bridge that humanity has been using to walk from our First Golden Age of oral culture to our Second. We undertook this journey to survive as a species. Six thousand to ten thousand years ago, lacking the ability to store and retrieve by memory the growing sum of survival information, our species faced two options: develop new storage-retrieval technology or self-destruct. That's when and why we created the written-language bridge.

As a species, humans have instinctively understood that any systematic failure in our ability to store and retrieve information is a threat to our survival. Now, we in the print-literate nations are instinctively reacting to the fact that written language--our stored-information accessor of choice--has hit its limits and is failing us.

It is failing us, first, because it is no longer able to do the tasks we created it to do and, second, because too many people are unable to use it. An example of the first: for most literate people, communicating, storing, and retrieving information by writing and reading is still far slower and more tedious than doing it by speaking.

Regarding the second, it's sufficient to remind ourselves that the great majority of the world's people, by conservative estimates 80% of humanity, including many living in the so-called print-literate nations, still can't use written language effectively. Most societies in the world today are still oral cultures, and very few of the world's societies--including the United States--possess either the enormous human and economic resources and/or the political will required to fully train their populations to write and read.

There's another reason--also related to evolution and natural selection--that we're leaving written language behind. In carrying out the historical commitment that we, in the print-literate societies, had made to written language, we have--largely unaware of our dangerous path--strayed too far away from our innate information-communication-storage-retrieval method: speech.

Our genes, nervous systems, muscles, and emotions have been sending us a crisis wake-up call, reminding us of our spoken-language survival mandate and telling us to return to our oral-aural roots, or else. Or else what? Or else the speech-deficiency-based physical and mental illnesses--similar in many ways to sun-, motion-, sleep-, and vitamin-deficiency illnesses--that began to strike the print-literate nations in the 19th Century and that became an epidemic in the late-20th Century, will continue to spread unchecked.

Since the late-1800s, we in the print-literate nations have been acting swiftly and positively--though mainly unconsciously--to avert this health crisis. We've been heeding the evolutionary mandate of our human physiology and psychology to reverse the widening gap between our present print-oriented selves and our innate, biogenetic, oral-aural selves. It seems clear to me now that the steps we have been taking to stem this epidemic include phasing out writing and reading entirely and phasing in speech-based devices including talking computers.

On some unconscious mental level, we seem to understand or believe that talking computers will help us to achieve the wellness and wholeness we seek. We seem to unconsciously understand that hooking ourselves up to these talking-computer I.V. units--IntraVIVOs?--will rid us of textual toxicity and pump us full of lifesaving orality. I am over-dramatizing again, but only a bit.

Located at the far end of the written-language bridge, the Second Golden Age of oral culture has been visible to us since the invention of the phonograph in 1877. We trekked the bridge toward our destination decade after decade through the 20th Century. By mid-21st Century, we will finally reach the bridge's end and step off into the future. Once across, we will never look back.

School children's declining literacy rate is a symptom of these deeper processes. As a group, young people in the electronically-developed countries have chosen oral-aural and non-print visual technologies--video, stereo, radio, film, telephone, and computer--as their preferred methods for accessing "live" and stored information.

These technologies, like written language, are external extensions of our brains' memory banks and our sense organs--mindparts located outside of our heads. But unlike written language, they allow us to communicate in the way that's most basic and familiar to us: through spoken language.

Most young people today instinctively understand this rock-bottomness of speech/spoken language. They are in touch with it. They feel it in their bones, their brains, their genes. Why should they read and write, so many young people ask, when they can listen and speak? They view the rules of writing as they view all rules imposed on them by adult society--as devices to dominate and control young people. And they're rebelling.

Students' refusal to go along with the program is causing our schools to develop a record of failure, as each twelfth-, eighth-, or third-grade class graduates with a weaker grasp of reading and writing than the prior year's twelfth-, eighth-, or third-grade class. Writing teachers are feeling discouraged and demoralized, and many have basically given up trying to teach it. The result: a downward spiral of writing-reading skills and stagnating test scores that became the school literacy crisis of the 1990s.

By 2050, if large numbers of students will have been able to gain access to talking computers, all this negativity and failure concerning writing and reading will be a distant memory. All education in the electronically-developed countries will be oral-aural and non-text visual. Students will use talking computers with optional monitors displaying icons, graphics, and visuals to freeze and thaw information.

Instead of the "three R's"--reading, 'riting, and 'rithmetic--students will focus on the "four C's"--critical thinking, creative thinking, compspeak, and calculators. I call it VIVOlutionary learning.

We won't have to wait until 2050. By *2005*, a student assigned to write an essay will be able to speak it into a VIVO computer, use VIVO's grammar-check to organize and correct it, "proofread" it by listening to VIVO repeat it, print it out, and submit it to the teacher for a grade.

The student will have proven two things. First, that any person--nonliterate as well as literate--with a talking computer will be able to produce a perfect written essay. Second, that *because* any person with a talking computer will be able to produce a perfect written essay, written language will have become obsolete.

Why should the student in the above example bother to print out a copy of the essay? Why should they bother with that final step of translating their spoken ideas into written language? Their teacher certainly doesn't need a written record of their ideas. Using their own VIVO, the teacher will be able to listen to the student's spoken ideas online and respond accordingly. Neither the student nor the teacher needs to write anything down in order for learning to occur and for education to take place.

In this scenario, the student and teacher are using their VIVOs exactly the way VIVOs are supposed to be used. Isn't that why we're developing VIVOs? Isn't that what they're for? Don't we *want* students to be able to input their ideas orally online and teachers to be able to access those ideas aurally? Voice-in, voice-out: simple.

We developed written language to store and retrieve information, and we are developing talking computers to perform the very same function. Because talking computers will do it more easily, quickly, efficiently, universally, and (ultimately) cheaply, they will replace written language. Simple.

We used to cut our grass with a scythe; then, we invented the push lawn mower and put the scythe in a museum; then, we invented the gasoline-engine lawn mower and put the push lawn mower in the museum. That's the way technology works, and the way we work with technology: we are forever replacing the old with the new.

In the case of written language, however, we are replacing a technology (written language) with a non-technology (spoken language), but we are giving the non-technology a new technological twist: an electronic echo, a gigantic memory capable of storing and retrieving an almost unlimited amount of information in the form of speech.

Written language was a technology created by our ancestors to help them deal with a specific set of historical needs and conditions in a specific historical period several thousand years ago. Today, we are creating VIVO technology to answer a different set of needs and conditions in our own historical period. Soon we'll be placing written language on the museum wall next to the scythe.

Just as some students today might join a choral group, karate club, or chess club as a pleasurable pastime, some mid-21st Century students might join a literacy club to learn written language for fun. But there will be no compelling reason why they would need to learn to read and write and, therefore, no compelling reason why they should have to learn it--or why their schools should have to teach it. Exit the school literacy crisis.

Not only education but also the arts and, possibly, international relations will be transformed in the shift from print to oral culture.

Imagine the literary arts without written language, and the musical arts without written music: a return to story*telling*, spoken poetry, and improvised music.

Imagine international relations without written language: dominant nations would no longer be able to force other nations to read and write in the former's "standard" languages--a traditional weapon of cultural domination--and would no longer be able to decide which individuals, in the dominated nations, would be allowed to become literate.

These are just two examples of areas in which VIVOs, or, more accurately, people using VIVOs, will reshape the world in the 21st Century. In this article, I take the viewpoint that *good* results *could possibly* come from the fact that talking computers will soon take over written language's job. Lovers of the written word--and I am one of you--I invite you to give the following ideas a hearing.

The creation of VIVOs will create new *potential opportunities* for people in three areas.

*** VIVOs will create new *potential opportunities* for the world's nonliterate and semiliterate people to be able to access--through speech or signing alone--the world's storehouse of information and knowledge. For the first time since the introduction of written language, people's nonliteracy or semi-literacy won't prevent their accessing all stored information.

Pre-VIVO electronic technologies have already actualized similar potential opportunities for millions, maybe billions, of people worldwide. Within a period of about sixty years, a huge amount of information that had been formerly inaccessible, because it had been stored in the form of written language, has become available to people who can't write or read. Radio, video, stereo, film, telephone, and computer have opened up an oral-aural and/or non-text visual universe of stored information for the non-readers and non-writers who have finally been able to gain access to these technologies.

Sixty years isn't a long time. The very existence of written language on Earth for sixty-hundred years or more has profoundly affected and reshaped all cultures and communities--even those that are still oral cultures. Now, even before VIVOs sprout from our wrists and lapels, radio, video, and the rest have been busily, and irreversibly, reshaping global reality once more.

*** VIVOs will create new *potential opportunities* for all people, whether literate or not, to instantaneously communicate *in all languages* with other speakers or information storage units. Using today's "old-fashioned" text-entry computers and text-translator software, a person can communicate in writing with another person who reads and writes another language. The problem is that both people must already be able to read, write, and enter text in at least one language, their own.

Using VIVOs, we won't need to know how to read or write, won't need to be verbally fluent in any language other than our own native language, and won't even need to understand a universal language like Esperanto. VIVO units will allow people around the world to speak easily with one another in their respective native languages, thanks to VIVO's simultaneous speech translation function. Electronic Esperanto!

*** VIVOs will create new *potential opportunities* to access stored information for many people who can speak and hear, or sign and see, but whose physical and/or mental disabilities make it difficult or impossible for them to write and/or read.

In these last three asterisked sections, I've italicized the words "potential opportunity" with good reason. The most that *the birth* of a new technology can possibly achieve is to open potential opportunities for people. These opportunities can only become actualized when people actually gain access to the technology and utilize it.

Here's a familiar example. Since most people in the world can speak and hear, they have the ability to use the telephone. But most of the world's people don't have access to telephones because of the high cost of service and/or the unavailability of service in their communities. The invention of the telephone has opened up the *potential opportunity* for everyone to speak across long distances, but using a telephone remains out of reach for the billions of people who haven't been able to get their hands on one.

The birth of a new technology, by itself, can't change anything. People having access to and using the new technology can create change and make history.

For the foreseeable future, which includes the VIVO Age of the 21st Century, the issue will continue to be: who controls the new technology and, therefore, who controls whom. As with all technology, talking-computer hardware and software will be developed, patented, copyrighted, programmed, manufactured, encrypted, sold, bought, leased, used, distributed, and shared--or not shared--by those with the wealth and resources to control these processes.

In my opinion, it would be great if all the nonliterate and semi-literate people around the world could actually start using VIVOs on January 1, 2010 to access the world's databanks. But it would be naive to think this will happen automatically just because the technology itself will exist on January 1, 2010. If people want access to talking computers, if we want to actualize the potential opportunities VIVO technology presents to us, we've got to figure out how to do it...and then do it.

The right to have access to the stored information, the collective knowledge, of our community, our society, and our world is a human right. The ability to read and write, print-literacy, is still the key that opens these information vaults. Yet, billions of people around the world are being denied access to this information because they remain nonliterate or semi-literate. Most of the world's people still haven't received their keys. Literacy has historically been treated as a privilege, rather than a right, by those who hold the master keys--and it's as true today as ever.

Most people in the world haven't even seen a library. If they were able to travel to a library, and if they were able to find its door open to them--for many libraries' doors would not be--they would still find the meanings of the sentences in the books on the library's shelves closed to them.

In this article, I say some negative-sounding things about writing and reading. For example, I say that they are about to become obsolete. This isn't intended as an attack on written language. It's merely an observation, part of a broader analysis presented here. And it's definitely not intended as an attack on, or a demeaning of, people worldwide who are striving to learn to write and read.

I have the greatest respect and admiration for children and adults around the world who are trying to achieve literacy. Today, a person's ability to write and read still raises for them new possibilities of communication, knowledge, social and political involvement, employment, enjoyment, self-esteem, creative expression, and much more.

The analysis presented here, rather than closing the doors of hope on those who lack and/or seek the literacy-key to information, communication, and knowledge, opens these doors wide for them. It says that the same VIVO-computer technology that will make written language obsolete will also create potential opportunities for the billions of nonliterate and semi-literate people throughout the world to tap into the world's store of information--without having to learn to read and write at all.

To all students and all others who wish to read and write, I still say: Go to school! Stay in school! Learn to read and write! We'll need it in our lifetimes!

I say this because written language isn't going to disappear overnight. It will take time: decades, two or three generations, maybe even a whole century. Yet, its eventual disappearance will be the end of a process that's already well underway.

It is ironic that, with the 21st Century's arrival, oral culture is growing in the print-saturated, electronically-developed countries at the exact moment that many electronically-undeveloped countries are earnestly launching literacy campaigns. The near-future course of literacy development in these latter countries is very difficult to predict. However, in the United States today, we need only to look around to confirm that a massive, rapid, electronically-aided decline in the number of writers-readers has begun.

We're witnessing the beginning of an earthshaking transformation of human society away from print culture toward oral culture. It will occupy and involve the energies of humankind from the beginning to the end of the 21st Century and will surely reshape every field of human activity. By 2050, in the United States and the other electronically-developed countries, the use of written language, of writing and reading, will mainly be a thing of the past.

One hundred years beyond, by 2150, all of the world's communities will again be oral cultures. VIVOs will link all of them--including those we build in space--into a single, oral-aural, information-access network: a true, worldwide oral culture.

There is a book, yet to be written, titled *The Future*, that is already *out-of-print*..

Teaching and Learning in a Network World
P. Hoffman and D. Lemke (Eds.)
IOS Press, 2000

Online Course Design Using the Teach/Learn/Assess Model

By Susan V. Crosson,
Santa Fe Community College, Gainesville, FL, USA
http://inst.santafe.cc.fl.us/~scrosson

What am I doing? Somehow my course needs to have a web presence. I am a teaching professional not a "techie". How do I go about going to distance successfully?

These questions and feelings are natural when beginning course design for the Internet. The purpose of this paper is to support you, the faculty, as you design successful web-based courses. First, you will cover the basics of designing a course whether it's on campus or online. The importance of having an overall design plan and course goals. Second, you will consider the specific teaching, learning, and assessment aspects of your course. How will you deliver or teach your course. What learning activity choices will you offer. How will you design assessment alternatives that link to your course goals. Finally you will complete the teach/learn/assess process by bringing together your various design pieces into your well-planned and designed course.

Basics of Course Design

On Campus and Online: The teach/learn/ assess process is common to both on campus and online courses. Whether the educational setting is on campus or online, faculty teach course material, students learn it, and together they assess the knowledge transfer to determine its success. The teach/learn/assess process is a continuous spiral. New knowledge builds on the knowledge base established in prior cycles. The T/L/A process is inherent in every course.

On Campus Course Design Basics

The T/L/A Process on Campus...

Do Homework, Participate
LEARN:
Activities to Gain Confidence

Write Papers, Exams
ASSESS:
Demonstrate Breadth and Depth

Read Book, Come to Class
TEACH:
Deliver knowledge, skills, abilities, attitudes, and values...

On campus, the teach/learn/assess process mostly occurs at a specific time and place--the class period and in the classroom. Faculty teach students in a classroom setting a certain number of minutes each week. Students learn by attending and participating in class, reading their textbook and doing homework. Finally, professors and students determine what has been learned through students demonstrating their knowledge on exams or in papers.

The advantages to on campus classes for faculty include:

- face-to-face interactions with students;
- immediate student feedback;
- student contact in class and during office hours can make grading easier;
- administrative convenience;
- easy access to libraries, labs, and tutors; and
- in person experience with a diverse, cross cultural student body.

The disadvantages to on campus classes for faculty include:

- hard to reach every student, especially shy ones;
- motivating students to do the work or come to class;
- class schedule constraints;
- on campus facility and technology constraints;
- in large classes, students can hide;
- student apathy and bad attitudes;
- redundant questions
- difficult to make course material real.

Think about what you enjoy most about teaching on campus. These are your non-negotiables when designing an online course. In other words, what matters most to you in teaching. They are your valuables in making the teach/learn/assess process uniquely your design.

Think about what you do not enjoy about teaching on campus. Can you out source them to the Internet based T/L/A platform? How can you do them differently? Stay alert to the possibilities and opportunities to keep the best of what you do and how you can rethink the rest!

Online Course Design Basics

The T/L/A Process Online...

Create Activities
LEARN:
Activities to Gain Confidence

Assess Outcomes
ASSESS:
Demonstrate Breadth and Depth

Identify Resources
TEACH:
Deliver knowledge, skills, abilities, attitudes, and values...

This course process of teach/learn/ assess must also be in a good distance learning course design. Being released from time and place constraints offers design possibilities not practical in an on campus course. Faculty can identify teaching resource strategies other than lectures and make them available to students in different formats i.e., text, video, Internet. Students can engage in a variety of learning activities created in a variety of mediums to gain confidence i.e., Internet, spreadsheet, paper, e-mail. Also, pre and post assessment opportunities can be expanded outside of the classroom using secure online testing and real world applications.

The advantages to adding an online component include:

- able to each more students on a one-to-one basis,
- flexible scheduling,
- on demand student learning,
- encourages technology skills,
- students held accountable for learning,
- variety of learning modes, and
- use of numerous learning resources.

The disadvantages to adding an online component include:

- course more time consuming for faculty to prepare and teach,
- student retention,
- harder to connect and maintain dialog with students,
- misperception of course workload by students,
- technical support for course,
- technical knowledge required to add and maintain an online component
- student online readiness.
- difficult to monitor exams or work, who's work is it?

From the advantages and disadvantages, it is clear that faculty who accepts the challenge of adding an online component to their courses will have much to consider and do. Before you begin adding online components, take time to develop your overall course design. In the long run you will save time and redesign headaches. A plan will allow you to thoughtfully add value to your course. Each component will have a purpose and enhance the overall T/L/A process. Consider adding a new feature or component periodically instead of rolling out a complete course. You will learn from each added feature and successive projects will build on your past successes. Having a systematic design plan is essential to keep the best of what you do and have reason to change the rest.

Faculty having on campus and online experience contributed to the following list of similarities and differences between teaching on campus and online:

Similarities and Differences

- Same Content
- Same Course Goals
- Same T/L/A Cycle
- Same Resources
- Still interacting with students

- Reach/Teach students differently
- Static v. flexible class schedule
- Communication less verbal more written
- On-line requires more advanced planning
- Technical headaches

Notice the similarities listed are really your comfort zone in course development. You already know the course content. You are aware of many T/L/A resources. You know how to deliver a course effectively. You are good at interacting with students. The differences are your challenges in online course design. You begin to think and challenge yourself to succeed in a different kind of classroom--one that requires a lot of advanced planning, can be full of technical glitches, requires more writing and less talking, and reaches students in new ways. Take a moment and record your impressions for your course's overall design. How can the Internet compliment your course design?

Begin with the End in Mind: When designing any course, it is essential to set curriculum, course, professor, and student goals. By establishing these desired outcomes at the beginning of the course design process, you will find it easier to identify appropriate teaching strategies, assign relevant learning activities, and tailor assessments to adequately measure clear appropriate outcomes. Also explicit goals will answer some of the externally driven performance expectations exerting pressure over your courses. Employers expect work ready employees. Governing boards and states are starting to fund education based on student performance outcomes. Other funding sources like grants and contract training demand measurable results. Thus, many are interested in what you expect in your courses. If you are able to put into words your goals, all will benefit from a clearer understanding of what your courses are designed to do.

Before examining your student goals, consider what your curriculum, course, and professor goals should be. They set your educational overview. The curriculum goal should establish the **context** of your course in the broader educational plan that leads to a job or higher degree. The course goal should express the "how" or **course structure** of your course. The professor's goal should express your **mission or vision**--the "why" a professor values what they do. Here are examples:

Begin with the End in Mind...

Curriculum Goal: *To create courses required for transfer to an upper division School in the state.*

Course Goal:

•*Teach Course Content,*

•*Create Learning Activities to Gain Confidence in Knowledge, and*

•*Assess Mastery*

Course content offers students a menu of learning approaches to master the course's learning objectives. Different learning styles are apparent in the various approaches. When the student is "prepared for class", they engage in the various learning activities. The learning activities encourage a variety of thinking processes and require students to integrate the learning objectives of the course. Assessment occurs both before and after teaching and learning to determine a measurable outcome of the learning process.

Professor Goal: *To create a learning process as individual as each student requires to master the course content and actively apply with confidence what's learned.*

Your Student goal should express the student **learning outcome** your course wants to achieve. Do not confuse a course's learning objectives for student learning outcomes. These learning objectives are curriculum goals. Your student learning outcome centers on what developmental stage of learning and knowing you want your students to achieve as a result of your course. This learning outcome metric is based on the well-validated developmental psychology theories of learning stages. One by Baxter-Magolda expresses the developmental stages of learning and knowing as follows:

Student Goal: *My Success is a student who...*

Absolute knowing: knows the facts and can answer questions like how, what, where, and when.

Transitional knowing: can apply the methods or knowledge to specified situations and can compare and contrast methods.

Independent knowing: uses the knowledge to form opinions in nonspecific situations and can answer the question why.

Contextual knowing: integrates their knowledge into a broad context and is able to evaluate perspectives to make reasoned decisions and policies using this knowledge.

Based on Baxter Magolda's Developmental Stages of Learning and Knowing

Take a moment and review your impressions for your course's overall design, what Curriculum, Course, Professor, and Student goals will you set? By declaring them, you begin your course design with your goals in mind.

Teach/Learn/Assess Model Specifics

Teaching: Teaching is shifting. Faculty responsibilities are expanding and the learning environment is changing. Remember when your primary purpose was to teach knowledge? Now you teach content, technical and thinking skills, writing and communication abilities, work ready attitudes, and ethical values, to name a few. The list keeps expanding. No wonder many faculty are counting the days to retirement. But it's exciting too. As the teaching/learning paradigm shifts, it is your challenge to thoughtfully manage the change in your courses.

What might it mean to teach differently? Traditionally, a course has been teacher centered and knowledge based. Now, the focus has shifted to learning and learning centered. Students are opting for learn anytime, anywhere with distance courses and with multiple educational providers. How can you address these students' academic needs and teach your expanding course responsibilities for content, skills, abilities, attitudes, and values?

One way to reach students is to recognize their learning focus or style may vary. Remember the student who says, "I don't get it, explain it another way." or the student who always tries to apply their new learning to a different situation? Students approach learning with different questions. Some learn by asking **why** is this important. Others want to know **what** the facts are. Another group is interested in the process of **how** it works. And still others take what is learned and ask **what if.** These questions indicate a student focus preference. Faculty too tends to have a personal teaching/learning preference. Being aware of your preferred focus and remembering to embed all four inquiries into your teaching and assessing will improve the educational experience of all your students. As you design your course materials remember to include Why? What? How? and What if?

Another consideration of the academic needs of your students is to recognize their learning modality differences. Some learn by reading the book and taking notes. Others prefer an audio or videotape of the course. Still others have to do it before they learn the material. The best way students absorb knowledge may not be the way you teach. So how can you design your online course to reach more students? Try to identify your various teaching resources by learning modalities. Does your course's teaching resources serve all of the learning modalities? Consider developing and offering teaching resources that address each learning modality. Then students can chose to see it, hear it, read/write it, or do it to learn new course material. They control the teaching menu to your course.

Take a moment and review your course's overall design and goals, record your thoughts on how you will teach your course.

Learning: Encouraging students to learn and master your course is challenging. Old student learning assumptions like "learning equals seat time" tend to muddy the expectation that the responsibility to learn is theirs alone. Fortunately, adding an online component shifts students into a new learning/teaching paradigm released from the old student assumptions. Consider adding value and relevance to your students learning activities of your online course, by linking your course assignments with your course's student goal. If you are able to categorize your student learning activities by Bloom's Taxonomy of Cognitive Objectives, goal appropriate learning activities can be created and assigned.

Creating Learning Activities based on
Bloom's Taxonomy of Cognitive Objectives:

Knowledge: identifying and recalling information

Comprehension: selecting and using facts or ideas

Application: using facts, rules, theories, or principles in specific situations

Analysis: separating the whole into parts to see relationship and discover the structure of an idea or concept

Synthesis: combining parts or facts to develop new,creative ideas

Evaluation: developing opinions or making decisions on materials, information, or problem situations

- For the student goal of Absolute knower, assign learning activities meeting Bloom's Knowledge and Comprehension objectives.
- For the Transitional student goal, learning activities that target Bloom's Application objective are appropriate.
- For the Independent student, learning activities meeting Bloom's Analysis and Synthesis cognitive objectives should be assigned.
- Finally, for the Contextual student goal, include learning activities that focus on Bloom's Synthesis and Evaluation cognitive objectives.

In addition, consider including learning activities and assignments in your course using all learning modalities (I see, I hear, I read/write, I do) to facilitate the learning/teaching exchange. What choices will your students have when learning and practicing course material? Do the activities match your curriculum, course, professor, and student goals?

Take a moment and review your course's overall design and goals, record your thoughts on what learning assignment choices your course will offer.

Assessing: The teach/learn/assess process is a continuous spiral. New knowledge builds on the knowledge base established in prior cycles. If you can have an accurate picture of what a student knows both before and after the learning/teaching exchange, it will help you determine if learning has occurred. Devising appropriate pre and post assessments of course mastery is challenging but doable if you focus on your course curriculum and student goals. Consider offering only outcomes based assessments. In other words, build your course learning objective assessment options using your student goal as your guide. Your students will appreciate your tests being at the same level as your teaching and learning activities.

Look again at the four student goal choices, try to match them with the four learning focus questions: Why? What? How? and What if?

- What question does the Absolute knower prefer? *What*
- What question does the Transitional knower ask most often? *How?*
- What question is the favorite of the Independent knower? *Why?*
- What inquiry does the Contextual knower pursue? *What if*

If you assess at the Absolute level then the recalling of facts and terms is appropriate. In other words, the "what" of your course. If you assess at the Transitional level then you would stress the application of course material or ask for students to compare and contrast course material. In other words, the "how" of your course. If you assess at the Independent level then students would be asked for their analyses and opinions of course issues. In other words, the "why" of your course. If you assess at the Contextual level then students would be assessed through multi-perspective case evaluations where they would offer well-reasoned decisions and policies. In other words, the "what if" of your course.

Take a moment and review your course's overall design and goals, record you thoughts about your assessment resources and student goal relevant testing methodologies.

Completing the Teach/Learn/Assess Process

Finally complete the teach/learn/assess process by bringing together your teach, learn, and assess elements into a cohesive course. Initially you will do this when you develop your overall course plan and goals. Then, as you add course design elements, you will repeat the T/L/A process. Remember...

Successful Online Course Design

- **No Turnkey Solutions**
- **Expresses You**
- **Continuously Challenges**
- **Delights Students!**

Teaching and Learning in a Network World
P. Hoffman and D. Lemke (Eds.)
IOS Press, 2000

Pedagogy-Based Technology Training

David P. Diaz[1] and Kevin F. Bontenbal[2]
Cuesta College, P.O. Box 8106, San Luis Obispo, CA 93403, USA
zaiddave@thegrid.net[1] kbontenb@bass.cuesta.cc.ca.us[2]

Abstract. This article examines the difference between technical- versus pedagogy-based training in preparing faculty to create and use technology-based educational products for the classroom. A discussion of the influence of learning theory on instruction and how this affects ones choice of instructional technology is also exemplified.

1. Introduction

The use of technology is an immanent concern at many educational institutions. More and more colleges are interested in providing training for their faculty that will enable them to create technology-based educational products and use them to aid the teaching/learning process. The technological field is a prime example of an area in which increasingly rapid external environmental changes will require more rapid responses than traditional training approaches can provide. Educators are in great danger of losing a competitive advantage in serving their students/clients if they are not able to respond quickly to the changing technological landscape. Further, unless the deficiencies of traditional training programs are successfully addressed, many institutions will find their faculty resistant to implementing instructional technologies.

Using technology to enhance the educational process involves more than just learning how to use specific pieces of hardware and software. It requires an understanding of pedagogical principles that are specific to the use of technology in an instructional setting. A model for training and development that emphasizes pedagogy-based training, and promotes team-based product development, is illustrated in Figure 1.

2. Technical- versus Pedagogy-based Training

Traditional technical-based training focuses on familiarizing the trainee with the mechanics of how a particular piece of hardware or software works. This type of training is hardware/software dependent and attempts to transfer specific technical skills to the trainee. For example, a technical-based training approach to learning about e-mail would focus on the specific mechanical aspects and features (e.g., creating and editing mail rules, or attaching files) of a particular e-mail application (e.g., Outlook, Eudora, etc.).

In contrast, pedagogy-based training focuses on preparing the trainee to implement technology skills and acquired knowledge in an instructional setting. It is hardware/software independent and attempts to educate the trainee on how to use newly gained technical skills in the teaching/learning setting. Pedagogy-based training would approach the e-mail scenario by focusing on how e-mail might enhance and/or support instruction, and how e-mail technologies can match differing student learning preferences.

The preceding should not be misconstrued as advocating pedagogy-based training over technical-based training; both types of training are necessary to promote comprehensive and effective technology-mediated instruction. However, to ensure good instructional practice, as well as student success, instructional goals should drive technology-training needs. Thus, pedagogy-based training should be addressed prior to, and separate from, traditional technical-based training.

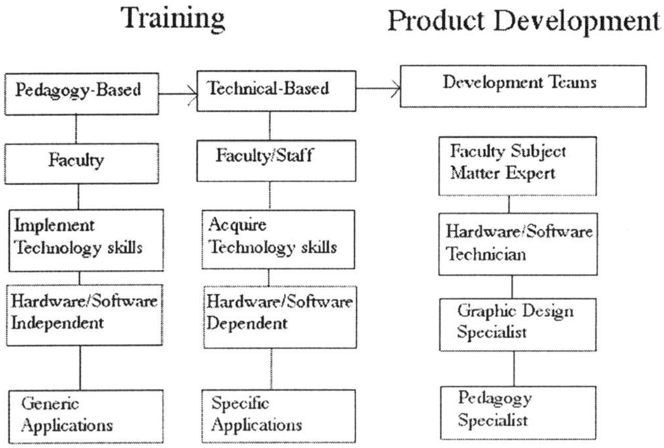

Figure 1. Training and Product Development Model.

3. Product Development Teams, a Realistic Approach

Traditional training/development approaches have placed the burden of educational product development on the shoulders of faculty. Most colleges offer technology workshops designed to help faculty acquire various technology skills. The purpose of these traditional classes is to teach faculty to develop their own technology products (e.g., web sites, multimedia presentations, etc.). Unfortunately for most teachers, the creation of these products requires multiple skills, more skills than can be practically mastered given the typical faculty workload. To create a multimedia presentation, for example, faculty would need to learn to use multimedia presentation software, digitizing hardware and software, have a knowledge of principles of graphic design, and even be acquainted with the unique pedagogy skills for using multimedia to enhance the learning environment. Product development teams are a way to bring innovative, high-quality products to the market (i.e., classroom) in a time-efficient, cost-effective manner. By using a team approach, institutions can distribute the workload of product development across individuals and departments. This is not only more time and energy efficient, but it also serves as an integrated training mechanism that helps team members to learn from each other.

These teams could be comprised of a faculty person, who would provide the product concept, and other specialists including digitizing technician, software specialist, graphic design specialist and technology pedagogy specialist. In a team approach, faculty would share their instructional concept with the rest of the team, who would then work together to bring the project to fruition.

4. The Influence of Learning Theory on Instruction

Pedagogy-based training begins by helping teachers understand the role of learning theory in the design and function of class activities, and in the selection and use of instructional technologies. The following brief summary will explain the prominent features of two main educational theories: "instructivism" and "constructivism," and discuss the implications for technology training. Though obviously an oversimplification of learning theory, the following discussion is meant to provide a simple and applicable "working theory" of learning. For a fuller treatment of learning theories, the reader is advised to look elsewhere [1-3].

The traditional, teacher-centered, "instructivist," learning theory reinforces a view that knowledge is attained passively by information transfer from a knowledgeable "authority" figure (teacher) to the learner. Knowledge (reality) exists independent of, and external to, the learner. Thus, an instructivist teacher assumes the responsibility for obtaining this knowledge and controlling the learning process through the "distribution" of knowledge. This approach clearly places the emphasis for learning on the dispenser of knowledge (i.e., teacher), and on the method of dispensing information. Instructivism leads quite naturally to a lecture format, a dualistic (i.e., "black and white") view of knowledge, and a passive learning perspective.

Though it has been shown that actively involving students in discussion fosters retention of information, application of knowledge, and development of critical thinking skills, between 70% and 90% of professors still use the traditional lecture as their instructional strategy of choice [4]. Why is this? In many cases, teachers teach as they have been taught. Since an instructivist learning theory has prevailed for quite some time, it is understandable why so many instructors have used a teacher-centered approach in the classroom, and also why most traditional students tend to exhibit dependent (passive) learning styles [5]. Perhaps many educators are simply replicating their own traditional instructivist training.

An instructivist view of teaching/learning promotes three predominate types of communication (Figure 2). According to instructivist principles, learning flows in a mostly unidirectional path, proceeding from the knowledgeable authority (teacher), or from instructional content, to the passive learner. Though many teachers employ methods that attempt to engage students, they often apply them in ways consistent with a predominately instructivist worldview. For example, an instructor may employ a "Socratic" or question/answer style in the classroom, however if the teacher is "leading" students toward pre-planned learning objectives, then this application of the Socratic method is still instructivist-based.

Educational theory has been changing throughout the 20th century [6]. Dewey, in the early 1900's noticed that students who were interested in their subjects applied more effort to their studies. This idea shaped the concept of "student learning preferences." So did the curriculum experiments of the 1930's, which promoted a curriculum designed to meet the future work needs of post-Depression-era students. In following suit, Thorndike encouraged "transfer training" that is, training that could be transferred to real-world workplace environments.

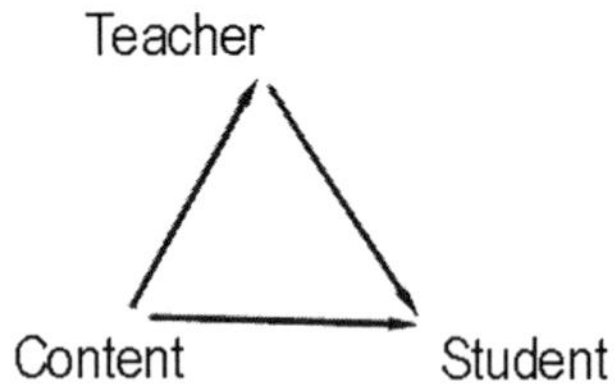

Figure 2. Facilitating Communication: Basic View.

These developments led to the current "constructivist" theory: that "learners are able to construct their own knowledge" with guidance from their teachers. Instead of being passive recipients of information and knowledge, students become more active in the learning process and are placed closer to the center of the instructional experience. The constructivist learning perspective asserts that the learner constructs new knowledge through a process of relating new information to prior knowledge and experience [7]. According to the constructivist approach, teachers become guides rather than dispensers of knowledge, and instructional practice places more importance on the role of the student in constructing knowledge. Thus, the adult learning theory paradigm has shifted from a teacher-centered towards a learner-centered environment [8, 9].

Constructivist learning theory paves the way to a multi-dimensional view of communication (Figure 3). Constructivist practice facilitates reciprocal communication and a more balanced participation between educational participants. Using this approach, teachers can employ collaborative learning techniques that allow students to combine efforts at solving a problem, or in task management. Further, teachers interact with other teachers, as well as with content, to facilitate professional and personal growth (i.e., staff development, conferences, etc.). Finally, "smart" technologies allow one application to interact with other applications (e.g., search engines) to cull data based on specific queries. This content-to-content interaction will become more commonplace and specialized as information management struggles to keep pace with the information explosion.

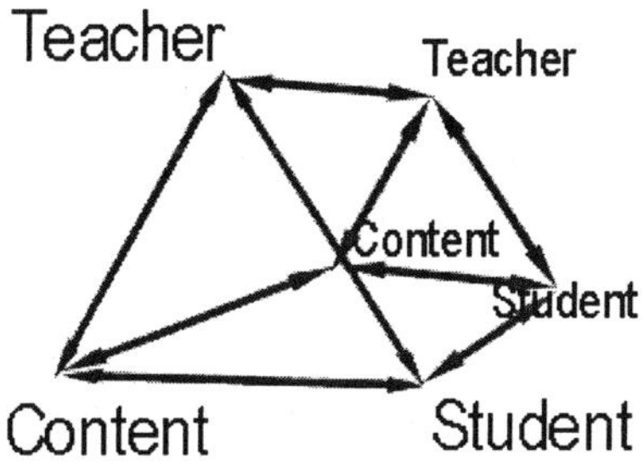

Figure 3. Facilitating communication: 3-D View.

5. The Influence of Learning Theory on Technology Selection

For practical purposes, we view learning theory as a continuum between instructivism on the one hand, and constructivism on the other. The extent to which teachers see themselves as instructivist versus constructivist, implicitly determines the extent to which classroom activities are based on teacher or student preferences, and guides the selection of instructional technologies. Instructional technology selection is based on the type of com-munication desired, which in turn is based on one's predominate learning theory (Figure 4).

Selection of Instructional Technologies

· Instructivist	· Constructivist
· Teacher focused	· Student focused
· Learning objectives	· Student learning preferences
· Activities support objectives	· Activities match learning preferences
· Technology selection	· Technology selection

Figure 4. Selecting Instructional Technologies.

An example of an instructivist implementation would be the posting of lecture notes on a course web site for students to read and/or study. Posting lecture notes would facilitate a passive, unidirectional information exchange from teacher to student. On the other hand, a constructivist approach might be to create a threaded discussion site or establish a listserv to facilitate communication and discussions on lecture topics covered in class. This approach is more active and expands communication in a multi-directional manner. Thus, a constructivist approach employs technology to engage the student, facilitate reciprocal communication, and foster an interactive learning environment.

6. Conclusion

In preparing faculty to create and use technology-based educational products for the classroom, a new approach to training is necessary. Technology training for faculty should at the very least include a discussion of learning theory. Instructors should be made aware of the two predominant learning theories (instructivism/constructivism), and should determine to what extent they ascribe to each theory. This process is essential for helping faculty understand the factors that determine the design of instructional activities and the choice of instructional technologies. In conjunction with a discussion of learning theory, instructors should also be aware of student learning styles and how instructional activities relate to and encourage these styles. And finally, an integrated approach to technology training should incorporate both pedagogy and technical skills, and should promote team-based educational product development. This comprehensive approach to technology training and product development will help ensure that faculty are favorably positioned to meet the demands of a changing technological landscape, as well as meet the unique needs and expectations of students in the 21st century.

References

[1] Duffy, T. M., & Cunningham, D. J. (1998). Constructivism: Implications for the design and delivery of instruction. In D. H. Jonassen (Ed.), Handbook of research for educational communications and technology. New York, NY: Simon & Schuster Macmillan.

[2] Miller, S. M., & Miller, K. L. (1999).. Using instructional theory to facilitate communication in web-based courses. Educational Technology & Society 2(3), 106-114.

[3] Ornstein, A. C., & Hunkins, F. P. (1993). Curriculum: Foundations, principles and issues (2nd ed.). Boston: Allyn and Bacon.

[4] Gardiner, L. F. (1998). Why we must change: The research evidence. The NEA Higher Education Journal, pp. 71-88.

[5] Grasha, A. F. (1996). Teaching with style. Pittsburgh, PA: Alliance.

[6] Tyler, R. W. (December 1986/January 1987). The five most significant curriculum events in the twentieth century. Educational Leadership, 44, (4), 36-38.

[7] Olgren, C. H. (1998). Improving learning outcomes: The effects of learning strategies and motivation. In C. Gibson (Ed.) Distance learners in higher education: Institutional responses for quality outcomes (pp. 77-95). Madison, WI: Atwood.

[8] Berge, Z., & Collins, M. (1995). Computer-mediated communication and the online classroom in distance learning. Computer-Mediated Communications Magazine [On-line], 2(4), 6-12. Available: http://sunsite.unc.edu/cmc/mag/1995/apr/berge.html

[9] Schuyler, G. (1997). A Paradigm shift from instruction to learning. ERIC Digests [Online], Available: http://www.gseis.ucla.edu/ERIC/digests/dig9802.html

Teaching and Learning in a Network World
P. Hoffman and D. Lemke (Eds.)
IOS Press, 2000

Maintaining Large and Small Corporate Websites: San Jose City College's Website Administration Program

Lucy Dodge
Title III Activity Director, CIS Department Coordinator
San Jose City College
2100 Moorpark Ave.
San Jose, CA 95128

1. Program Goals and Objectives

San Jose City College's two programs, Web Site Administration and Web Application Solutions, will offer classes designed to give students the necessary skills in administering a Web site and in creating applications for the Web to compete in a rapidly changing job market. In keeping with the range of new technologies associated with the growth of the Internet, San Jose City College provides courses that cover a variety of skills necessary to support enterprise-wide intranets, internets, and extranets. These two technical degrees include classes that cover both the programming and networking skills necessary to implement interactive, dynamic technologies supported on many corporate Web sites. Students will be able to obtain a degree in either:

- Web Site Administration - managing a Web site and configuring a Web server
- Web Application Solutions - writing application solutions for a Web site

Students will also be able to obtain certificates of competency, specialization, and achievement by taking a combination of subject-related courses.

Web Site Administration

Upon successful completion of the Web Site Administration program, students will be able to:

- Configure and customize different Web servers on various platforms
- Troubleshoot Web applications and Web server software
- Establish evaluation standards for different types of Web servers and Web software applications running on different platforms
- Use Web server extensions to incorporate support for applications into a Web server
- Integrate interactive forms and database applications into Web pages
- Identify the required browser plug-ins and customization required for client and server browsers
- Integrate various Web technologies used within corporate environments to distribute information, obtain feedback from customers, and publish Web pages
- Identify the structure and content of metadata used for representing information about a Web document
- Create a secure Web application that accepts and submits e-commerce data to a Web server
- Understand basic networking concepts as applied to the Web, e.g., TCP/IP, domain names, clients and servers, and authentication.
- Use and evaluate various types of Web security systems, proxy servers, and firewalls
- Load, maintain, edit, publish and download files on different systems

- Create Internet e-mail lists and assign aliases and manage Web log files
- Debug and fix Web application client and server errors
- Set up, customize, and maintain site navigation and search tools
- Write Web searches to access database files on a client computer

Web Application Solutions

Upon successful completion of the Web Application Solutions program, students will be able to:

- Use JavaScript with tools such as plug-ins and Java
- Identify security holes and common bugs
- Use JavaScript to design interactive applications that can access data in a database management system (DBMS)
- Build ActiveX components and write CGI scripts for Web mailing and customer feedback forms
- Write programs using scripting languages such as Perl and JavaScript to supplement server- or client-side CGI programs
- Develop customized components for applications
- Extend pages with third party and custom-built controls
- Develop code safety techniques
- Use proven debugging techniques
- Write customized courses for online distribution
- Compile scripts with OLE automation objects
- Create Web applications using Perl libraries available on the Web
- Write CGI scripts to send information to Web browsers
- Build databases, bulletin boards, and e-mail response applications
- Identify ways to avoid security holes and unsafe practices
- Use forms to transfer information from a Web browser to a CGI program
- Use Perl to analyze log files, manage cookies, and assign passwords

2. Course Descriptions

Table 1. Web Programming Courses

Course	Title	Description
CIS 23	JavaScript Programming for the Web	This is an introductory course in the use of JavaScript. In this course, students learn how to use a cross-platform scripting language such as JavaScript to create interactive Web pages. The course covers forms, communicating with other Web tools, and customizing Web pages.
CIS 24	CGI and Perl Programming for the Web	This course is intended for students who have a preliminary knowledge of programming and HTML. The course teaches students how to write CGI scripts using Perl, to work with forms, searchable databases, and e-mail responses. Students will use CGI scripts to retrieve and manipulate data in Web pages and Web page databases. This is not a complete Perl programming class; it covers only the commands in Perl that are necessary to make Web pages interactive.
CIS 25	VBX and ActiveX Controls	In this course, students build components that enable interactive content for the Web. Students design their own ActiveX controls, develop property sheets, and learn debugging techniques. They also incorporate ActiveX tools such as document containers and OLE automation objects into applications designed for the Web.
CIS 26	Designing Web-Based Courses and Training Materials	This course covers local vs. public Web site presentations, users' expectations from online courses, chat-rooms, evaluation of effective Web-based training materials and ways to promote interactivity on the Web. This course provides those who are involved in designing online courses hands-on experience with the basic requirements for creating a successful course. It covers various online tools devoted to this purpose. Students will learn the advantages and disadvantages of creating online applications and the special requirements of these courses. This course is designed for instructors, writers, editors, illustrators, and any individuals who need to create online, interactive tools.
CIS 27	Web Application Solutions	This is a second level course which provides an in-depth discussion of Internet file formats such as HTML, VRML, XML, DOM, RDF, and CSS used for documents, video and sound clips. It also covers data encryption procedures, e-commerce applications, Internet file formats, and the use of Java applets in creating Web solutions for corporate and academic Web sites.
CIS 28	Web Site Administration #1	This is a first level course that covers the basic information and tools required to establish a Web site in a business or academic environment. The course covers Web servers, Internet tools, CORBA, networking protocols, and Web-based formats such as MIME, HTTP, host and proxy servers. The course also addresses the issues of data warehousing and database tools used to access pages on the Web.
CIS 29	Web Site Administration #2	This course is intended for students who are already familiar with programming and HTML. The course gives students an understanding of operating systems and site administration tools as they relate to Web site programming, design, and publishing. The course covers advanced Web site management using CORBA applications, client-server solutions, and network performance monitors. It gives students criteria to use when evaluating the effectiveness of firewalls, media backups, server performance tools, and various security solutions such as packet-filtering. This course is designed to help prepare students to pass the International Webmasters Association certification exams.

3. Program Rationale

The Internet continues to increase in popularity driven by the rapid growth of these factors:

- A healthy and competitive Internet access provider market
- Enhanced bandwidth becoming available to businesses and homes
- Development of inexpensive standardized tools for publishing on the Web

At the same time, more sophisticated software and technology, such as future generations of browser software (Java, VRML, etc.) are developing. Because of these trends, we need to provide additional courses that offer students the skills necessary to support sophisticated enterprise-wide intranets, internets, and extranets. The need for web masters who are skilled in client/server programming is increasing dramatically. Because of this demand for programming expertise, we also need to offer our students courses in using Java, Visual BASIC, and Perl-based CGI scripts that support the following interactive procedures available on many corporate web pages:

- Feedback forms such as those found on Technical Support web pages
- Credit card order forms
- FTP and SMTP e-mail systems
- Password-protected technical information pages
- Automated web publishing procedures that enable employees to use a standardized template when submitting web pages

4. Community Support

Community resources have provided input into the development of the curriculum. Those in industry who are directly involved in establishing web sites have been contacted for information related to the proposed curriculum and the skills we need to teach students who plan to become web site administrators. As a result of our having solicited input from our industry contacts, the curriculum will more than likely serve the needs of our students who will be seeking employment as either interns or full-time employees during or after they have completed their training at SJCC.

For students to achieve the goal of being hired as interns or full-time employees, we must not only provide state-of-the-art skills to our students but also work-experience opportunities. The SJCC Workforce Initiative Network (WIN) Program staff members have expertise in marketing our students so they can compete in Silicon Valley's ever-competitive job market. The WIN program, which maintains a database of potential employers, will continue to ensure that internships and job placements are maintained so that successful results can be tracked for program evaluation and modification. Furthermore, regional community college job placement organizations are currently meeting to develop ways of increasing job placements and enhancing regional employer partnerships.

As the Web Site Administration program grows, the services of the WIN program will be used to increase relationships with employers and opportunities for student internships and job placements. Documentation of internships and job placements will continue to be maintained to sufficiently measure successful results. In addition, a regional community college job placement consortium is currently meeting to increase job placements in this area and enhance employer partnerships regionally.

This curriculum will not only prepare students for employment in industry but also in the academic area. Currently, community colleges hire individuals to manage Web development in both the instructional and administrative areas. Often, the instructional web master manages faculty and student web sites while the administrative web master works for Computing Services, the administrative division of the campus. Job opportunities in both these areas will continue to increase according to current predictions.

5. Employment Information

According to California Employment Development Department Labor market industry Trends and Outlook for Santa Clara County for 1995 to 2002, data processing occupations, including "computer programming services and the development and production of prepackaged computer software, will continue to record some of the fastest job growth in the country." In addition, business services, which includes not only computer programming services but also advertising, security, personnel supply services, "...will grow by 60,3000 jobs during the seven year period." In general, the entire services area will add "97,600 jobs and account for 50 percent of the overall non-agricultural growth in Santa Clara County." [1]

Detailed trends from America's Career InfoNet indicate that database administrators, computer support specialists, and other categories of computer scientists will increase by 141% from 1996 to 2002. This is the fourth highest increase ranked by states throughout the United States.

Companies such as Exodus Communications in Santa Clara, the Los Angeles Times, Microsoft, Manpower, and Hewlett Packard list openings for jobs that require Web site administration skills. (Refer to the individual company Web sites and America's Job Bank for the most recent information on available jobs.) Although these jobs are currently listed as Network Integrator/Software Engineer or Professional Internet Technologist, Data Warehousing Consultant (Microsoft), Backend Web Developer (Manpower), Tech Support/Applications Specialist (Hewlett Packard), the skills required are those taught in our Web Site Administration and Application Solutions programs. For example, the Tech Support/Applications specialist at HP must "develop expertise in Web-based client/server development tools/techniques, security tools, and distributed application tools and techniques." The Backend Web Developer (Manpower) must support Internet-based electronic bill payment systems and know Perl, Java, and SQL. The Data Warehousing Consultant (Microsoft) who participates in the design and implementation of data warehousing must have experience using SQL, C, Java, client/server technologies, and Visual Basic. Microsoft is also seeking Applications Development consultants who know Inter/Intranet application development using IIS, IE, ASP, VBScript, Java, HTML, and DHTML. (Consult the JOBTRAK™ Job Listings for additional information.) In the area of audio and Web music distribution, companies such as Liquid Audio are seeking Web Developers, Web UI Designers, and Web Development engineers proficient in Unix, Perl, Java, C++ and SQL databases. (Refer to the http://www.liquidaudio.com site for additional information.)

Although many of these employers may prefer a candidate who has a BS in Computer Science, candidates with several years experience and demonstrated subject matter knowledge will also be interviewed. An Information Architect/DBM for Exodus Communications needs to know how to design, develop, and manage information architecture and solutions for all business areas and ensure that customers can find information about the business enterprise on the Web. Experience with Web-based architectures for information access and storage is a must for this job. Other jobs with titles such "Professional Internet Technologist," require skills such as knowledge of most Internet-related technologies and familiarity with Windows NT and databases such as SQL server.

6. Job Market Analysis

California Salaries

Salary depends on job and experience although software engineering jobs in the Web area pay $36,000 to $48,000 as beginning salaries. Web site administrators with experience in multi-platform tools can earn a beginning yearly salary of $55,000 to $60,000. Web page designers and HTML programmers earn $15.00 to $20.00 per hour. According to JOBTRAK and the Monster Board, jobs in Web-related fields are increasing more rapidly than in almost any other area. For full-time employees, the salary depends on skills and experience; for part-time employees the salary averages $15.00 per hour. In addition, interns working in various companies can earn a minimum of $8.00 per hour.

Summer and part-time jobs are also available in the field of Web Site Administration. A part-time Web Site Developer at Merlin Media, Inc. in San Jose can earn $12.00 per hour for no experience to $17 per hour for 2 or more years experience. This particular individual is expected to not only to create Web pages but also to maintain client Web sites for international customers.

The Interactive Salary Guide sponsored by Pencom Inc. offers comparative salaries based on years of experience and programming skills. According to their data available on their Web site, Web-based Applications Developers earn $35,000 with 0 to 1 years of experience and up to $51,000 with 1 to 2 years of experience. Skills required for this job include a knowledge of Java, Javascript, Perl, Intranet/Extranet applications, Apache Web Server, CGI, ActiveX, NetScape server, and Web-based languages such as HTML and XML. Computer software developers with a knowledge of Web servers, Web-based programming languages such as Perl and Javascript can earn from $41,000 with 0 to 1 year of experience to $46,000 with 1 to 2 years of experience. Computer programmers who become systems or network administrators can increase their first year salaries by $2,000 from $51,000 to $53,000 by knowing Web server technologies. (Refer to the Interactive Salary Guide Web site, the SuperSite: Intra/Internet Web Master, and individual company Web sites for the most recent salary and job information.)

California Employment

In the area of Web Site management, in addition to current requirements for skilled Web Site managers, employers predict that employees capable of performing the following tasks will soon be in demand:

- Load balancing among servers
- Synchronizing multiple servers in diverse locations
- Optimizing database-driven Web sites capable of cross-browser support

If the current employment trend continues, the demand for full-time employees in the area of Web Site management will increase and the need for those whose skills include only Web page design will decrease. Increasingly, companies are hiring full-time employees to manage their Web sites and multimedia specialists who are under contract with companies such as 3DG to design their Web pages. (Refer to the Monster Board and JOBTRACK for the most recent employment and salary information.)

7. Commercial Web Certificates

The San Jose City College Web Administration program is designed to help students prepare for the following commercial exams. The curriculum includes materials and objectives students are expected to know to be able to obtain certificates and pass certification exams offered by the International Webmasters Association (IWA) and Microsoft.

IWA Certified Web Professional (CWP) Certificates

- Site Designer: Implements and maintains Websites using authoring and scripting languages, content creation and management tools, and digital media
- Internetworking Specialist: Defines network architecture, identifies infrastructure components, monitors and analyzes network performance, designs and manages TCP/IP networks
- Enterprise Developer: Builds n-tier database and legacy connectivity solutions for Web applications, using Java, Java application programming interfaces (APIs), Java Database Connectivity (JDBC) solutions, middleware tools, and distributed object models.
- E-Commerce Specialist: Demonstrates expertise in standards, technologies and practices in electronic commerce. Understand and manage the relationships among credit cardholders, issuers, merchants, acquirers, payment gateways and third parties. Understands the uses of Secure Electronic Transactions (SET), cryptography standards, Certificate Authorities, and electronic services.
- Security Specialist: Implements security policy, identifies security threats and develops countermeasures using firewalls and attack-recognition technologies. This individual is expert in transaction and payment security solutions.
- Server Administrator: Manages and tunes E-Commerce infrastructure including Web servers, FTP, news, and mail servers for midsize to large businesses. Server administrators configure, manage and deploy e-business solutions servers.
- Application Developer: Builds client- and server-side Web applications using Rapid Application Development tools and component technologies to implement two-tier database connectivity solutions.

Refer to the IWA Web Site or contact the organization directly at 119 E. Union Street, Suite #E, Pasadena, CA 91103 for additional information.

Microsoft Certificates

Although the Microsoft certificates and courses are subject to change, one of the more recent courses (as of October, 1999) of interest to Web technicians is course 1125 which prepares engineers for passing Exam 70-056, Implementing and Supporting Web Sites. Using Microsoft Site Server 3.0. The course (and, by extension, the exam) covers search capabilities, content management, security strategies for users and servers, capacity planning, backup-and-restore strategies, installation and configuration, component access, publishing documents to a Web site, and analyzing Web site content and usage. Another new Microsoft Certified Professional exam is the Designing and Implementing Commerce Solutions with Microsoft Site Server 3.0.

In addition, an exam currently under development, which our students might be prepared to pass as a result of enrolling in our Web Site Administration program, is the Implementing and Supporting Microsoft Internet Explorer 50 by using the Microsoft Internet Explorer Administration Kit. (Refer to the Microsoft Web Site for further details concerning certificates.)

8. Knowledge, Skills, and Abilities

During our Industry Advisory Board meetings, employers have indicated their support for our program. Course descriptions and prerequisites have been distributed and discussed. Employers continually indicate interest in hiring SJCC students enrolled in these programs as either interns or full-time employees.

Companies that list additional knowledge, skills, and abilities (KSAs) that are desired for computer programmers specify knowledge of processors and chips, knowledge of telecommunications systems, and facility with the English language as knowledge required to succeed. Skills include:

- Active learning
- Ability to work with new material
- Operations analysis
- Testing
- Critical thinking
- Equipment selection

Abilities include

- Written comprehension
- Oral expression
- Speech clarity
- Written expression

(Refer to America's Career InfoNet for additional information on KSAs for computer scientists.) These are the tools we also include in our curriculum and the qualities that students gain by taking a well-organized logical curriculum leading to an Associate of Science degree with a specialization in Web Site Administration or Web Application Solutions.

References

[1] California Employment Development Department Labor Market Information, Industry Trends and Outlook, 1995-2002, Santa Clara County.

Technology Leadership Through Innovation and Example

Jay Field
Center for Advanced Technology in Education
Santa Rosa Junior College
1501 Mendocino Ave
Santa Rosa, CA 95401
jay@santarosa.edu

Abstract

The Center for Advanced Technology in Education (CATE) at Santa Rosa Junior College provides SRJC with technological leadership through it role in creating and providing online educational resources, including online courses. CATE endeavors to be an entrepreneurial, technology providing organization in its own structure for product development. Being a part of a larger organization that does not see itself necessarily aligned with the goals of technological leadership or entrepreneurial organization lessens the impact that CATE has organization wide at SRJC.

History

The Center for Advanced Technology in Education (CATE) at Santa Rosa Junior College was established in the Spring semester of 1995 with the teaching of Business Administration 54 (Doing Business On The Internet) as an online course. This occurred simultaneous with, though independent of, the teaching of another SRJC online course, Art 299.35 (Online Art Using The World Wide Web). Together, these were the first two fully online California Community College courses offered. CATE's history provides an opportunity to explore what role technology leadership and innovation can play in an educational institution as well as what some of the limitations on that role can be. CATE has provided SRJC with valuable technological leadership. Online enrollment has increased from those two classes of 40 online students to over 800 students in the Fall semester of 1999. It is now commonplace for faculty to put their course information for traditional courses online. Use of the World Wide Web to support traditional courses has also become fairly routine. CATE's early use and advocacy of the Web as a legitimate tool to support learning has been one impetus, among many others, at SRJC for these changes to occur.

Organizational Influences

CATE, like many other technology-based organizations, can be described as an "emergent organization" [2]. This means that CATE is continually in the process of discovery, definition, and implementation. This fits our less formal style of continual development through prototypes. We have come to recognize that we will likely never be "finished". As technology continues to change and as faculty and staff expectations of what they can accomplish using Internet technology increases, our work is better defined as adapting to each of these influences. Requirements are dynamic, not static. Specifications tend to be ambiguous. They need to be open-ended and modifiable. There is also no fixed point of obsolescence at which an entirely new system will be developed from scratch. Rather, enhancement and modification are continual. Our systems and organizational architectures are only as good as they allow us to work within this continually changing environment.

Leadership Characteristics

Peter S. Cohan postulates "four sources of advantage that drive leaders' success". [1] His ideas are targeted at the marketplace and thus lose some of their realism when applied to bureaucratic and political entities such as institutions of higher education. While these bureaucratic and political realities may mean they will not be readily applied at institutions such as SRJC, they remain valid nonetheless. They are:

- Entrepreneurial Leadership
- Open Technology
- Boundaryless Product Development
- Disciplined Resource Allocation

In his book, Cohan draws the distinction between companies that have become technological leaders and those that are merely "peer" companies. The leaders are the ones that capitalize on the four "advantages" cited above. CATE has tried within its limitations to follow similar principles. It is difficult to directly influence leadership and resource allocation outside of CATE. The reality of life in the community college system is that being "entrepreneurial" is not often seen as a benefit and resource allocation follows a unique discipline not directly related to most business models.

Technology and Product Development

CATE did have the ability to control which technologies we chose to create ourselves and which we chose to incorporate into our model. A core technology represents an organization's single, main focus. We determined that CATE's core technology was creating online courses. Initially, this meant that our staff of one and a half programmers and systems administrators (with occasional student help) built the web sites for our classes "by hand". A large component of this core technology was working with each faculty member to organize his or her class materials and structure so that it would translate to the online medium. This was accomplished by trying to assimilate what the current and changing technology could offer and then using that knowledge to work with the instructor and his material. Once we reached a critical mass of courses, we could no longer afford the time to build new ones and update current ones in such a labor-intensive manner. "Sisters", our own courseware product, was the result.

In 1996, our study of the available courseware tools left us feeling that we would not be able to effectively use any of them to realize our vision for online courses. The online courseware industry was in its infancy then. However, once we decided to create our own software we still remained open to incorporating many "Open Source" tools. This meant that we did not have to waste valuable resources "re-inventing the wheel" for significant parts of our product. "Not Invented Here" was not a problem for us if the tool could accomplish the task and be easily incorporated into Sisters. One example is our use of MySQL as our database management system. Many courseware products have created their own proprietary databases. Another is our use of the Majordomo mailing list management software. Incorporating these and other tools considerably lessened our development time and allowed us to focus more intently on our core technology of creating online courses.

CATE has functioned with a very small staff and because of that "boundaryless product development" has been the norm. Our small staff is a cross-functional team. It has included at various times administrators, faculty, classified staff, and student staff. We have tried to involve our early adopters in product development. In fact, CATE survived at SRJC because of its early adopters. After a year of grant funding, CATE went through a year of virtually no funding. Yet, our early adopters stayed involved because they knew they were a major force in what we were doing. They were our customers and we listened to what they said about their experiences teaching online. CATE staff and the faculty teaching online through CATE often appeared together at SRJC staff development and training functions to discuss our mutual experiences in developing content, putting courses online and teaching those courses. This integration of faculty, staff, and administrators was itself somewhat unique in our environment.

Prototypes figured large in our development and in fact, Sisters is still considered more of a prototype than a finished product. We do not have a formal R&D cycle of proposal – review – development. Instead, new features are prioritized either by overall system design requirements such as database enhancements for better module integration or by customer feedback.

Concurrent engineering occurs between the application programming and the underlying systems architecture. Prototypes in each area constantly under revision and these efforts are then coordinated. This flexibility has allowed us to move forward with a very small staff. As progress is made in each area, the results are then integrated into the whole. Concurrent prototype development has allowed us to have failures as well as successes without the former costing us so much in lost time or resources as to cripple our overall endeavor.

Our last component of this development style has been the involvement of our early adopters. This was a lesson that we had to learn along the way. By keeping the CATE faculty involved in the development of Sisters and our online courses, we made "customers" who became committed to not only our product, but to our organization as well. They became advocates for CATE as a resource on campus that deserved significant institutional support. We have tried to understand our customer's needs, develop product attributes that fit those needs the best, and then develop our technologies to accomplish those goals. This is a continual process and at times has caused us to reconsider our commitment to some prior key technological decisions and directions.

Our faculty needed to create high-quality content-based online course web sites. We translated these needs into product attributes such as a web-based set of integrated modules for content creation, testing and other forms-based interactive input, mailing list management, and student record management. Our evaluation of competing products in 1996 left us thinking we could do a better job as well as one more tailored to SRJC faculty. From this analysis, we started developing Sisters. It is currently still very much a prototype system and will continue to be one. We continue to incorporate our own programming with several Open Source technologies into our own architecture.

Understanding our faculty's needs has been an evolving process for us. In areas of new technology, our early adopters can also be early adopters of technologies that we might not be quite as enthralled with. We sometimes struggle to not let ourselves get so locked into our vision that we can't hear what our customers need. At other times, our needs and our faculty's needs have nicely merged. For example, they needed to control their content and to be more in control of the production of their own web sites. This was similar in result with our need to hand over the maintenance chores of course web sites to the instructors.

Success and Failure

In a more global view, CATE has seen both successes and failures. The greatest failures have come from the disparity between the entrepreneurial-like goals of technological innovation and the larger system in which CATE functions. Higher education is not inherently entrepreneurial. It is not based on understanding student's (customer's) needs, developing product characteristics to best fit them, and then developing new technologies to meet them. CATE is but one group on campus that tries to take this approach, even though some of the other groups do not focus on what they would consider technological solutions.

Michael Hiltzik, in Dealers Of Lightning – *Xerox PARC And The Dawn Of The Computer Age* [3], suggests several reasons why Xerox was unable to take full advantage of the research and product development coming from Xerox PARC. They seem applicable to higher education as well. For example, Xerox is faced with an enormous challenge in trying to remake itself into a computer company. This is a challenge that most corporations could not successfully tackle. He further suggests that when other companies started to make inroads into Xerox's market, it was unable to move from its original business model that was the result of being in sole possession of a technology that brought the world to its door. This reliance on what became an outdated model made it increasingly difficult for Xerox to embrace new technologies and new models of research and development as well as organization. This led to Xerox losing much of its lead in key technology fields.

To be innovative leaders, in technology or any field, higher education needs the flexibility to rethink its basic model. This is very difficult to accomplish. Changes occur very slowly in its current organizational scheme. Similar to the story of the many technologies developed at Xerox PARC but never turned into fully supported products by Xerox, community colleges can favor "innovation" without institutionalizing the "products" that are developed. CATE was more easily able to get non-continuing, one time funding for personnel and equipment on a year-to-year basis *for five years* than it was to become established as a base budgeted operation. It took four years to turn the key programmer position into a permanent classified staff job as opposed to a "temp" position. It took a similar amount of time to create a "coordinator" position and even that was only half time, sharing its responsibilities and time with Staff and Faculty Technology Training. Yet in that time, SRJC was never hesitant to point with justifiable pride to CATE's many accomplishments. For example, virtually every "techie" visitor to campus was brought through CATE for a tour.

Another frustration Hiltzik mentions was the difficulty Xerox researchers had making their corporate sponsors interested in what amounted to "alien technologies". Higher education is itself slow to embrace technological advances. There are administrators and faculty who view technology with great suspicion and see it as "alien" to the teaching and learning process. Some see technology as a threat to their view of education or to their job security. Many see technological innovations as threatening to take over what they do, not as an additional tool to be used if appropriate. This "all of nothing" view is not one taken by CATE, yet it is one that has been voiced to us repeatedly as a concern. New technologies break new social and organizational ground and this is uncomfortable for many people. Online education at SRJC was one impetus for working out an Intellectual Property Rights policy statement. It continues to bring up other areas of potential controversy such as workload issues.

Conclusion

CATE tries to provide technological leadership for SRJC through its innovations in software development, through its direction in using Internet technologies for instruction, and by attempting to be an example of organization that adapts to, incorporates, and promotes a continually changing technology. Being a part of a larger organization that does not see itself necessarily aligned with the goal of technological leadership definitely lessens the impact that CATE has had organization wide. In fact, each minor victory such as creating a full time programmer position actually constitutes a major accomplishment within the constraints of the community college environment. Resource allocation at the institutional level is mostly a political process. While there are many dollars spent on resources such as computer equipment, there are too many political pitfalls for resources to be spent on human resources such as permanent staff. Programs such as CATE and other new initiatives that can directly influence the fiscal health of the institution, for instance through the addition of new FTES (full time equivalent students) are typically allocated non-permanent resources such as temporary staffing and "one time" budgeting. This will continue to lessen the effectiveness of these programs.

References

[1] Peter S. Cohan, The Technology Leaders, Jossey-Bass Inc, 1997. ISBN: 0-7879-1072-4

[2] Duane P. Tuex, Richard Baskerville, Heinz Klein, Growing Systems in Emergent Organizations, Communications of the ACM, August 1999-Volume 42, Number 8.

[3] Michael Hiltzik, Dealers of Lightning: Xerox PARC and the Dawn of the Computer Age, Harper Business, 1999. ISBN: 0-88730-891-0

Teaching and Learning in a Network World
P. Hoffman and D. Lemke (Eds.)
IOS Press, 2000

Technology and Multiple Intelligences: The Praxis of Learning Intelligences in the Classroom

Ray Gen
English Department Chair, El Segundo High School, 640 Main St., El Segundo, CA 90245
Doctoral Student, Pepperdine University, 400 Corporate Pointe, Culver City, CA 90230

Abstract. Practical applications of the theory of multiple intelligences are presented and discussed. The implementation of multiple intelligences strategies can be instituted in the classroom through project-based learning via the utilization of cyber technology.

1. The Failure to Implement the Theory of Multiple Intelligences

Howard Gardner's seminal theory of multiple intelligences was widely hailed and accepted since Gardner presented the theory in 1983 in his book *Frames of Mind: The Theory of Multiple Intelligences*. Educators around the world immediately recognized the truths contained within the concept of multiple intelligences as evidenced from their own learning experiences and from those of their students. People and educators can straight away recognize the salient truths underlying multiple intelligences by simply recalling how they learned to recite the alphabet by way of Wolfgang Amadeus Mozart's melodic tune. The fact that some people, even into adulthood, cannot recite portions of the alphabet without breaking forth into song only serves to underscore the validity of the concept of multiple intelligences.

Gardner has come to recognize eight learning intelligences. The logico-mathematical intelligence suggests that some people learn best through the manipulation of numbers or through a series of logical precepts or through syllogisms. The person who learns best by utilizing the logico-mathematical intelligence is not necessarily destined to become a scientist, mathematician or an accountant. This person merely learns best through the manipulation of logical precepts or numbers. An effective example of the exploitation of this intelligence by teachers would be to have students investigate the cause-effect relationships of the American Civil War or by analyzing the differences between the economies of North and the South.

The learners who favor the verbal-linguistic intelligence learn best through the manipulation of words and their concepts. Thus mathematics teachers who employ the multiple intelligence strategy have had their students write out in words the processes and theorems involved in solving equations. Narratives have been created that illustrate certain historical periods. The stories of personal struggles against the institution of slavery make alive historical events of the Civil War for learners who favor the employment of language arts in the acquisition of knowledge and facts.

For the learners who are inclined towards the musical intelligence, studying the cultural influences of musical compositions like the "Battle Hymn of the Republic" or "Dixie" would bring understanding of the cultures that influenced this period of American history. Similarly, the visual-spatial learner would be profoundly moved by the compositions of the Civil War photographers or painters. The aesthetic qualities found in films, photographs and paintings create mental images for the spatial intelligence learner. The visual-spatial intelligence learners make meaning for themselves through these visual images. For the kinesthetic learner, participation in re-enactments of specific battles would prove to be enlightening. The visitation of Civil War period plantations, museums and forts would enliven the history for those who wish to experience history tactually, optically and acoustically. To actually walk through the activities of the daily lives of the people of the period would be the best learning the kinesthetic learner could have.

Interpersonal intelligence students learn best through personal interactions with others. Small group activities that investigate the Civil War period would stimulate such a learner. A good simulation in which the students take on roles would bring to light the human factors surrounding the Civil War period. Taking part in the debates that of that period would prove to be a powerful learning experience.

The intrapersonal intelligence students favor personal, reflective learning. The reading and reflection of a Confederate or Union soldier's diary or an abolitionist's pamphlets would be educational for these students. These students need time to reflect and ponder the lives, arguments and philosophies of that day.

The naturalist intelligence is Gardner's most recent addition to the original seven intelligences introduced in 1983. The naturalist intelligence students are able to recognize large, overarching patterns or structures in nature and in concepts. For example, the ability to see a pattern in a seemingly set of random numbers is key to the understanding of fractals. Similarly, the study of taxonomies and classifications and the construction of hypotheses involving macro-systems are further examples of the naturalist intelligence at work. For the students of the Civil War, the naturalist intelligences learners may investigate phenomena of slavery throughout American history or its antecedents in order to understand the institution of slavery in the Ante-bellum South.

Of course, none of these intelligences exist in isolation from the others. Astute learners will use effective combinations to reinforce their lessons. Thus verbal-linguistic intelligence learners might reinforce their book-acquired understanding of the Civil War with a kinesthetic walk through the battlefield of Gettysburg with period music playing in the background. Such a combination of learning intelligences would create an indelible impression of the period.

The truths underlying Gardner's multiple intelligences are self-evident. Learners favor different intelligences and use different combinations in their acquisition of material and knowledge. This being so - the question must be asked, "Why isn't multiple intelligences being effectively implemented throughout all departments and through the K-16 curricula?" What we see in practice is either total denial of the existence of multiple intelligences or half-hearted attempts at one or two collateral intelligences but no genuine attempt to utilize all eight intelligences in our teaching practices. It also appears that the higher the academic ladder a student ascends, the fewer learning intelligences are made available for that student. Perhaps the best examples of multiple intelligences learning taking place in the K-16 arena is in Kindergarten. The Kindergarten room is filled with wonder and surprises to be explored through every learning intelligence. There is singing, story telling, personal-discovery activities, group-discovery activities, number manipulations, jumping, running and sitting learning games, the exploration of patterns, and finger painting. But by the time children reach eighth grade, most students only experience the learning intelligence most conducive to the discipline itself. Students create art in art class, but not in science. Students employ numbers in math but not in English. Thus a student dares to ask the question in an eighth grade science class, "Does spelling count? This isn't an English class, Ms. Smith!" Students and teachers have relegated certain skills and intelligences to be used only in certain disciplines. There is very little transference.

The creative teacher who dares to employ a "foreign" intelligence in her class is looked upon with academic suspicion by the time of high school. How can any self-respecting honors senior English teacher allow her students to write a song in place of writing a term paper? The musical intelligence may be used in a music class but is practically taboo in any other discipline in high school. By the time students reach the college level, any idea of multiple intelligence learning has been largely ignored – even by the discipline that exploits the intelligence the most. How many art departments have relegated the "performing arts" to a status below that of the academic study of art? Art history or music history classes are often considered to be much more serious, rigorous and "academic" when compared to their performing counterparts. At the college level, there emerge only two primary learning intelligences: logico-mathematic and verbal-linguistic. The others are largely abandoned. The traditional mid-term, final and a paper only allow a narrow choice of learning intelligences.

Nearly as appalling a situation are teachers who attempt to utilize multiple intelligences in their disciplines but only through the most unnatural and convoluted means. The singing of the periodic table or the singing of Shakespearean sonnets do not inspire most students. It may at times do something for the musical intelligence students; however, by the time the other learning intelligence students have denigrated the lesson as being insipid, even the musical intelligence students have rejected the lesson.

Most teachers do not even attempt to incorporate the other intelligences into their teaching strategies. The reasons are clear enough to discern. First of all, the established curriculum and the time-honored approaches to the disciplines do not lend themselves to other intelligences in a natural manner. As an example, to teach astronomy through a kinesthetic intelligence seems a bit far-fetched and unnatural to the discipline. How would the average teacher or lecturer begin to design a lesson with musical considerations that would be readily assimilated by all students in the class? Collaterally, standardized and traditional assessments do not utilize nor recognize any of the intelligences except the logical-mathematic or the verbal-linguistic. And with the recent resurgence of teacher evaluations resting on these high stakes scores, there is little hope that teachers will design many lessons with multiple intelligences in mind. A second reason why teachers neglect multiple intelligences lies in the pragmatic fact that there is inadequate time to prepare lessons utilizing more than one learning intelligence. With inadequate time to cover even the basically mandated elements of the course, teachers will not "waste" time by covering the same material for students who prefer to learn through another intelligence. Hence the ubiquitous lecture predominates at the higher educational levels. In addition, teachers, not only lack the time in their classrooms to utilize other intelligences, they also lack the time to prepare for such lessons. Thirdly, and perhaps the most important explanation why teachers largely ignore multiple intelligences is that it is simply wrong-headed. Teachers do not have the expertise in the other intelligences to produce meaningful lessons using multiple intelligences. It would take too much time and effort to plan and implement such lessons.

However, the concept of multiple intelligences is not about what a teacher does in the classroom, although most pre-service and in-service programs tend to make it so. The concept of multiple intelligences should be about how a person learns not about how a person teaches. The misplaced emphasis on teachers to teach lessons using different intelligences is well intended but practically unattainable.

2. The Implementation of Multiple Intelligences

Teachers should not abandon the implementation of multiple intelligences even though it is impossible for teachers to implement by themselves. The solution rests in the hands of the learners. The emphasis of multiple intelligences needs to shift from teacher to learner. The idea that teachers control multiple intelligences within their classes is nonsensical. Students should be empowered to learn in the method conducive to their learning intelligence. The job of the educator is to supply the opportunity, context and framework in which learning is to take place. The job of the student is to learn by utilizing the intelligences that best suits them for the task at hand. Teachers may utilize multiple intelligences in their class by allowing students to employ the intelligences of their choice in the acquisition of the material. The instructor supplies the context and outlines the content to be covered by the learners. The learners utilize the intelligences of their choice to obtain the material.

As an example, a literature instructor has assigned the novels *Brave New World* by Aldous Huxley and *1984* by George Orwell. The instructor plans to cover not only the literary constructs of the novels but also the concepts of utopianism. The political, social, economic, cultural, educational, and religious aspects of societies will be the topics of discussions as well. The instructor utilizing multiple intelligences will assign a variety of projects from which learners will choose. Each project will be required to cover a basic set of requirements, for example, each project must define the concept of utopia. Each project might be asked to demonstrate an understanding of either the political, social, economic and cultural aspect of societies and to create a model. Each project could be required to either create a utopia or argue the conditions under which a utopia might be possible.

The traditionalist learner who is also probably a verbal-linguistic intelligence learner will choose to write a term paper. The logico-mathematical intelligence learner might choose to create economic models of a utopia illustrating perfectly controlled economies of supply and demand. The naturalist intelligence learner may choose to create a paradigm of how utopian ideas have come about in the past and why they have failed. The musical and kinesthetic intelligence learners may pool resources and utilize the companion interpersonal intelligence to create a musical play based upon one of the novels. The intrapersonal intelligence learner may choose to investigate the writings of Thomas More's *Utopia* and create a comparative study of More's writings with the two novels. Or perhaps the intrapersonal learner may wish to explore the history of utopianism through film. The visual-spatial intelligence writer may attempt to design architecturally the hatchery building so described in *Brave New World.* By using projects, students may choose the intelligence best suited for their learning intelligence and determine the projects that will demonstrate their understanding and mastery of the subject. Educational institutions need to break away from the standardized and traditional assessments of exams, essays, and term papers.

3. Technology as a Means for Implementation

Technology is a way to allow the utilization of various intelligences. Technology can provide students with the proper medium through which they may demonstrate and present their mastery of the subject through technology-based project learning. With so many media available in today's classrooms, the utilization of technology as a means to demonstrate mastery of content becomes not only convenient but also effective as a teaching/learning tool. The learners become teachers in their presentations and teachers become true advisers and mentors to student learning.

The verbal-linguistic intelligence students today may create not only the traditional term papers, but they may also present their learning and papers on the Internet through web pages. The papers and projects created on the web becomes a resource for future students who will also investigate these topics. Web pages may be created and archived through HTML or the traditionally generated papers may be stored on the Internet through Adobe Acrobat's PDF for convenient, universal accessibility. The sharing of knowledge and the management of knowledge becomes a necessary skill for the modern-day teacher and learner. The Internet is a means to begin to manage this deluge of information.

For the logico-mathematic intelligence student who will demonstrate economic models, the use of spreadsheet or statistics programs will become essential to illustrate economic scenarios based on certain market factors. The results of these models may be shared on various presentation programs such as PowerPoint, Hyperstudio, or Corel's WordPerfect's presentation maker program. Presentation programs may also be stored on the Internet as well.

For the kinesthetic and musical intelligence learners, they may produce their musical play in animation or with real performers. Either of these performances may be captured on CD-ROMs. There are a number of animation programs that may be utilized. A currently popular animation program is Macromedia's Flash. Performances with human actors may be digitized with digital cameras or analog tapes may be digitized by computers. These digital images are conveniently stored on CD-ROMs, which can be inexpensively reproduced. The kinesthetic and musical intelligence learners may also organize and create virtual tours or presentations of their topics.

The naturalist intelligence learners may need to catalog historical utopian ideas and group similar ides together and yet note their differences as well. These past ideas may be created and indexed with various programs. A popular, powerful program is Adobe's

Acrobat. Once these ideas have been collected by the learner, indexes and catalogues may be created for quick searches to compare and contrast ideas. From these indexes, the naturalist intelligence learners will be able to discern patterns of ideas and recognize commonalities between various thoughts of utopianism throughout the history of thought.

The interpersonal intelligence learners will be able to collaborate effectively by utilizing groupware programs. Various group programs are available that facilitate small group work. Groupware allows each member of the group to share his or her ideas while still retaining a workable structure and timeline.

For the visual-spatial intelligence learners who wish to design the hatchery building described in the beginning of the novel *Brave New World*, programs such as a Computer-Aided Design (CAD) would be very useful. Various drawing programs such a Adobe Illustrator or Macromedia's Fireworks will also assist these students.

The intrapersonal intelligence learners may wish to compile various films of utopian concepts and narrate their own documentary of utopianism. This may be performed through either analog or digital technology. Modern technology will provide these reflective learners access to resources beyond the traditionally printed media.

4. Conclusion

The use of multiple intelligences in classrooms is the choice of instructors and their institutions. Instructors must first recognize the need to go beyond the verbal-linguistic and logico-mathematic intelligences. While these two intelligences have dominated academe traditionally, the other intelligences should not be ignored. Once having recognized the need to reach out to learners who favor the other intelligences, instructors need to release and empower their students to learn according to these intelligences. While modern technology is not essential for the utilization of these learning intelligences, technologies can certainly make the demonstration and implementation of these learning intelligences more accessible for the classroom setting. Institutions must also adapt to the age of information and recognize academic work in iterations other than the traditional ink and paper forms of essays, term papers and exams. Authentic academic work can take many creative forms in the age of information and cyber technology.

For examples of student work using multiple intelligences in project-based assessments, please see http://www.genconnection.com/students/welcome.htm.

Teaching and Learning in a Network World
P. Hoffman and D. Lemke (Eds.)
IOS Press, 2000

Developing a National Grid for Learning in the UK

Dr M J Herbert
Head of Technology Research and Development
British Educational Communications and Technology Agency (Becta),
Science Park, Coventry, CV4 7JJ, United Kingdom
Tel: +44 2476 416994, Fax +44 2476 847120
Email: malcolm_herbert@becta.org.uk

Abstract
The National Grid for Learning (NGfL) is one of the key education policies of the current UK Government, placing an emphasis on Information Communication Technology (ICT) in terms of commitment and funding that has not been present in previous initiatives. This paper describes the main features of the NGfL, its achievements so far, the key issues for the development of a national network and concludes by looking at the possible areas for future development. This includes details on the network and computing infrastructure, policy for ICT training for teachers and development of content.

1 Introduction

The National Grid for Learning (NGfL) has emerged as a major Government policy since it was elected to power in May 1997. The outline proposals for the NGfL, *Connecting the Learning Society* [1], were issued in the October of that year, with consultation with industry, commerce and education taking place in the autumn. From this a challenge document [2], was published in 1998 providing details for proposed NGfL.

There are around 23,000 schools in the UK, with a pupil population in excess of 8 million and over 450,000 teachers. The NGfL has a number of targets to be achieved by 2002, including connecting all schools, providing email accounts to all teachers and the majority of pupils over the age of 9. It also makes a commitment to ensure that all teachers are Information Communications Technology (ICT) literate and confident.

The NGfL has received funding from a number of sources, including from central and local government (through matched funding programmes) and the New Opportunities Fund (NOF) of the National Lottery. This latter funding has concentrated on teacher training provision for Information Communication Technology (ICT). In all, there will have been in excess of £1 billion provided between 1998 and 2002 for the development of school and Local Education Authority (LEA) infrastructure. This will be in addition to existing expenditure by schools and LEAs and should be put in the context of an IT market for this sector that was worth less than £150m in 1995.

The paper often refers to Primary and Seconday schools, which can be related to Key Stages 1-2 (up to 11 years old) and Key Stages 3-4 (11-16 years) respectively.

2 Computing Equipment

Up to 1997, the development of computing infrastructure in schools had been varied and diverse, with a range of national, regional and local procurement initiatives.

Educational computing equipment in the UK has traditionally been an eclectic mix, with little reference to current commercial trends. The majority of machines are now standard desktop PCs, with a fewer Mac's or Acorn Risc PCs. However, there is still a large number of older machines in primary schools in particular, such as pre-Pentium PCs and even BBC Bs from the early 1980's.

There have been a number of significant national initiatives. The CDROM for Schools initiatives during the early 1990's provided up-to-date multimedia desktop machines for over 25% of primary schools in the UK, giving widespread access to an increasing range of educational CD-ROM titles. These projects were managed by the National Council for Educational Technology (NCET), the British Educational Communications and Technology Agency (Becta) predeccesor, which also managed the £30m Portables for Teachers projects which ran from 1996-8. Current national schemes include the procurement of laptop machines for numeracy and literacy consultants and the Computers for Teachers project[1]

There are around 150 Local Education Authorities (LEAs) in England, Scotland, Wales and Northen Ireland, each with regional responsibility for education in their area. They vary greatly in size and organisation, have markedly different geographical regions and demographic make-up. Through them, central Government delegate responsibility for delivery for teaching and learning, for the schools and lifelong sectors. The differences between the LEAs is also reflected in variations in equipment and management methods used. In some areas IT planning and procurement is delegated completly to individual schools, whereas some LEAs still provide a central guidance and advice service.

At a local level, the level of IT provision prior to the NGfL had been patchy. Schools have been notoriously poor procurers of Information Technology, with poor value for money and quality of service being obtained. This has been partly due to a lack of long-term planning and the neccessary funding, but also due to having no expertise in this area in the schools. While the larger secondary schools usually have a IT teacher or technician, this is especially rare in the smaller primary schools where they rely on a combination of help from the LEA function (where there is one) and from parents, governors and other people in the local community.

3 NGFL Managed Services

To enable schools and colleges to procure ICT well, the Department for Education and Employment have introduced National Grid for Learning Managed Services [3]. These provide both a fully integrated service, which includes all IT components, in addition to guarentee a minimum standard. Becta has arranged a series of tests and checks to ensure

[1] More details on the Computers for Teachers project can be found at http://cft.ngfl.gov.uk.

that certified providers can meet the expectations of schools and other educational institutions.
NGfL Managed Services consist of the following components:

- Equipment
- Local Networking
- Internet Service Provision
- Intregrated Support
- Initial Training and Commisioning
- Servicing and Maintenance

Telecommunications are not included as part of the service, due to the variety available and the varying needs of the organisations (see Networks section below). In the first round of certification which took place between October 1998 and June 1999, 12 suppliers have were approved for the delivery of NGfL Managed Services and have signed framwork contracts.

As well as ensuring that schools have single point of contact for ICT and that all the system components work together, Managed Services also allow for flexible procurement methods, making it possible for schools to have predictable expenditure on ICT.

The suppliers of Managed Services are very enthusiastic about the process, as not only does it give them a mark of approval if successful, they also it see it as clear statement of Government policy, one that they can develop and plan for.

Currently, it seems that the suppliers are taking the successful Managed Service models used in the commercial sector and adapting it for education, but as has been seen with other ICT developments that can take time before it is fully evolved and therefore popular with schools. Also, schools and education authorities have approved of the process of certification and the procurement confidence that it brings, but it is currently too early to comment on the uptake of the Managed Services themselves.

4 Network Infrastructure

The network infrastructure for the NGfL is made up of a mixture of commercial, academic and local authority networks.

The Internet service provision in schools is dominated by a few, commercial providers, with much of the connectivity (where it is available) using ISDN2. Nearly all of this is provided by the main telecommuncation's company in the UK, British Telecom (BT) and their Schools Internet Caller (SIC) service. This provides a schools with 128Kbps connection for £790 per year, with no call charges between 8am and 6pm during school term times and has no installation charge. Calls outside this period are charged at the normal, local call rate. This provides schools with another predictable tariff, along with the Managed Service charges. Recently BT have added a Public Institutions Internet Caller service, which provides fixed charge, 24 hour access and there is also an immeient annoucement of a 2Mbps tarrif for schools.

BT claim to have connected in excess of 18,000 customers to the Schools Internet Caller (SIC) service, but this current figure has not been confirmed by the regulator, OFTEL. A similar package is also available for people wishing to use dial-up services (PSTN), although it is not clear the extent uptake of this service.
However, while the communications charges are not cheap, the ISP costs are not, as typically they charge per connected workstation (or allocated IP number) rather than just

the bandwidth. As they do not claim revenue from the SIC in terms of interconnect fees they argue that claim that schools can use it as a semi leased line. This 'worst case' pricing makes a commercial package beyond the reach of many schools.

In some urban areas, such as Liverpool and Birmingham, the LEA has been able to make use of the infrastructure provided by the local cable company and this allows for cost-effective 2Mbps connectivity to each school as a charge similar to that of ISDN elsewhere. Other LEAs are also looking at other delivery media, including wireless, and are developing their infrastructure alongside local government offices, libraries and other public organisations.

The universities have their own network[2], made up of a high-speed backbone connecting clusters of institutions via Metropolitan Area Networks (MANs). The collective procurement of the backbone and the MANs means that connectivity costs are relatively inexpensive compared to the equivalent commercial provision. A new project, the New Learning Network (NLN), is now in the process of adding all Further Education (FE) colleges to the MANs and hence the network backbone, with a local connection of 2Mpbs or greater.

As part of the development of the NGfL funding of £50m has been earmarked for the development of a number of Regional Broadband Consortia [4], to provide high-speed networks between LEAs and therefore provide connections of 2Mbps and above to individual schools. This project is in its early stages (the funding for the 2000/01 financial year has just been allocated), but the indications are that many of the projects will look to make use of the existing infrastructure that is in place for the MANs and JANET. The existing nodal structures (see figure 1) are already in place and in some areas there is already high-speed connectivity to local institutions (mainly in urban areas with cable services).

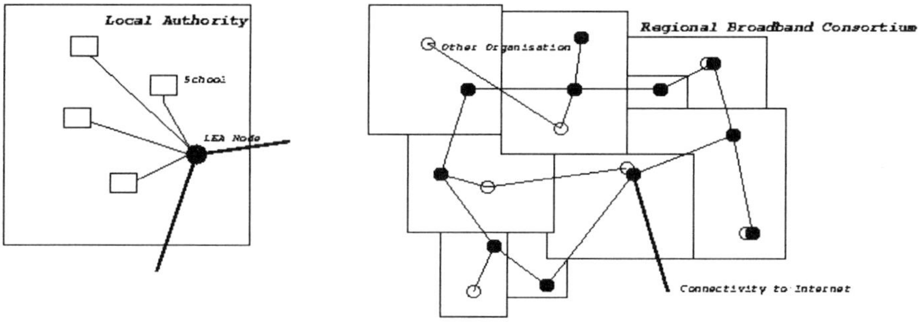

Figure 1 – Regional Broadband Consortia network

While it was never intended that the NGfL actually have its own identifiable physical infrastructure it seems that this may occur by default, from the bottom up. As the regional consortia and local education authorities look to obtain best value, network interconnectivity and quality of service, it will be only a small number of teleco's and Internet Service Providers who will be able offer the services required.

---

[2] The Joint Acadmic Network (JANET) is run by UKERNA, more information via their website , http://www.ukerna.ac.uk.

5 Content

The NGfL has also been about creating online resources for education, both through direct funding and through collecting together individual developments under a single umbrella. While Government and its agencies (such as the Department for Education and Employment, Becta[3] and the Teacher Training Agency for example) have developed and maintained sites like the NGfL portal, the Virtual Teacher Centre and the Standards Site directly, the NGfL has also collected other educational resources together. Currently, there are in excess of 250,000 indexed pages, provided by people like the British Broadcasting Corporation (BBC), Museums and Galleries and LEAs. These have all been subject to some form of quality control and hence provide a 'guarenteed' educational resource, covering a range of areas. For example, the appropriateness of the content is considered and the amount of commercialisation is tolerable (especially for sites with a student audience) . From a technical standpoint, the site links are checked, as is its robustness.

Hence the NGfL has a distributed content framework operated at national, regional and local levels. While some of the high profile content is hosted by DfEE and Becta directly, including the portal NGfL site, it also has a rich source of distributed content that is hosted by local education authorities or by individual schools. This distributed content framework is complementary to the emerging physical network, with a backbone, rather than a hub construction.

6 Training

The DfEE's annual report, the ICT Survey in Schools 1999 [5], indicates that 68% of Primary and 61% of Secondary teachers feel confident in using ICT in the curriculum. This survey was carried out before the New Opportunities Fund (NOF) initiative started, which is providing £300m for the training of teachers and school librarians (£230m) and librarians (£20m) [6], as well as the digitisation of library and museum content (£50m). This is being delivered by a number of providers who have been approved by the DfEE and Teacher Training Agency and will increase confidence figure significantly.

The Managed Service providers also have a requirement to provide initial training as part of their contract with the educational institutions. This will include technical training for potential system administrators, *power* users and other lead people in the organisation.

7 Future Developments

This will continue to look at both aspects of the NGfL, infrastructure and content with the aim of increasing performance and connectivity from schools.

Becta's remit includes continuing technology research and development is continuing to look at IT developments and assess their potential impact on the NGfL. Communications tariffs are changing constantly and new delivery media are also emerging, such as xDSL, Satellite and Digital Broadcasting. Satellite delivery in already the subject of a trial in over 100 schools and now offers a predicatable, fixed monthly charge tariff, while

[3] http://www.becta.org.uk.

ADSL is about to be rolled out by British Telecom. Other DSL technologies are also in the process of being trialled, some as part of Regional Broadband Consortia.

Becta is also looking at the growth of Open Source software and content and assessing how it is already being used in delivering the NGfL [7]. Open Source applications, such as the Apache web server[4], are already extensively used to run and deliver Internet functionality and are highly suitable for a distributed network infrastructure, as is evolving for the NGfL.

Alongside application development, document and information standards such as XML are already being used to provide the mechanism for the adaptable retreival of content.

Becta will also be undertaking an evaluation of leading edge ICT projects up to 2002, along the same lines as the Education Department's Superhighway's Initiative (EDSI)[5], which ran until 1997 and provided much of the evidence for the NGfL.

On the content side, Becta is aware of the need for the construction of good 'content-rich' sites as well a dynamic portal for the NGfL, with searching and conference functionality. The NGfL Learning Resource Index (LRI) provides an easy-to-access database of educational resources, which also has a map-based search function.

Other content is being submitted for inclusion in the NGfL all the time, including a number of 'Community Grids for Learning', which provide regional and local online resources, but which also increasingly have valid national content.

8 Conclusion

The National Grid for Learning (NGfL) has already enabled 63% of Primary and 93% of Secondary schools to be connected to online educational resources. It is also increasing ICT confidence and competence amoungst teachers and hence the student population.

To assess the benefits to education, evaluations of the impact of the various areas of the NGfL have been set up. These cover the technical and procurement aspects, as well as assessing the learning benfits. Although these evaluations have only just started, it is hoped that it will significantly improve the overall standard of learning in UK schools.

References

[1] Department for Education and Employment, Connecting the Learning Society http://www.dfee.gov.uk/grid/consult/, 1997.

[2] Department for Education and Employment, Open for Learning, Open for Business, http://www.dfee.gov.uk/grid/challenge/, 1998.

[3] British Educational Communications and Technology Agency (Becta), NGfL Managed Services, http://managedservices.ngfl.gov.uk, 1999.

[4] Department for Education and Employment, Standards Fund Grant 1999-2000 – Circular 16/99, http://www.dfee.gov.uk/circulars/16_99/, 1999.

[4] Further information at http://www.apache.org

[5] EDSI, http://www.becta.org.uk/projects/edsi

[5] Department for Education and Employment, Schools ICT Survey Bulletin, http://www.dfee.gov.uk/sfr/sfr23.htm. 1999.

[6] New Opportunities Fund, ICT Training for Teachers, School Librarians and Librarians, and Digitisation of Learning Materials, http://www.nof.org.uk, 1999.

[7] Herbert, M.J., Open Source: a new flavour for education, http://www.ose.org.uk/papers, 1999.

Using Interactive Multimedia to Promote High Level Science Skills

John J. Hirschbuhl Ph.D.
Professor and Manager, Instructional Development
University of Akron
Akron, OH

Abstract

This study examines the effects of Interactive Multimedia instruction upon the variables of achievement and problem solving skills on non-science majors in an Environmental Science course at a mid-western university. The findings indicate that the Interactive Multimedia had a significant effect on both of the variables. The findings are discussed in terms of the impact on self-study when students are learning outside of the classroom in a distance learning environment.

Introduction

During the 1990s critics and supporters alike have been questioning the effectiveness of science education within the American Education System. Pearlman [1] states, "In the United States alone, education costs $450 billion a year. It is a huge burden, yet almost everybody agrees that schools are failing." Pearlman believes schools have not taken advantage of the teaching and learning enrichment that technology tools provide and it is one of the major reasons they are failing.

Perhaps schools are having some difficulty in catching onto many of the new opportunities that technology tools offer, but computers are widespread in the schools and some good things are happening. This presentation examines how schools are now using interactive computer-based multimedia as a tool to develop thinking skills needed to assimilate and transform massive quantities of information into solution for today's fast paced changing society.

Case Study

One of the problem areas for schools today revolves around the lack of student interest in science. Enrollment is down and performance is low. However, today's generation shows an interest in things pertaining to the environment. In this study a package entitled *Environmental Science: Computer Lab Simulations,* [2] an interactive multimedia (IMM) program based on actual geological field studies, was used by undergraduate non-science majors at a mid-western university. For this study these simulations were added to one section of an environmental studies course and compared to a section that used only the traditional method of instruction (classroom lecture).

According to Trollip and Alessi [3] one of the purposes of adding computers to classroom instruction is to facilitate learning for students by improving the quality and quantity of what they know. Schwier and Misanchuk [4] believe an advantage of interactive multimedia instruction is the creation of meaning developed by the learner's interaction with the new information in the program.

At the time of this investigation there was very little empirical evidence regarding the use of interactive multimedia instructional technologies in higher education [5]. Most articles were anecdotal describing outstanding research (Heller [6]; Park [7]; Park and Hannafin [8]; Preece [9]; Zachariah [10]) regarding the effects of a self-paced interactive multimedia computer simulation on students' learning, motivation, and attitude. Reeves [11] stated for a worthwhile study of interactive multimedia, a diverse population spending several hours in purposeful study should be examined.

Purpose of the Study

This research examined the impact on students' grades and higher level thinking skills when computers were added to the classroom. Interactive multimedia simulations of "real world situations" (actual field trips of a geology professor with 22 years' experience) were incorporated into one section of an environmental geology course. The interactive multimedia modules, which promoted participation and interaction, were designed for students to gain scientific knowledge and concepts, and develop problem-solving skills without the heavy use of mathematics.

Research Design

The research design was quasi-experimental because it combined the use of "naturally assembled" intact groups [13] pre-test and post-test, and the use of a control group. The control group research design is shown in Table 1.

Table 1: The control group research design

O_1	X_C	$O_{2\text{-}3}$
O_2	X_{IMM}	$O_{2\text{-}3}$

Where
X_C = Control — X_{IMM} = Interactive Multimedia
O_1 = Pre-test — O_2 = Post-test
O_3 = Course Grade

Sample

One hundred and fifty-two students were involved in the study in the spring of 1996. The control group (113 students) received the traditional lecture of instruction, while the interactive multimedia replaced part of the traditional instruction for the treatment group (39 students).

GALT Instrument

The Group Assessment of Logical Thinking (GALT) [14] was designed to measure student cognitive development. The instrument has been used by many as a predictor of student's mathematics and science achievement [15], [16], [17]. Roadrangka *et al.* [18] reported a coefficient alpha of 0.85 for the total test and validity was reported with a strong correlation (0.80) between the GALT and Piagetian interview results.

The GALT consisted of 21 questions of which 18 questions not only required the student to pick the most appropriate answer, but also the reason the student chose that answer. For the question to be considered correct the student must correctly choose both the answer and the reason. Students are classified as concrete thinkers with a GALT score of 0 to 8, transitional with a GALT score of 9 to 15,k and those with GALT scores of 16 to 21 are recognized as formal thinkers.

Interactive multimedia instruction

Multimedia can be loosely defined as computer-based technology integrating some, but not necessarily all, of the following: text, graphics, animation, sound, and video [19]. There are several definitions of IMI (interactive multimedia instruction) [20] and, as the multimedia environment changes rapidly, so may the meaning of interactive multimedia instruction. According to Schwier and Misanchuk [21] IMI is "instructional, multiple-sourced (i.e., multiple media sources are involved) intentionally designed, and coherent"(p.4).

Interactive multimedia modules for environmental geology

The topics of the eight units of interactive multimedia are: 1) Introduction to Environmental Science, 2) Energy from Coal, 3) Geology of Homesite Selection, 4) Minerals for Society, 5) Legal Control of the Environment, 6) Stream Pollution, 7) Streams and Floods, and 8) Radiation in the Environment. All of the modules are based on actual field studies, and the student assumes the role of investigator, with each module presenting a different environmental problem.

All modules have a consistent screen format and each module consists of: an introduction to the problem to be addressed, the role that the student must play in the investigation, a means for the student to collect data relevant to the problem, a modeling book where the student enters, reviews and draws conclusions based on the collected data, a multiple choice test and an essay test. The essay test puts the responsibility of solving the problems on the shoulders of the student, who takes on the identity of an official in charge, who must make critical decisions based on the problem and data collected. The student is always in control and may access additional data, recheck data collected, access a glossary of appropriate terms, listen to audio associated with the problem, and may elect to take or repeat the multiple choice test. From the menu page a student can access any one of the eight modules, the progress report, or send the instructor email. Students must make some data collections before they are allowed to take the test or write their essays; thus forcing active participation and preventing students from rapidly paging through the modules and declaring themselves finished.

Procedure

For the treatment group five weeks of classroom instruction were replaced with eight unites of environmental science computer lab simulations (interactive multimedia). The GALT was used as a pre-test prior to use of the interactive multimedia and after use as a post-test (Figure 1). The GALT was computerized and available at the university-computer-based-testing center. The treatment group was told it was a required part of the class while students from the control group were given extra credit for participation. Forty-eight students in the control group and 26 from the treatment group completed a pre-and a post-test GALT.

The mean of the pre-test GALT scores was 9.08 for the treatment group and 8.92 for the control group giving a difference of only 0.16 between groups which suggests both groups' cognitive level of knowledge were similar. The GALT was used as a pre- and a post-test to determine if there had been a change in the students' formal operational cognitive level of knowledge.

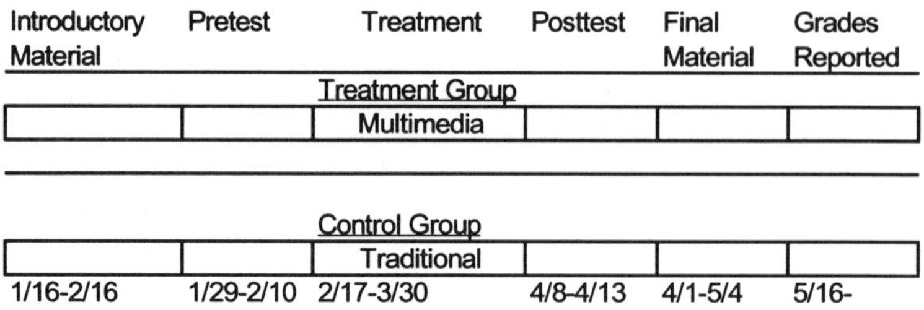

Figure 1: Timeline of the experiment

Results

First validation of the GALT as a predictor of student success was examined. Students in all groups who attained a GALT score indicating a cognitive level of development equal to transitional level or higher (score of 11 or above) performed significantly better than those who did not when grades of B or better were compared to those below B (see Table 2). The continuity adj. Chi-square value = 10.808, and p = 0.001.

Next the GALT scores were found to be significantly higher for the post-test over the pre-test for those students using the treatment (IMM). When the difference in the treatment group GALT score was compared to the difference in the control group score no-significant difference was found, F = 2.58, p = 19.

Finally the proportion of students with a passing grade d(B or better) was significantly higher for those students in the treatment group when compared with those in the control group. The continuity adj. Chi-square value was 30.9922 with a p = 0.001.

Seventy-four percent of the experimental group received a passing grade (B or better), while only 27% of the control group received a passing grade. This result is comparable with the findings of Massaro [22] where he found 74% of students who chose to use four modules of interactive multimedia as an independent study attained grades of B or better compared to 55% of the students who chose to attend regular lectures and scheduled tests.

Table 2: GALT vs. grade

GALT vs Grade	B or Better	Less than B
≥ 11	29	4
< 11	20	21

Table 3:Treatment vs. grade

Treatment vs Grade	B or Better	Less than B
Treatment	29 = 74%	10 = 26%
Control	26 = 23%	87 = 77%

Conclusions

The following conclusions were drawn from this study:

1. Those students in all groups having attained a GALT score indicating a cognitive level of development equal to transitional level or higher (score 11 or above) performed significantly better in a course for non-science majors than those with a GALT score less than 11 when grades of B or better were compared to those below B.
2. There was a significant difference in pre-and post-test GALT scores for the treatment group.
3. The proportion of students with a passing grade (B or better) was significantly higher for those in the treatment group when compared with those students in the control group.

Discussion

Overall, this study validates the effectiveness of the IMM treatment significantly increasing student achievement and problem solving skills in environmental science. The following statements support this claim:

First, this study appears to validate the use of the GALT as a predictor of student performance because the probability of those students with a GALT score of 11 or above receiving a passing grade (B or better) was significantly greater than those with GALT scores less than 11.

Next, both groups had post-test GALT scores gains over the pretest. The treatment group showed a significant reasoning gain while the gain for the control group did not. When the gains of the GALT scores between groups were compared the difference was not significant. Part of the increase in the GALT scores might be attributed to students taking the same GALT tests for both the pre-and the post-test.

Finally, the proportion of students with a passing grade (B or better) was significantly higher for students in the treatment group when compared with those in the control group. This increase was so significant it is hard to suggest uncontrollable variables normally attributed to the difference such as: classes meeting at different times of the day, different days of the week, being taught by different instructors, grading standards or student attendance could account for all of the variance. This result is supported by the findings of Massaro's [22] study.

According to Wills and McNaughton [23] educational software using interactive multimedia must actively engage the student, which is exactly what we witnessed one morning when not a sound could be heard as students were intensely engrossed interacting with the computer program in the Multimedia Lab.

This study validates the effectiveness of the use of interactive multimedia as field trip simulations for an environmental geology course. However, future studies should be conducted using different research design, methodologies, disciplines and quality software to determine the long-term consequences of the use of interactive multimedia.

References

[1] Gandolfo R, Will technology alter traditional teaching? *Christian Science Monitor* (1993) 9-12.

[2] Hirschbuhl J, Bishop D and Jackson J, *Environmental Science: Computer Lab Simulations* Falcon Software Inc, Wellesley, MA., 1996.

[3] Trollip S R and Alessi S M, Incorporating computers effectively into classrooms *Journal of Research on Computing in Education,* 1988.

[4] Schwier R A and Misanchuk E R, *Interactive Multimedia Instruction* Educational Technology Publications, NJ, 1993.

[5] Spots T H and Bowman M A, Faculty use of instructional technologies in higher education *Educational Technology* 35 (1995) 56-64.

[6] Heller R, The role of hypermedia in education: a look at the research issues *Journal of Research on Computing in Education* 22 (4) (1990) 431-441.

[7] Park O C, Hypermedia: functional features and research issues *Educational Technology* 31 (1991) 24-31.

[8] Park I and Hannafin M, Empirically-based guidelines for the design of interactive multimedia *Educational Technology Research and Development* 41 (3) (1993) 63-65.

[10] Preece J, Human-Computer interaction in the informatics curriculum *Educational Computing* 8 (4) (1993) 295-301.

[11] Reeves T C, Pseudoscinece in computer-based instruction: the case of learner control research *Journal Computer-Based Instruction* 20 (2) (1993) 39-46.

[12] Zachariah S, The effects of multimedia-based instruction on the academic achievement of students studying economics (Doctoral dissertation, University of Akron, *Dissertation Abstracts International* 57-03pg. 1108 UMI # AAI9623176, 1995.

[13] Campbell D T and Stanley J C, *Experimental and Quasi-experimental Designs for Research* Rand McNally, Chicago, IL, 1963.

[14] Roadrangka V, Yeany R H and Padilla M J, *GALT. Group Test of Logical Thinking* University of Georgia, Athens, GA, 1982.

[15] Bitner B L, *The GALT: A measure of logical thinking ability of eighth grade students and a predictor of science and mathematics achievement* Paper presented at the annual meeting of the National Association for Research on Science Teaching, San Francisco, CA, 1986.

[16] Bitner B L, *Logical and critical thinking abilities of sixth through twelfth grade students and formal reasoning modes as predictors of critical thinking abilities and academic achievement* ERIC Document Reproduction Service No. ED 293 715) 1988.

[17] Bitner B L, Formal operational reasoning modes: predictors of critical thinking abilities and grades assigned by teachers in science and mathematics for students in grades nine through twelve *Journal of Research in Science Teaching* 28 (1991) 265-274.

[18] Roadrangka V, Yeany R H and Padilla M J, The construction and validation of group assessment of logical thinking (GALT) Paper presented at the annual meeting of the National Association for Research in Science Teaching, Dallas, TX, 1983.

[19] Barron A E and Orwig G W, *Multimedia Technologies for Training* Libraries Unlimited Inc, Englewood, CO, 1995.

[20] Galbreath J, The educational buzzword of the 1990's: multimedia, or is it hypermedia, or interactive multimedia, or ..? *Educational Technology* 32 (4) (1992) 15-19.

[21] Schwier R A and Misanchuk E R, *Interactive Multimedia* Instruction Educational Technology Publications, NJ, 1993.

[22] Massaro D A, A multimedia geology program for non-science majors with distance learning capabilities. (Doctoral dissertation , University of Akron) *Dissertation Abstracts International* 56-05 pg. 1745 UMI # AAI952845, 1995.

[23] Willis S and McNaughton C, Evaluation of computer-based learning in higher education. *Journal of Computing in Higher Education* 7 (2) (1996) 106-128.

Anytime, Anywhere: The Power of Video Streaming

Dianne Hoff, Ed.D.
33 Merrill Hall, The University of Maine, Orono, ME 04469
Doug Marchio
28 Shibles Hall, The University of Maine, Orono, ME 04469
Justin Hafford
122 Chadbourne Hall, The University of Maine, Orono, ME 04469

ABSTRACT

With advances in compression, media streaming is now a powerful educational tool that can facilitate distance learning and enhance classroom instruction. Presentations are easily produced using QuickTime, an enabling technology that supports video, audio, virtual reality, and animation. These "movies" can then be streamed live to recipients at remote sites via the Internet, or archived for student access on their home computers whenever the information is needed.

Streaming uses either RTSP (Real Time Streaming Protocol), designed to deliver live Internet broadcasts, or HTTP (Hypertext Transport Protocol), which requires the viewer to download the file. Each type of streaming has its own production process and strengths for specific situations. Steps for creating and streaming QuickTime movies are discussed along with suggested hardware/software configurations.

QuickTime and streaming have the power to immerse students in a multimedia environment that addresses a wide range of learning styles and abilities. Students can retrieve information whenever they need it, in a non-linear fashion, and at their own pace. When the streamed information is combined with other interactive technologies (such as email, hyperlinks, and computer bulletin boards), students are able to collaborate as they view. And perhaps most importantly, students can be part of live or recorded events, even when they cannot be in attendance, truly making learning possible "anywhere, anytime."

1. Introduction

It is no longer difficult to empower students to watch live events as they happen, to access archived presentations, or to review segments of recorded lessons – all from their home computers. Within this multimedia environment, students can explore a virtual world and absorb information in non-linear, non-sequential ways. This is possible and affordable using QuickTime which, when delivered via streaming, becomes a tool for learning "anytime, anywhere."

QuickTime is an enabling technology that can provide important multimedia features of video, audio, and animation for easy use in distance education. The problem in the past has been that QuickTime movies needed more delivery bandwidth than was available. Now, with advances in compression and streaming, it has become a viable teaching tool.

Media "streaming" is a method of data transfer through the Internet that allows information to be sent one piece at a time so that the end user does not have to wait for the entire material to be transmitted. It allows a complex, multimedia presentation to be delivered from a server to any authorized recipient. Streaming can be done live to distance learners, or recorded for viewing anytime. This means that students may access the file, draw upon any lesson or video you want them to see, view any portion of it, and repeat it as many times as needed. Since the student does not necessarily have to download the file, there is little delay, nor are there issues with hard-drive space. And perhaps most importantly, the instructor controls who has access to the presentation, which protects intellectual property from unauthorized redistribution.

This paper will familiarize you with the advantages of video streaming and QuickTime for multimedia instruction and distance learning. It will explain the steps needed to stream presentations, discuss educational applications, and provide a list of suggested hardware and software.

2. *Streaming*

The first step for streaming, as with any multimedia project, involves identifying the audience and selecting content that could be enhanced with a technological presentation. Armed with this information, your next step is to make a choice in how to stream the media. Streaming uses either RTSP (Real Time Streaming Protocol), or HTTP (Hypertext Transport Protocol) to deliver its content to the viewer. Each type of streaming has its own production process and strengths for specific situations.

Introduced in 1998, RTSP streaming is the newer of the two protocols, and it is primarily designed to deal with live transmissions over the Internet, although it can be used to stream archived material. The way in which RTSP can accomplish the best results for your streamed content is through a transmission protocol (UDP) that sends the data without checking to ensure that the information has arrived at its destination. RTSP focuses on maintaining a real-time stream of information and assumes that the end user will receive a continuous flow that maintains an acceptable broadcast reception. When the network is busy, RTSP ignores the fact that some data are missing and keeps the rest of the media delivered at the correct time. Because information is sent on an as-needed basis, one of the benefits of RTSP is that the viewer is always prevented from saving the information being streamed. (In an educational setting this can assist in obtaining copyright clearance on desired materials.) If a student wishes to review any segment of archived media, it can be replayed. The stream will pick up from that point and continue forward.

One of RTSP's advantages is that it uses a QuickTime Streaming Server program to broadcast the stream while managing and conserving bandwidth. The stream is controlled by the server, not by the speed of the receiving modem, leaving plenty of bandwidth for other uses. This makes RTSP a good choice for avoiding network infrastructure issues.

RTSP offers two methods to stream the broadcast to the viewer, using either a multicast or unicast scenario. If you choose to have your RTSP stream multicast, one stream will be shared and split as often as necessary among all the viewers making requests for this media. Multicast, therefore, enables you to prevent network congestion when a whole host of streams are requested at once. With unicast, a unique stream is created for each viewer that matches the viewer's connection speed. However, this could yield high volumes of stream demand that can overwhelm a network. Combinations of stream delivery methods can also be used. For instance, unicast can send a stream to several reflector computers, which in turn redistribute to viewers via multicast. One word of caution, however, multicast is not always compatible with all network routers.

The other protocol for streaming, HTTP, normally requires the presentation to be saved to the viewer's hard drive. This is also called progressive downloading. The viewer must wait for enough of the media to be transferred before any playback can commence. When compared to RTSP (real time streaming) HTTP can be choppy. Once the media is completely downloaded, however, the playback quality is excellent. If copyright issues are important, there is a method to disable saving of HTTP movies if embedded in a web page.

3. *QuickTime*

Although there are other applications on the market that incorporate streaming technology, such as MS Media Player and RealPlayer, QuickTime is an exceptional choice for the following reasons:

- It is standards based and the core of the emerging MPEG-4 standard.
- It is easy to use by authors and students.
- It is very affordable for institutional infrastructure and authoring.
- It is a royalty free streaming solution for any number of recipients.
- It supports 3rd party development via plugin software.

Media produced with QuickTime are called "movies," which are actually storage documents that can import over 30 different multimedia formats including video, audio (e.g. MP3, MIDI, Karaoke), 3D, virtual reality (VR), still images, animation, sprites, and graphics (bit mapped or vector). The process to produce these movies is described below.

4. *Quick Time Movie Production For Real Time Streaming (RTSP)*

Although there are many hardware and software choices available for capturing, creating, and delivering streamable media, we suggesting one possible combination for live streaming (See Table 1.), and another for non-live. (See Table 2.)

Table 1. QuickTime Movie Production Process for LIVE Streaming

Steps	Products Used In Process (A portable computer is recommended for all steps.)
Capture Content	Camcorder for Video, Analog Capture Card
Compress and Encode	Sorenson Video 2, Qdesign Music Program, Sorenson Broadcaster program
Deliver (Stream)	Sorenson Broadcaster program, Mac OS X Server program, QuickTime Player

The combination of products in Table 1 will enable you to stream a live event to your desired audience. First, you must connect your camcorder and auxiliary microphones (if needed) to your broadcasting computer. A Sorenson Broadcaster program will take the video/audio from your sources and compress the information down to the connection rate of your target audience. They receive each encoded packet all at once to recreate the event real-time. The Sorenson Broadcaster program then encodes this compressed information to create a stream that is sent to a second computer, which uses the Mac OS X Server program to send the stream to viewers. Each viewer receives the stream simultaneously to recreate the event real-time.

The Sorenson Broadcaster program features convenient preset compression settings that are activated by simply choosing a target audience connection rate (i.e. 28.8, 56k). It also has simple menus for selecting your previously connected audio and video sources. The last step is to enter the IP address of your MAC OS X streaming server and select either multicast or unicast from the menu. After making all of these choices, the Sorenson Broadcaster program sends an email announcement to your recipients that includes a link to the movie (you can also embed the broadcast in a WebPage). Now you simply go back to Sorenson Broadcaster and hit start to begin broadcasting.

You would use live streaming to deliver important events to students who cannot be in attendance and as an alternative mode of delivery for instruction. It allows you to step outside commercial broadcasting's scheduling constraints. Live events can also be archived for delivery on demand.

Table 2. QuickTime Movie Production Process for NON-LIVE Streaming

Steps	Products Used In Process (A computer with FireWire ports is required.)
Capture/Create Content	DV Camcorder for Video, Digital Camera, Scanner, Software Graphics Program, Final Cut Pro
Compress and Encode	Media Cleaner Pro Suite
Deliver (Stream)	Mac OS X Server (computer and programs), QuickTime Player

For non-live broadcasting, you would first use a DV camcorder to record the video content you wish to stream. Final Cut Pro is then used to import your media via a FireWire connection from the camera to your hard disk. You will also use Final Cut Pro to edit the movie and export to a QuickTime format uncompressed. We recommend you use Media Cleaner Pro to compress your movie to a streamable format. It is then uploaded to a Mac OS X Server, which handles the delivery.

Non-live broadcasting has definite advantages because it can be edited to meet specific needs. It can be embedded into a web page where you can creatively combine it with other forms of interaction. And, like live broadcasting, it is also valuable for enriching instruction by providing a multimedia experience that accommodates different learning styles.

5. *Enhancing the Learning Process*

Today's students are accustomed to media-rich learning environments, using the Internet for finding knowledge, for communicating, and for entertainment. To meet student expectations, even traditional institutions are increasingly delivering some instruction over the Web, both for enhancing the classroom curriculum and for distance learning. Furthermore, incorporating multi-media instruction immerses students in an environment that addresses a wide range of learning styles and abilities.

There are numerous advantages in using media streaming for instruction. Students can find segments quickly and in a non-linear fashion. They can retrieve information at their own pace and in accordance with their own time schedule. And, when streamed information is combined with other interactive technologies (such as email, hyperlinks, and computer bulletin boards), students are able to collaborate as they view.

Accessibility to this technology is critical in order for it to be successful and equitable. Since many students do not have access to high-end computers, an instructional delivery system must be software-based and operable through a web browser. QuickTime meets all these requirements because of its multimedia capabilities, and because it is readily streamable to a home computer.

Additionally, most students will find QuickTime very easy to use, since movies can be easily navigated with VCR-like controls, including slow motion, frame advance, pause, fast forward, and reverse. Students can go anywhere within a movie by using the chapters menu or by searching for text within a text track. The following QuickTime features allow students to receive multi-sensory images, which gives them access to complex information and facilitates learning.

- Picture in picture
- Side-by-side movies
- Layered animation
- Text track, which can provide sub-titles for movies and hyperlinks
- Text annotation that begs to be clicked or simply read
- Embedded objects, which can be explored, rotated, zoomed, or linked

There are other important features that make QuickTime a powerful tool for education. On the production side, movies can be embedded into a web page, PowerPoint presentation, or email message, which facilitates communication and shared learning. Different languages are accommodated on different text tracks, and unused ones can be disabled. PowerPoint presentations, which many instructors already have produced, can be imported and streamed. Additionally, movies can be made more interactive with the animation features of Electrifier or Flash, and they are scriptable.

For ease of delivery, QuickTime works well over the Internet, on CD's, and kiosks and it works cross-platform. Finally, students on the receiving end may bookmark favorite movies without having to save to their hard drives, and they can extract still images from movies as handout documents.

6. Getting Started

As the appeal of taking courses over the Internet grows, it becomes increasingly important to develop the core competencies to compete. QuickTime streaming now produces acceptable multimedia viewing over the Internet, and the quality of the delivery will continue to increase. In a few short years, the delivery "pipes" to students will become very large. The tools for preparing multimedia will become increasingly easier to use on one hand, and more extensive on the other, to meet the rising expectations of our students. Virtual reality environments will become even more real, adding to the value of the student's learning experience.

The important thing is to get started now. As you become more familiar with the advantages of streaming, keeping up with advances will be exciting and challenging, yet not overwhelming. You may find that streaming causes you to change dramatically the way you deliver instruction, both in traditional settings and for your students at a distance. Additionally, media segments may be reused, both for your own classes and for institutional uses, perhaps in other curriculums. This is what you can do today:

- Plan ways your curriculum could be enhanced through multimedia instruction.
- Join a list serve of teachers with the same interests.
- Start experimenting with advanced multimedia techniques such as embedded objects and virtual reality.
- Be sure to produce multimedia in the highest quality possible so it can be used for other purposes. (For example, use a digital video camcorder to capture video instead of a VHS-quality camera.)
- Within your institution, make decisions about how to index and record media assets in databases. Keep a list of multimedia assets that you have created or that you have found on the Internet. Provide "poster movies" as previews so viewers can decide which to select. You may want to develop a rating system for your list to assist users. It's also important to consider rules for use (including copyright procedures, usage log, royalty policies, etc). Passwords will facilitate your distribution if you want to restrict use.
- Meet with your Instructional Technology organization to plan the delivery infrastructure. (Will you use reflectors or off-campus servers?) Also discuss how to integrate QuickTime with your email system, BBS, and courseware-authoring environment (such as WebCT or Blackboard).
- Start a list of experts who you can turn to for information or advice.

7. *Conclusion*

QuickTime and streaming create a powerful combination that can deliver instruction efficiently and affordably to learners using their own home computers. It is an important educational tool because it immerses students in a multi-media environment that addresses a wide range of learning styles and abilities. Students can have the benefit of experiencing live events, even when they can't be in attendance, or they can access all or part of the presentation later for review. Since the instructor controls who has access to the presentation, streaming protects intellectual property from unauthorized redistribution.

With improvements in compression and streaming technology and with the versatility of QuickTime, the possibilities for delivering instruction over the Internet are now virtually endless. Learning truly can be "anytime, anywhere" with the power of media streaming.

For more information, contact: Dianne Hoff (email: Dianne.hoff@umit.maine.edu)
Doug Marchio (email: Doug@umit.maine.edu)
Justin Hafford (email: Justin.Hafford@umit.maine.edu)

Teaching and Learning in a Network World
P. Hoffman and D. Lemke (Eds.)
IOS Press, 2000

Vons/Pavilions Teach the Teachers Collaborative at the Thacher School

Kurt Meyer
The Thacher School
5025 Thacher Road
Ojai, CA 93023

In 1999, Teach the Teachers Collaborative (TTTC), a unique partnership of public and private schools, the retail food industry, technology companies, and a strategic philanthropy advisory group, was formed to address the critical need in southern California for teacher training in technology, creating the first professional development project of its kind.

The TTTC mission is to deliver the finest possible teacher training in research-based teaching practices and classroom technology use, in order to accelerate teachers' effective use of technological tools to improve student motivation, achievement, and employability. In our first year, the Teach the Teachers Collaborative was established as a California non-profit organization and developed a six-year strategic plan.

We secured a $6.1 million commitment from our primary funding provider, VONS/Pavilions, Inc., as well as more than $650,000 in technology loans, discounts, and donations with commitments for future seminars.

We launched a highly successful summer residency professional seminar program, a web site (http://www.teachtheteachers.org), and received recognition from California Secretary of Education Gary S. Hart, Texas Governor George W. Bush, and Los Angeles Mayor Richard Riordan.

Although recent investments in educational technology in the United States have topped $6 billion per year, there has not been a comparable investment in teacher technology training. In January 1999, the National Center for Education Statistics found that only 20 percent of teachers surveyed reported feeling "very well prepared" to integrate educational technology into the classroom. The study also found that the most effective teacher training incorporates mentoring by another teacher and sustained training over a period of time of more than 8 hours.[i] In southern California, it is estimated that only 10% of teachers have received enough training to be technologically proficient.[ii] Teachers are pushed to use technology without embracing its potential, so the potential for innovative technology use to improve education is not being realized. Teach the Teachers Collaborative seeks to redress these deficiencies.

The Teach the Teachers Collaborative offers six-day residential intensive training seminars at no cost to qualified K-12 teachers in southern California (from Fresno to San Diego). Each weekly seminar is held at The Thacher School in Ojai, California, and focuses on a particular curriculum area with workshops on curriculum/technology integration tied to the California Academic Content Standards.

Teachers participating in the program have exclusive use of a laptop throughout the week, and 24-hour access to e-mail, the Internet, and other network services via wired and equipped classrooms, dorm rooms, and study areas. They use the computers to take notes, practice lessons, and create a learning activity for publication on the web site (http://www.teachtheteachers.org). Teaching Assistants in every classroom capture the lessons in electronic journals and post the day's activities, presentations, and links to the archives section of the TTTC web site. Technology experts support the communications infrastructure by providing tutoring and hands-on demonstrations. Evening speakers, technology productivity training, introduction to an online educational discussion forum, and extensive individual instruction fill out the weekly routine. The intensive focus of the TTTC program enables participants to return to their schools emboldened not only to implement what they learned in their own classrooms, but also to become mentors to other teachers in their schools and districts.

In 1999, over 700 classroom teachers, representing over 450 schools in 14 southern California counties attended TTTC's first summer professional development seminars. During the 1999-2000 school year, these 700 will train 7,000 additional teachers and provide new opportunities for thousands of students in their own classrooms. Through contact with principals and school district administrators, TTTC ensures that teachers will have local support for their efforts. In summer 2000, TTTC plans to host an additional 1,350 teachers who will then each train ten teachers.

As an incentive to complete their 10-teacher training commitment, successful teachers receive college course credit, technology discounts from companies such as Gateway Computer, Inspiration Software, The Learning Company, CSG Visual Communication, Inc. and AlphaSmarts, and publication on the TTTC web site. At the conclusion of our first two years, we will have trained more than 22,000 teachers.

TTTC personnel maintain a year-round office and communicate regularly with participants, both collectively and individually, using the TTTC web site, discussion groups, a bi-weekly e-mail newsletter, school site visits, and personal communications. The searchable archives section of the TTTC web site includes comprehensive notes from each seminar and a compendium of teacher-made lesson plans, all of which are aligned with the California Content Standards. Scheduled online discussions give participants an opportunity to reconnect and share their successes and challenges.

Newsletters and e-mail highlight achievements of participants, offer tips and advice, list special discounts, and target sections of the web site. The wide base of support offered to teachers who attend the program allows them to go back to their schools ready to be effective mentors in technology to other teachers in their district. They form the core of an online community that can serve non-participant educators as well.

This unprecedented collaboration brings together diverse partners who have a strong commitment to the southern California community and to the futures of our children.

The nonprofit operates with a board of directors, president, and advisory groups in the major program areas (residency, web site, communications, and business development). Representatives from each of the major partners bring their expertise and organizational resources to the Collaborative to create a unique and successful partnership. Each partner brings the message of Teach the Teachers Collaborative to a larger audience, educating the community in the importance of teacher training.

The Thacher School, a nationally recognized private boarding school, offers professional expertise, training experience, and state-of-the-art facilities for teacher training. The school has a five-year history of summer teacher training programs that have been recognized by the New York Times, Popular Science, and, through a $280,000 grant, the W. M. Keck Foundation of Southern California. Using the full campus facilities: dormitory, dining room, state-of-the-art technology and recreational facilities, the Thacher School staff treat teachers as professionals performing critical tasks, and cultivate a professional atmosphere in which teachers become fully immersed in six days of training. Thacher School also serves as the "hub" of the TTTC information network, providing staff, equipment, and facilities to house the TTTC web site, email lists, and electronic newsletters.

The Los Angeles County Office of Education (LACOE), one of the largest public school agencies in the country, provides leadership in curriculum development to retain master instructors, to recruit a substantial number of qualified K-12 teachers and ensure the alignment of TTTC training with the California Academic Content Standards. Los Angeles County contains 1,700 schools, 81 school districts, and one third of California's student population. The county office provides the latest findings in educational research, and expert trainers to deliver it. Their commitment to integrating technology and curriculum, exemplified by the Technology For Learning Initiative, has been evident in popular and highly acclaimed training programs. Since 1997, TFL has created, in a program recognized by Vice President Al Gore, a county-wide core of technology teacher-leaders who work with teachers to develop personal and professional proficiency in technology, and with subject-area leaders to integrate technology use into their programs. The Los Angeles County Office of Education provides G-3 laptops for each participant to use during the training, ensuring every teacher's intensive hands-on experience throughout the week.

Menashe and Associates, a strategic philanthropy advisory group, brought the message of TTTC to the corporate community, securing the VONS/Pavilions partnership and developing sustainable business and funding models for the nonprofit. By offering potential investors an opportunity to touch millions of teachers and students through a single program, Menashe and Associates raised more than $650,000 in technology partner contributions for summer 1999.

VONS/Pavilions, a Safeway Company and a leading food retailer in southern California, partnered with manufacturers to underwrite the program with a $6.1 million commitment. They also provide a connection to the community through their stores and an education-related advertising campaign. Supported by the corporate office, individual store managers promote the program to neighborhood schools, and highlight local teacher participation in their stores. These partners have pooled their resources and lent their expertise to create a unique program designed to deliver free, content-based technology training and support to thousands of southern California K-12 teachers.

A study by the Office of Technology Assessment estimates that "it can take up to five years to effectively infuse technology into schools and that all teachers need to be trained and supported over that period."[iii] TTTC's program creates a unique blend of the best pedagogical practice, technology support, residential living, and information network access so that teachers achieve a level of mastery unattainable in other workshop settings. The broad partnership ensures that, on a year round basis, the entire community becomes engaged in the effort to improve student motivation, achievement, and employability.

---

[i] Laurie Lewis, Basmat Parsad, Nancy Carey, Nicole Bartfai, Elizabeth Farris Westat, National Center for Education Statistics: *Teacher Quality: A Report on the Preparation and Qualifications of Public School Teachers*, (U.S. Department of Education: Office of Educational Research and Improvement NCES 1999-080).

[ii] Technology for Learning Initiative, Inventory Analysis, 1997-1998, p. 22.

[iii] Glennan, T. and Mesmad, A., *Fostering the Use of Educational Technology: Elements of a National Strategy,* http://www.rand.org/publications

Teaching and Learning in a Network World
P. Hoffman and D. Lemke (Eds.)
IOS Press, 2000

But Do They Learn? Connecting Technology and Learning

Judith Neill, Director
Robin Curoe, Associate Director
Instructional Design and Planning Division
Wisconsin Technical College System Foundation, Inc.
Waunakee, WI 53597 (800) 821-6313 www.wids.org

Abstract. A rewarding learning experience involves more than a shiny CD-ROM or trip to a snazzy website. Careful instructional design lies at the heart of any learning experience, online or not. Practical strategies for designing learning in any environment support the learning process (motivation, comprehension, practice, and application). Accommodating varied learning styles in course development and examining tools for designing full learning-centered online courses.

In distance learning it is particularly tempting to become so engaged in figuring out how you can use technology to deliver information to your learners that you neglect the front-end design of the *what, how,* and *when* of the learning. Up-front organization, clear communication about performance expectations, outcome driven assessment, and imaginative learning strategies are even more critical to successful distance learning than they are in a classroom setting. When you and your learners are not physically in the same place at the same time, careful instructional design, based on what we know about how people learn, provides a map that guides you and your learners toward successful completion of a learning experience.

1. Methods and Media

Differentiating between media and methods is the first step toward ensuring that learning and distance are not contradictory. Instructional methods cause learning. Media deliver methods. Ruth Clark, Business and Industry Training Consultant, describes methods as "Techniques that support cognitive processes that lead to learning." Examples of instructional methods include practice, simulation, discussion, presentation, demonstration, role-play, questioning, debate, etc.

Dr. Clark goes on to define media as "Delivery devices or strategies that carry methods." They do not cause learning in and of themselves. Examples of instructional media might include audio, video, computers, Internet--in the high tech arena. More traditional examples are transparencies, print materials, and even presenters or instructors.

Studies show that though media and delivery format may affect accessibility and even satisfaction, given equivalent instructional methods, media do not impact the effectiveness of the instruction. When we design learning activities, we want to first concentrate on methods for helping learners learn. When we address the selection of distance learning media to deliver instruction, we may need to adapt some of our learning activities, but in doing so we need to be carefully creative to minimize any compromises that negatively impact the effectiveness of the learning.

Only after you have determined *what* your learners need to be able to do and how you will know *when* they have achieved the *what*, is it time to plan *how* your learners will get there. Though it is tempting at this point to focus on the delivery of content information, your learners' success depends on your resisting that temptation to first consider what methods (strategies that cause learning) you will build into the distance learning experience.

2. How Does the Learner's Mind Work?

Noted leader in adult education, Patricia Cross reminds us that "how learners are taught lies at the heart of quality education. It makes the difference between a lifelong learner and a grade grabber, between enthusiasm for learning and indifference to it, between an educated society and credentialed one." We know that most learners learn better when they are actively engaged in the learning process. In distance learning it is even more important to abandon a "Telling as teaching" mode for learning methods that support the human thinking and learning process.

The Three Memories

Before you launch into the design of learning activities, you may find it helpful to consider how learning works within the learner's mind. In his book, *A Celebration of Neurons*, Robert Sylwester compares the organization of the memory system to the organization of an office. In the office we process vast amounts of information that compete for our attention. To cope, we label some information "Junk mail" and discard it. We handle or process other information immediately and forget about it. Some information we store to be handled later; some we put into permanent files with related information; and other information we incorporate into new or existing procedures for operation.

Our brains have three memory systems that deal with information processing and storage: the sensory memory, the working (or short term) memory, and the long-term memory. The sensory memory takes in enormous amounts of information. This memory system has a large capacity, but a very short duration (visual as little as .2 of a second; audio a maximum of 4 seconds). It selects a subset of the information that comes in (junking--ignoring the rest), transmitting the selected bits directly to the long-term memory for storage or to the working memory for processing.

The working memory receives data taken in and selected by the sensory memory. The working memory then processes the selected information. It is our center of consciousness--our center of thinking. Though the working memory is very powerful in its ability to process information, it is also very fragile. Its capacity for quantity of information is limited to 5 to 9 chunks. Chunks are units of information that vary in size depending on the expertise of the individual. We know this as the rule of 7 +/-2.

The working memory also is limited in duration. Without rehearsal (practice), a chunk of information will last about 12 seconds. Thus the alternative label "short-term" memory. The working memory continually monitors the data being delivered by the sensory system, simultaneously prioritizing, editing, focusing, and shifting attention to important, interesting, and familiar information. It continually allows us to shift chunks of information between the foreground and background so that we can experience and respond to the current situation.

The third memory system is the long-term memory. It is considered permanent memory and serves as our repository for storing information. The long-term memory has immense capacity.

Five main processes control the flow of information through the memory systems: attention, encoding, rehearsal (practice), retrieval, and metacognition. Attention allows learners to select a sub-set of information that comes into the sensory memory for processing in the working memory. Encoding allows the learner to store information in any of the three memories. During rehearsal/practice the learner processes information in the working memory. *It is only through rehearsal/practice that learners can encode information to long-term memory.* Since the information in working memory lasts only up to 12 seconds, learners do not learn anything until they have stored it in their long-term memories. *In other words, learners cannot learn without practice!*

In order to process information in our long-term memories, we need to retrieve it, bringing it to the working memory--our conscious mind. How many times have you seemingly "Forgotten" a name that you are sure you know? You know the frustration—"It's just on the tip of my tongue." Actually, you have not "forgotten" the name; it is still in your long-term memory. Your problem is retrieval. In humans our working and long-term memories function together. As Robert Sylwester points out, "Short-term (working) memory allows us to experience the present, but we would become a prisoner of the present without the two interrelated forms of long-term memory."

The fifth process, metacognition, is not sequential, but functions as a monitoring system. The learner uses metacognitive process to set goals, select strategies, monitor progress, and adjust learning strategies.

Cognitive Overload

Cognitive overload is what learners sometimes refer to as "fried brain syndrome." It happens when the fragile working memory cannot process information in the quantities or at the speed with which it is being presented. *Nothing is learned until learners encode it into long-term memory.* Before entering the long-term memory, knowledge must be processed by the working memory; that is--practiced. Since the working memory can handle only so much material, a logical strategy for avoiding cognitive overload and maximizing its use is to clear out the clutter with meaningful practice that moves information from the working memory to the long-term memory.

Learning Styles/Processing Preferences

Research tells us that people learn in different ways. In distance learning environments it is easy to fall victim to a teaching-centered, rather than a learning-centered approach. When we focus on teaching, we often try to mold all individuals into reflective, abstract, analytical, sequential learners. More over, teaching methods that focus heavily on giving information are easier to adapt to distance learning than are more learning-centered methods. In this teaching-centered environment the active, concrete, feeling, holistic learners struggle to adapt, but many of them just cannot succeed. They need to learn by doing.

3. Designing Effective Learning Methods

Surely distance learning is fertile ground for the application of numerous theories rooted in educational psychology and teaching methods. However, you may not have the luxury of returning for four to six credits of graduate work prior to designing your distance learning experience. As you plan your next distance learning course, these five strategies will help you move a long way toward ensuring that distance teaching also means distance learning:

- provide learning plans
- design with a bias for learner-centered methods
- insert frequent practice
- support all stages of the learning cycle
- vary the format of learning activities

Provide Learning Plans

Metacognition is the learner's internal process for monitoring learning. Learners use metacognition to consciously apply study skills and to reflect on the process that they have used to solve a problem. Learning plans lay out a road map for learning one competency or two-three related competencies by spelling out performance expectations--*what* learners will learn; explaining assessment--*when* you will know they have learned; and identifying learning activities and materials--giving learners a plan for *how* they can learn. A learning plan gives learners an advanced organizer that helps them consciously set goals, select strategies, regulate their progress, and adjust personal learning behavior. Though learning plans are very helpful in traditional, instructor-led learning environments, they are critical in distance learning situations where learners do not have frequent, in-person access to teachers.

Design With a Bias For Learner-Centered Methods

Learners learn best when they are actively engaged in the learning process. Though learning activities fall on a continuum somewhere between teacher-centered and learner-centered, the best measure is the level of passivity or involvement on the parts of the learners.

It is obvious that teacher-centered learning activities such as lecture and demonstration place the teacher in an active role and learner in a more passive role. What may not be as obvious, however, is that common distance learning activities such as reading teacher-selected texts and teacher-produced materials, viewing teacher-selected videos, and performing highly structured drill and practice are also predominately teacher-centered.

In learner-centered learning activities, teachers play a facilitation role, while learners play an active role. There are countless varieties of learner-centered learning activities such as role play, chat room discussions, interview, solving case studies, researching information--perhaps on the Internet, performance of a skill, reading learner-selected materials, developing learner-designed job or learning aids, and so forth.

Well-designed learner-centered activities cause critical and creative thinking. Because they involve learners, they also assist in the process of encoding learning into the long-term memory. Learner-centered activities hold learners' attention, support multiple learning styles or processing preferences, and provide metacognitive opportunities as learners are required to set goals and solve problems. Learner-centered activities make learners full partners in the learning process, teaching them how to learn, and requiring them to take responsibility for their own learning.

Insert Frequent Practice

Learning activities do two things--help learners acquire information or cause learners to practice. The simplest strategy for helping learners avoid cognitive overload is to chunk instruction into short, informative lessons that are punctuated by frequent, meaningful practice. When you provide feedback to practice, you do more than just clear the working memory. You support metacognition by providing continuing improvement assessment that helps learners rate their learning success and helps instructors judge their teaching effectiveness when they can still make needed adjustments.

There are two types of practice--maintenance and elaborative rehearsal. Maintenance rehearsal involves repetition and memorization. It uses a great deal of energy, and may require as many as 500 repetitions before many learners can perform the skill or use the knowledge automatically. Though maintenance rehearsal serves to keep information active in the working memory, it also clutters this fragile, short-term memory. Consequently, it is not very efficient.

Elaborative rehearsal causes learners to interact with the content. This type of practice connects the new content or skill with what learners already know, applies practice to the solution of real problems, creates something new. Elaborative rehearsal is the more efficient way to encode information into long-term memory. Though examples of elaborative rehearsal are unlimited, we might include solving a case study problem, engaging in hands-on practice, examining how prior personal experience relates to the current content, creating a scenario that applies the new knowledge, taking and defending a position, synthesizing multiple ideas and perspectives, etc.

Support the Learning Cycle

When you develop learning activities for a competency or several related competencies, you are creating a plan that guides learners through the process of learning. We represent the learning process as a cycle (Figure #1). There are four major stages: motivation, comprehension, practice, and application. Each stage supports one or more of the five thinking processes: attention, encoding, rehearsal, retrieval, and metacognition. When you select the learning activities for a learning plan, choose activities that provide a framework guiding learners all the way through the cycle.

At the motivation stage you facilitate the attention process by inspiring learners to learn and answering the question, "Why do I want to learn this information or skill?" During the comprehension stage you facilitate encoding and processing in the working memory by clarifying performance expectations and helping learners access the information they need to perform the target competency. In the practice stage you need to provide guided practice—elaborative rehearsal, giving feedback to facilitate encoding to long term memory. Finally, the application stage fosters retrieval from the long-term memory to enable working memory processing on demand. During the application stage learners need to show that they can apply what they have learned to real world problems and decision-making. It is during the application stage that you build in assessment.

When you design learning plans, move learners through the cycle: motivation, comprehension, practice, and application. However, learners need to swing back and forth between the comprehension and practice stages before moving on to application. By doing this you help them avoid cognitive overload by chunking the learning into manageable pieces and punctuating it with frequent practice.

Vary the Format of Learning Activities

The way individuals learn depends on how they typically take in and process information. You can make your distance learning course friendly to differing learning styles and intelligences by varying the method (the learning strategy), media (the delivery mode), environment, interpersonal context, feedback, and givens.

You can choose from a limitless variety of learning methods by using various combinations of presentation, simulation, investigation, guided practice, projects, feedback, memory aids, graphic organizers, information seeking, information receiving, teacher-directed reading (textbooks or course materials), learner-directed reading, and so on. You can also vary the learning environment by creating learning activities that call for them to go into the community, centers for culture such as museum, or workplace.

You will enrich the variety by designing individual and collaborative learning activities that call for pairs, small or large groups. Even though distance learners may be learning via Internet, video, audio, etc., you can direct them to construct small groups on their own, or you can form discussion groups via E-mail, phone, or even snail mail.

Givens (what you provide for learners as prompts, information or tools) provide any number of options for varying learning and practice. You may provide a case study or a scenario as a prompt; you may give learners a particular problem to solve or topic to address. In guided practice you might provide a product or piece of equipment with flaws or errors that must be corrected. An even more effective variation is to have learners bring in or construct their own "givens" drawing on their experiences for relevant examples and problems.

One type of media may be dominant in your particular distance learning situation, but you can reach a broader range of learners and learning styles by incorporating different types of media to deliver the instruction. If you have access to some of the newer technologies, you may use computer simulations, computer-based lessons, computer-based practice, satellite conferencing and even the Internet to deliver a portion of the learning.

Even in a "low--tech" environment you can vary *media* with a rich combination of auditory learning (lecture, audio tape, radio), visual learning (transparencies, slides, flip charts, video, demonstration, and tactile learning such as manipulatives, models, hands-on practice). You can vary *delivery* of information by giving learners access to guest speakers and panel presentations, and by filling different roles as instructor, such as coach, facilitator, learner, presenter, and questioner. Remember, you are media too.

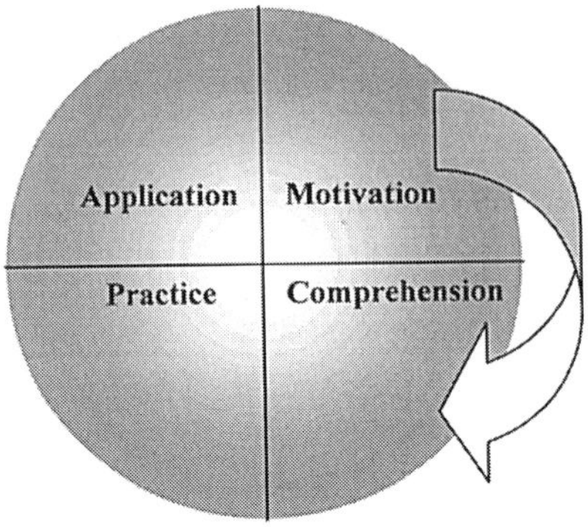

Figure 1. The Learning Cycle

References

Clark, Ruth C. (1994). *Developing Technical Training*. Phoenix, AZ: Buzzards Bay Press.

Cross, Patricia (1987, February 12). "Teaching 'For' Learning." [Paper] Raleigh, NC*: North Carolina State University Centennial Year Provost's Forum.*

Sylwester, Robert (1995*). A Celebration of Neurons: An Educators' Guide to the Human Brain.* Alexandria, VA: Association for Supervision and Curriculum Development.

Teaching and Learning in a Network World
P. Hoffman and D. Lemke (Eds.)
IOS Press, 2000

Hybrid Courses: Determining the Effectiveness of Using the Internet

Sandra E. Poindexter
College of Business, Northern Michigan University, Marquette MI 49855
Bonnie S. Heck
School of Electrical and Computer Engineering,
Georgia Institute of Technology, Atlanta GA 30332
Tawni H. Ferrarini
Dept. of Economics, Northern Michigan University, Marquette MI 49855

Abstract. This cross-disciplinary study identifies several of the benefits and costs associated with using the Internet to complement not compete against, the chalk-and-talk learning environments of instructors.

1. Introduction

Since the early 1990s and birth of the Web, instructional experimentation with Internet integration has been undertaken. It is time now for educators to identify the benefits and costs associated with utilizing the Internet to complement the solid educational structures tried and tested by so many traditional instructors. By relying on the Internet to complete previously time consuming tasks, can instructors reallocate their resources toward improving their educational environments in fashions valued by their disciplines?

While efforts are varied, usage of the Internet can be grouped into three general categories: communication supplements, course management aids, and course content supplements. Communication supplements are those which enhance the interaction between instructor and students, and between students. The latter is particularly true in courses where teams are a large part of the course structure. Course management aids provide organization and a computerized mechanism for both delivery and collection of course material. They also serve as an interactive study guide vehicle. Course content supplements add outside readings and materials to contribute to and enhance textbook subject matter.

From a cross-disciplinary perspective this paper highlights how the Internet use can be used to increase learning and the interest to learn, and reduce the costs of course management, research, locating educational information, and communication. Experiences in business, economics, and engineering courses will be relayed and generalized to other disciplines.

2. Internet Integration in Information Systems

By most measures, information systems is a discipline still in its youth with little more than 25 years of existence. From the standpoint technical innovativeness in teaching this youth has been a distinct advantage. Without a legacy of tradition to overcome, faculty are more likely to experiment with new techniques. The discipline's computing emphasis further adds to the likelihood of instructional technology use, and the Internet was a logical and early step.

2.1 Communication Supplements

Notifying students of announcements using a group email list has proven much more effective than maintaining an announcements web page. Students typically check their email daily, so class email taps into an already active medium. Less effective was a class announcement web page that students were to visit on their own initiative. Since daily announcements rarely occur, students quickly abandoned a daily check-in routine and missed announcements.

Online office hours can be conducted in two ways: preset times during which email will be answered immediately or replies sent whenever the instructor is online with a minimum email check of once per day. Much like getting a paper letter out before the postal carrier arrives, using a preset time lets students know what time of day their email will be read and to make that deadline. This simulates physical office hours the most closely, but also has its disadvantage of limited availability. Online, anytime office hours can become an intrusion to the instructor; it is near the equivalent of saying, "here's my home phone number, call me anytime." When the instructor doesn't reply quickly, students criticize availability even when email is answered within 12 hours. The solution is a balance of setting expectations while meeting the needs of students in a particular class—some classes simply need more instructor availability than others.

In situations where student teams are heavily used, student-student email with file attachments, bulletin boards, and chat rooms expand team meeting time outside of class. Students with class, work, and home schedules typically have little common time to meet on class projects. Training team members to regularly use these features has meant the difference between success and mediocre team performance.

2.2 Course Management Aids

Distribution of course materials via the web continues to be one of the first points of web integration [1] and has a quick return. Putting a course syllabus, handouts, and assignments in a website for student retrieval reduced some paper copies, eliminated problems of lost papers and obtaining replacements. The website became a course portfolio and helped students with their own organization. By keeping the site active, students were also more apt to relook at the syllabus on a regular basis. Many students indicated that other paper-based syllabi remained buried in their notes after the first week of classes, but the active online syllabus was reviewed at least weekly. Photos taken during class of team presentations and exercises were added to the course website to make the growing portfolio have some visual student ownership. An example is shown in Figure 1. It is not clear whether this was perceived as a gimmick or appreciated as a personal touch, but no complaints have been voiced regarding either the photo taking or postings.

Two additions to the course website have been successfully used: posting class minutes, shown in Figure 2, and grade retrieval. Class minutes, taken by students in rotation, summarize the content and announcements of a class period. These written notes are posted to the website by date and used by students who miss a class period as well as attending students who want to verify their own notes. If the instructor confirms the content (and adds notes in italics) these minutes serve as documentation and a source of reference in case of dispute. Grades can be posted for individual query by password or as a class list with anonymous posting ids. Some students prefer the individual postings for better privacy while many others like to measure their performance against the rest of the class. Use of grade postings is dictated by objectives, university policy, and instructor technical skills (individual posting querying requires more sophisticated software), but students definitely want to see their official grade standings.

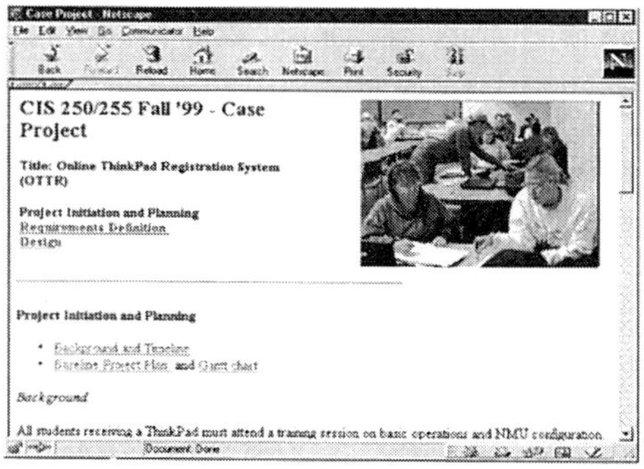

Figure 1. Course Portfolio

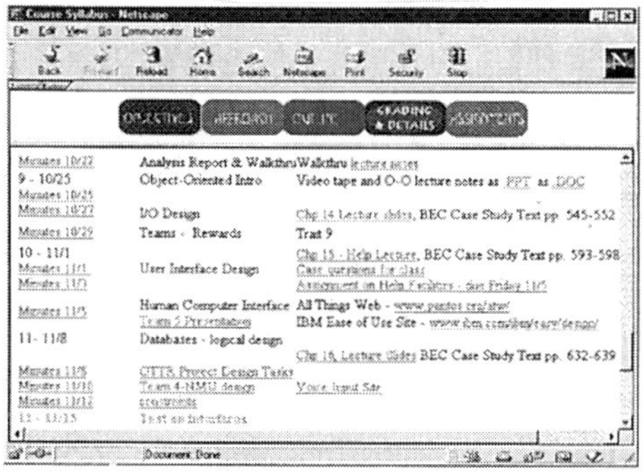

Figure 2. Material delivery and minutes

Course websites moved past a passive delivery to a feedback device when interactive features were added. Assignments collected online as file attachments or sent with ftp to a dropbox folder can be electronically graded (instructor comments in alternate font) and returned. This was especially true for team assignments as all teams members received a copy the graded file. Beyond this, posting select submissions or solution files to the website provided students with accurate models.

Online testing is a second avenue for student interaction with several levels of complexity: simple posting of prior exams, online practice tests with immediate feedback, and actual testing. While students indicate they want these features, it may not be the best return on time invested for two reasons. Many students do not actually use these practice test features, even though they request them. Others limit their studies to just the practice test questions and ignore the overall subject. These are the same limitations of paper practice tests used for decades. Objective questions seem a crucial part of both practice and online tests in order to provide immediately scored feedback. Many instructors prefer essay questions and online tests are not a well-suited medium. However, for take-home examinations the ability to download the questions, type answers in a word processor, and electronically submit the completed exam worked well.

2.3 Course Content Supplements

From a technical standpoint, creating a course web page containing links to online references relevant to course content is not difficult. Providing quality outside readings, whether journals on reserve at the library or selected online sites, has always required care. The added caution needed in validating website content takes extra instructor time and is hard. Once an instructor locates a quality source, the task becomes easier, however, some disciplines have more volatile content mandating more effort in site selection. In information systems, currency of content is a continuous problem that use of valid websites can overcome. Assigning readings from online journals for classtime discussion keeps both instructor and students abreast of new technologies and trends.

If students are expected to include web references as part of a research project, student training on effective web use is critical. Often incorrectly assumed, is that students are web literate and easily able to locate and critically assess information. Surfing the web may be well understood, but knowing how to get the best results of search engines and evaluate them is not. Instructors should provide a training session of web research that includes query command language, evaluation criteria, and copyright infringements. If the instructor is not qualified to provide this training ask the library staff for this service. Ignoring this issue results in frustrations, lost time, and poorly written research.

3. Internet Integration in Engineering

Engineering by definition is a discipline whereby the principles of math and science are harnessed to make products that are useful to mankind. Thus engineering education entails two specific tasks: teaching basic scientific and mathematical principles and teaching students how to design products. Learning these skills requires students to make complex calculations, simulate the behavior of complex processes, and test the effectiveness of numerous design approaches on a product—all of which are facilitated through the use of computers. As a result, computers have been an integral part of the engineering curriculum for twenty-five years—since the days of the card punch machines. In the 1980s and 1990s, computer usage was dominated by dedicated computer labs with local area networks set up for students studying computationally intensive topics. More recently, the Internet has made it possible for students to gain access to educational materials from their dorm rooms or any other computer site. The use of the Internet in engineering education is discussed in detail in [2] and is reviewed below.

3.1 Communication Supplements

The Internet provides a timely means to supplement courses with out-of-class announcements and questions and answers. These can be accomplished through e-mail, bulletin boards or chat rooms for simple announcements or simple questions. It generally takes little effort for students to ask questions via email and for instructors to answer them. Students can send email at any time of day (even at night when it would be inappropriate to telephone) and expect answers within a reasonable time frame. However, text-only formats, such as used in email, have limitations. Much of engineering homework requires analysis using mathematical and scientific expressions. Some of this can be translated into text using expressions such as x^2 for x2 and "alpha" for the Greek letter α, but complex equations cannot be transmitted over email or posted to standard bulletin boards or chat rooms. Some people have been experimenting with whiteboards for students to enter equations into a chat room [3]. The technology requires some additional software or hardware on the user side, but it does have potential for electronic communications in engineering courses.

3.2 Course Management

The basic elements in just about any course are the syllabus (including a list of required and recommended course materials, schedule, readings, course policies, instructor contact information), homework assignments and solutions, tests and test solutions. A Web server makes a wonderful storage place for these elements. It can be accessed by students at any time and it helps to organize the course. PDF format and postscript are the preferred methods of storing tests, homework assignments and solutions in engineering applications.

Online tests can be given using a course management package such as WebCT where the test can be graded automatically. For example, an online test using WebCT was given in a junior-level course at Georgia Tech. One goal of the course was to teach students how to use the software package MATLAB for analyzing system responses. The online test required students to open WebCT in one window and MATLAB in another window. The questions were given in WebCT and required students to perform some complex calculations using MATLAB to find the answers, which were then entered into WebCT. The test was given a time limit and could only be taken during a specified time window. The benefit of this type of testing is that it could ask questions that were more complicated than could be asked in a traditional classroom setting where students used only scientific calculators (rather than a computer), and it tested their knowledge of MATLAB. There are

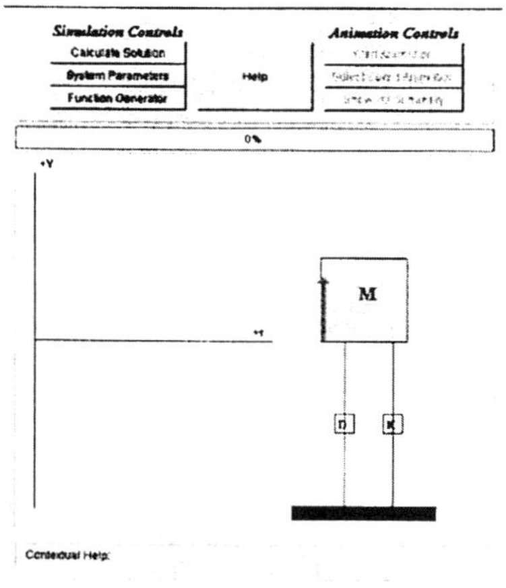

Figure 3. Initial configuration

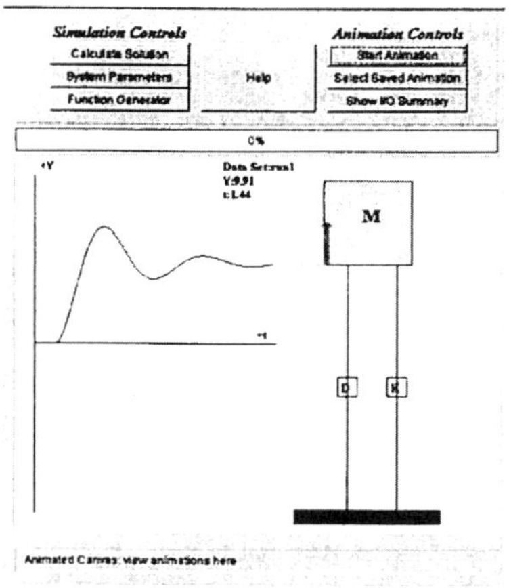

Figure 4. After student simulation

several drawbacks to this type of test. One is that it is unsupervised and may entice some students to cheat (as would any take-home test). Another is that the communication link may not be dependable. If a student starts the test and then loses the connection, how do they get back into the test environment? How is the time allotment handled in such circumstances? Students should not be able to voluntarily break the connection to work on problems off-line and then reconnect. Lastly, students have had over ten years of experience taking pencil and paper tests and in many cases are reluctant to taking any other type of test (especially one given on line). They need plenty of practice before a test is counted. This brings forth a new benefit to online testing software. A bank of practice test problems can be made available for students as a means of studying the material and working problems quickly. Their practice quizzes can be graded automatically giving students immediate feedback on their answers.

3.3 Course Content Supplements

One of the most challenging issues in engineering is for students to be able to visualize complex behavior of systems. Consider the mass-spring-damper system shown in Figures 3 and 4. This is a simple model that can represent the suspension in an automobile, the vibration of heavy equipment, or some other complex system. The mass moves up and down when a force is applied (such as when an automobile goes over a bump in the road). A JAVA applet is available on line for students to simulate the behavior of the system [4]. Figure 3 shows the applet in its initial configuration, and Figure 4 shows the applet after a simulation. Students can change the values of the mass, spring and/or damper and select different types of inputs (sudden jolts versus oscillatory inputs) using the simulation controls menu shown in Figure 3. The JAVA program computes the response mathematically and then animates the motion as well as displays a graph showing the history of the motion, see Figure 4.

Such interactive demonstrations have become very popular in teaching science and engineering. For example, the junior-level electrical engineering textbook by Kamen and Heck [4] has a Web site that is highly coupled with the text. The examples in the text contain detailed mathematical derivations. The web site has corresponding simulations and animations for the examples, such as the mass-spring-damper example described above. Students are free to change parameters in the simulation and see what happens. The animations provide more insight than mathematical analysis or even static pictures. The web site for this book also provides a bank of worked problems as a reference for students, a tutorial for the software used in the course, and downloadable software. All of these can be kept more up to date than a traditional textbook. The challenge for instructors is to entice students to view these demonstrations. If testing material does not cover questions about the online demos, then students may not spend the time necessary to review them.

Another trend in engineering education is the use of virtual and remote laboratories over the web. Virtual laboratories are simply elaborate demonstrations of the sort mentioned above. They generally involve use of JAVA programs and may even use a virtual reality program to simulate a real laboratory environment. A remote lab is a real lab experiment that is connected to the web. A remote user can set the parameters of the experiment and start it up. They can receive the data from the experiment. If bandwidth is not a problem, then a camera and microphone can be set up so that students can get streaming video and audio of the experiment as it is running.

4. Internet Integration in Economics

Recent studies show an increased demand for economics degrees, possibly indicating that students do not find this oft-labeled “dismal science” as being so dreadful [5]. As students return to the economics classrooms, they find that the Internet has been integrated into their learning environments. Economist instructors now use the Internet to bring students instantly to the economic data and news released by government agencies, policymakers, world organizations and business professional. The Internet allows instructors to connect their students immediately with key economic events, to communicate electronically with their students in a short period of time, to support bulletin board activities posting revised explanations of complex economic principles, and to direct students to electronic resources created, maintained and updated by economists. The electronically-supported learning environment increases the speed in which economic principles are taught and connected to real world events. Students appear motivated to learn more if instructors complement their class time with Internet components.

4.1 Communication Supplements

Electronic messaging proves efficient and effective in the economics learning environment. Students check email daily, complete electronically delivered assignments in a timely fashion, ask in-depth questions, and appear motivated to retrieve current economic information to complete assignments requiring them to do so. One clear advantage of using electronic messaging to answer commonly asked questions is that instructors can group similar questions, answer them as if they were one, and then distribute the answer to the class as a whole. Students comment that they appreciate quick responses from instructors and find value in knowing that classmates face the same types of questions.

Students use electronic office hours considerably more than traditional office hours. During the winter 1999 semester, students enrolled in a hybrid macroeconomics course used electronic office hours daily while students in a traditional macroeconomics course used them only eight times during the span of the semester. Electronic office hours demand little student time or energy in locating instructors’ offices or arranging schedules to fit office hours held by instructors and help minimize formal communication barriers between students and instructors. Hybrid students do contact instructors more frequently and they do ask questions more freely than traditional students. One distinct disadvantage does exist, however, as some students email trivial questions about class status and other issues that they could easily answer themselves; email can become a crutch preventing self-solution.

From the instructor’s standpoint, responding to electronic messages can be time consuming. To manage response time effectively, instructors may wish to set designated times in which electronic messages will be addressed. This allows instructors to specialize in responding to emails while helping students form expectations about when to expect responses from their instructors. To address technical problems, instructors may want to establish a short period at the beginning of their courses in which students may bring technical issues to the instructors' attention and expect assistance from their instructors and/or their assistants.

Creating electronic mailboxes for each course to filter email messages help instructors efficiently manage their email. Instructors can require students to use preset subject-heading phrases in the subject fields of their electronic messages can filter emails by class, section, and assignment and/or topic. For example, students enrolled in Economics 101 – Section 1 submitting assignment one may be required to place EC101-1: Assn 1 in the subject field of their emails. Electronic filters can then send all messages sent by EC101-1 students to a specific course electronic mailbox where messages can then be sorted and addressed by assignment. Organizing activities like these permit instructors to address similar student questions, exercises, or issues at one time, increasing instructor productivity.

Student to student interaction outside of class increases with the use of email and bulletin boards. Students often ask each other questions about assignments, organize study groups, and ask fellow classmates for assistance in understanding difficult concepts. Electronic devices are available to allow instructors to track and record these types of student activities, a task difficult to document in a traditional learning environment.

4.2 Course Management Aids

Electronically posted course syllabi, reading assignments, exercises, past tests and class outlines help students organize course materials. Students have ubiquitous and low cost access to these materials that are deemed important by their economics instructors. This access provides students with a useful educational structures that will help guide students down their learning paths. Students appear to be self-motivated to spend the required resources needed to learn various economic concepts when their economics course syllabi contain active hyperlinks to real world organizations, consumer groups, and businesses which actively use economics principles, models, and theories to conduct activities described in economics textbooks.

Students facing long download times on the Internet or who do not have Internet access can use computer-generated exercises located on disks. Often instructors and students will use these exercises to create dynamic learning environments in economics courses. Students need to be encouraged to complete these exercises and instructors need to test students over the material learned while completing them. Otherwise, students do not possess the proper incentives needed to learn how to use the software and to complete the accompanying exercises. To teach students how to use the software and to address user issues, instructors must invest time in learning how to use the software themselves. Depending on their level of computer expertise and what must be sacrificed in order to learn how to use the software, this investment may or not pay off for instructors.

4.3 Course Content Supplements

Many electronic resources are available on the Internet for economics instructors and their students to utilize. Some economic websites help economics instructors and students locate quickly economic data and information on key economic policies, organizations, journals, trade organizations, and societies. Some websites provide interactive exercise modules that take supply and demand graphs, static in textbooks, and make them dynamic over the Web. These sites often provide links to a wealth of information on various manipulations of demand and supply models. Using these interactive websites students gain from being able to manipulate graphs first hand, to make incorrect choices without penalty, and to receive instantaneous feedback on choices made. Still other websites provide inflation calculators and econometric models. Of course, educational objectives, instructors' teaching preferences, and level of students will influence which electronic resources will best complement the economics classroom.

5. Summary and Conclusions

Table 1 summarizes the effectiveness ratings of the Internet features as integrated into traditional courses in three disciplines. While the course content supplement features vary by discipline, there are some common threads of value in the communication and course management areas that might be generalized to most academic fields. Most significantly are group email and online postings of syllabi, handouts, and assignments. All of these take little effort or technical knowledge and provide a high return. The next level of integration with ratings of 3-4 are found to be useful, but require more skills / time on the part of the instructor. When the instructor has those skills or institutional support, these features can be of value. For a new user of instructional web technology, it may be wisest to begin with the features most related to their discipline or of general effectiveness. Use of the Internet as an integral component of a course and its delivery does not guarantee more time for other academic endeavors; however, it can result in an improvement in the quality of delivery and currency and some consistency and time savings in course management.

Table 1. Comparative Effectiveness

Internet Feature		Effectiveness rating for time spent		
		Info. Sys.	Econ.	Engineer.
Cmmun-ication	group email announcements	5	5	5
	electronic office hours	5	4	
	student-student email	5	5	
	chat/bulletin board		2	4
Course Management	online syllabus	5	5	5
	online handouts/assignments	5	5	5
	posting grades	5		5
	assignment collection via web/email	4	4	3
	interactive assignment sites (problems)	3	5	3
	practice tests	3	5	3
	actual tests			3
	web-only course		2	
Content Supple-ment	links to outside online readings	5	5	
	required reading of online journals	4		
	required web references in research	4		
	virtual lab for simulations			4
	ftp site for downloading software	5		
Rating: blank = not used, 0 = not effective for time spent, 5 = highly useful for time spent				

References

[1] Ferrarini, T.H. and Poindexter, S. E. Web Integration in Courses: Which Factors Significantly Motivate Faculty?, *Proceedings of ED-MEDIA International Conference,* Seattle, June 1999.

[2] Poindexter, S. E. and Heck, B. S. Using the Web in Your Courses: What can you do? What should you do? *IEEE Control Systems* **19:1** (February 1999) 83-92.

[3] Aktan, B., Bohus, C., Crowl, L., and Shor, M. Distance Learning Applied to Control Engineering Laboratories. *IEEE Transactions on Education* **39:3** (August 1996) 320-326

[4] Kamen, E.W. and Heck, B. S., Fundamentals of Signals and Systems with MATLAB, Prentice Hall, 1997.

[5] Mabry, T. Economics Enjoys a Bull Run at Colleges. *Wall Street Journal* (Monday Nov. 30, 1998) A2

Teaching and Learning in a Network World
P. Hoffman and D. Lemke (Eds.)
IOS Press, 2000

Strategy, Motivation and Incentives in Information Technology Diffusion and Adoption

Stephen K. Pollard, Director of Academic Technology Support
KH D140, 5151 State University Dr. California State University, Los Angeles
Los Angeles, CA 90032 spollar@calstatela.edu

Explore strategies and incentive based policies to increase both the spread and adoption of information technology across a broad spectrum of campus users.

1. Introduction

The purpose of this paper is to explore strategies and incentive-based polices to increase both the spread and adoption of the use of the information technology across a broad spectrum of campus users at California State University, Los Angeles.
California State University, Los Angeles is one of the 23 campuses of the California State University System. Cal State LA has over 20,000 students enrolled with a full time of equivalent (FTE) of 14,000.

Academic Technology Support (ATS) is one of the divisions of Information Resource Management (IRM). ATS oversees network services, email for faculty and students, faculty and student desktop services (hardware and software), technologically mediated classrooms and labs, open access labs for students, help desk, and informational technology consultants. ATS employs 60 FTE staff and over 80 student assistants. A complete organizational chart and description of services can be found at http://www.calstatela.edu/ats.

2. Historical Overview

A list of major technology milestones that have occurred at Cal State LA are set forth in Appendix A. It should be noted that from 1993 to 1997 a technology gap developed on campus. Windows 3.1 was the main operating system on campus along with a myriad of PCs (286s, 386s, 486s, and low level Pentiums). There was no strategic planning for technology during this period as well. The campus used "soft" funding for technology such as Innovative Instructional/Research Awards and Lottery Fund Awards. The ATS budget was used primarily for support of the network.

The CSU developed in 1997 the Integrated Technology Strategy (ITS) to utilize technology to improve: 1) the personal productivity of students, faculty and staff; 2) the quality of learning and teaching; 3) the quality of the student experience; and 4) administrative productivity and quality. Cal State LA put together a strategic technology plan so that it could participate in the ITS and access funding opportunities under the ITS. This plan was called the Baseline Hardware/Software Access, Training, and User Support (BATS) and was designed to cover the 3 year period FY 1997/98 to FY 1999/00. The University was to utilize funds to provide the members of our campus community with 24 hour access to appropriate hardware, software, network connectivity, training, and user support services to improve the quality of instructional delivery and overall University efficiency and effectiveness.

CSLA goals under the Campus Baseline Plan included: 1) basic information competency; 2) Campus wide training program; 3) Campus wide Help Desk; 4) a set of foundation support services appropriate to the campus mission and programs; 5) LAN and remote access capabilities; 6) a campus email system; 7) an ongoing planning process addressing 24 hour access; 8) standards for staff, faculty and student workstations, messaging, operating systems; and 9) campus network infrastructure developed and implemented. The complete details of the plan can be found at: http://www.calstatela.edu/ats/baseline/

3. Achievements and Accomplishments under the Baseline Plan

ATS is the unit within IRM that is charged with the implementation of most of the projects under the campus Baseline Plan.

The leasing of new workstations has allowed the campus to upgrade all faculty and staff workstations to Baseline level by June 30, 1998, one year ahead of schedule. Three fourths of all student workstations are now at Baseline level and a total of 14 Technologically Enhanced Classrooms (formerly known as Smart Classrooms) are available for technologically mediated course instruction. Approximately 100 faculty and student stations were upgraded to support Windows NT. The campus also began to address the lack of workstations for part-time faculty use by issuing low-end Pentiums. The low-end Pentiums were upgraded with memory and expanded hard drives to run e-mail and current software applications. Additionally, an Adaptive Technology Center (ATC) was established to provide assistive technology to students with special needs.

Software accomplishments include the upgrade of faculty, staff, and student workstations to Windows NT required for Y2K compliance, and the migration to Microsoft Exchange and Outlook as a tool to unify e-mail and messaging systems under one shared system. In addition, to offer low cost software to students, the CSU-Microsoft Campus Enterprise Agreement has been successfully implemented and offers the most widely used software applications to students at a discounted price.

A major goal of this project is to improve access to the campus network resources. A proxy server that allows access to proprietary library databases and other campus computing resources was also implemented. Negotiations began with Internet Service Provider Earthlink to provide discounted Internet service access to all students, faculty, and staff at Cal State L.A.

The increased access to new technology has also been accompanied by expansion of training programs for both faculty and students. The Student Scholar Training Program has grown rapidly and has provided opportunities for students both to teach and learn new applications of productivity and Internet software. Faculty training has been enhanced by the success of a lab for faculty to learn how to use new software and develop applications for innovations in instruction, research, and scholarly activities. Consistent with system-wide ITS/TII vision to increase computer literacy and provide professional development to the campus community, the deployment of Computer Based Training (CBT) course titles was initiated. More than 650 titles representing 2,500 hours of training are now available to all Cal State L.A. faculty, staff, and students 24 hours a day, seven days a week.

This past fiscal year, 1998/99 also saw the establishment of Cal State L.A.'s Computer Help Desk as a single location for providing technological information and support to the entire University. Through a partnership between the Associated Student Inc. (ASI) and Information Resources Management, a program to offer notebook computers to students was launched in Winter 1999. Also, the EagleLink Remote Access Toolkit CD was available to faculty and students to enable easy configuration from home computers to remotely connect to campus resources. This has dramatically simplified the process of accessing the campus network from remote locations.

One of the ongoing objectives of the Baseline project is to maintain user support services and continually communicate and promote those services and other campus news through on-line documentation and the quarterly newsletter, as well as generating instructional handouts to assist users with their computing needs. Our primary goal is always to educate the campus community about the many technological options offered to them to enhance their educational environment.

4. ATS: Internal Polices and Incentives

ATS, as a unit, had undergone a transformation during the period 1993-1997 that was not conducive to being a leader or implementer of technological change. The ATS director had retired in 1996 and was not replaced until 1998. Budget cuts had negatively impacted resources and there were internal disputes over existing resource allocation. ATS was consistently place under the "magnifying glass" by faculty, students and academic administrators. The perception was that ATS was not responsive to campus technology needs. As a result, ATS staff morale was extremely low and most felt under attack. An atmosphere to enhance technology diffusion and adoption was not present.

A new director was named in 1998. Policies and procedures were put in place to reverse the above trends. The staff morale issue was addressed immediately. A new mission and vision statement were put in place after much consultation with all staff and managers. A contest was held among the staff with respect to constructing and selecting the vision statement. Monthly open staff meetings were instituted where staff could express concerns/issues to management, trade project outcomes and discuss campus issues. Attendance at these meetings is optional, but about 2/3 of the staff attend regularly. All staff members wear name badges identifying them by name, division within ATS and bearing the ATS vision. Staff have received t-shirts, which are worn by all once a month, and most recently a tote bag displaying the ATS name and vision.

Customer service has been strongly emphasized. Managers and staff have attended customer service and team building workshops. A customer service credo has been established and customer service surveys are a part of ATS culture.

Each group develops an annual work plan. The ATS budget is allocated to support these work plans. The budget is allocated to not only support the baseline plan, but to meet the needs of faculty and students. Managers of the groups are given budgets for operating expenses and small projects over which they have control. Empowerment is extended not only with respect to financial resources, but with respect to the staff and their duties. A team approach is taken and the result is employees work on projects that are of interest to them and also meet campus wide needs as well. ATS managers work hard to avoid being the pointy haired boss of Dilbert fame. Managers and staff have undergone cultural change (and shock) which have led to new ways of work and organizational structure [3, 4].

5. ATS External Relations

An important factor for technological diffusion is the acceptance of the technical organization by external "customers". ATS management and staff have also worked diligently at improving relations with faculty and students. The ATS director is a guest at the twice monthly Academic Senate committee on Academic Information Resources to apprise faculty of technology/computing issues, plans and accomplishments and to hear faculty views. ATS management and staff participates actively in the campus wide Technology Roundtable. IRM publishes INFOBITS, a quarterly newsletter for all faculty, students and staff on technology issues, plans and information. A service booklet based on the ATS web site is being distributed to all faculty.

ATS and IRM have developed a partnership with the Associated Students Incorporated (ASI), the official student government group on campus. This has greatly enhanced training opportunities and the spread of new software for student use (as described in detail below).

ATS/IRM participated in the recent Health Center Fee Initiative. ATS/IRM was actively involved in surveying student needs for technology and in focus group discussions of students. Students responded positively with respect to computing resources they would like to receive if a reallocation of funds with respect to payment of a health center fee was required. ATS is working towards meeting these needs and will undertake additional focus group meetings during the year 2000.

6. Changes in the Use and Diffusion of Technology

6.1 Faculty

Data on changes in the use of computing technology by type is presented in Table 1. Substantial growth in all of the main computing use areas has occurred over the period from June 1997 (pre-baseline implementation) and December 1998 (baseline standards achieved for almost all faculty). The implementation of the campus baseline plan, new internal ATS policies and improved external relationships with the campus community have led to these increases. Moreover, there have been changes in the relationships between faculty and ATS with respect to support of computing resources.

In January 1997, the campus became a beta test site for WebCT, a web based course management and curriculum delivery system. Currently, there are over 340 faculty WebCT users/developers. Additionally, there are 140 "stand alone" instructional web sites that faculty have instituted. The Faculty Instructional Training Center and ATS provides continuous support to faculty who wish to use the Web to deliver their curriculum to students.

ATS works with faculty with respect to multimedia needs, which has also accounted for the increase in presentation/multimedia use. ATS provides complete services for instructional video production including scripting, casting, set design, direction, video editing, and production; as well as consulting services for such video production. Additional services include audio and video recording of special lectures, lab demonstrations, media duplication and format conversion, and training on the use of media equipment. Multimedia support also includes Graphic and Photographic services. Presentations in PowerPoint can be set up for delivery in the class or on the web (including Real Media). We can help prepare illustrations, photos or other graphics for use on the internet.

ATS has successfully partnered with faculty through our faculty mentor program. One of the first outcomes was to introduce audio/video streaming technology. ATS provided professional training in workshops presented by Real Networks Staff, hardware, and software to undertake encoding and streaming activities. Twelve faculty members participated and were partnered with an ATS staff person. This allowed for one to one collaboration and development of a classroom project. These faculty in turn will be putting on workshops for other faculty members and become "resident experts" for their respective school.

Finally, faculty have the latest and up to date software on their desktops, such as MS Office 2000, Outlook 2000, FrontPage 2000, Personal Web server, FTP server/client, telnet, web browsers, MS Electronic Reference Books, MS Training Advantage, CBT Systems courses, and multimedia tools (for a complete listing visit: http://www.calstatela.edu/ats/desktop/winsupport/dss_fac.htm)

Table 1. Percentage Distribution of Faculty using Computing Technology by Type 1997-1998.

Year	Email	WWW	Productivity	Presentation
CSLA 1997	40.5%	67.6%	64.9%	38%
CSLA 1998	95%	88%	79%	49%
National 1998	87%	59%	85%	38%

Source: Campus Computing Survey; HERI Faculty Survey, CSLA Surveys (various years).

6.2 Students

There are over 1,000 student workstations in 48 computing facilities. These workstations are deployed in computer classrooms, department labs, experimental labs and studios, instructional areas (classrooms and lecture halls), and open access labs. All, but a handful, of these workstations have been replaced and/or upgraded under the campus Baseline Plan at the end of 1999.

Student computing facilities at Cal State L.A. are currently used at near capacity. The Open Access Computer Labs on campus have seen a dramatic rise in usage since 1995. In Winter 1995 there were a total of 38,079 student visits to the labs. In Winter 1996 that number increased by 10,000 to 48,649. By Winter 1997 the figure had grown by over 30,000 to 65,510 visits and reached 70,000+ by Fall 1999. This increase coincides with the opening of new facilities, the general increase in the use of computing nationwide, the increase in computing in instruction, and the software (which mirrors that for faculty) that is available for student use (for a complete listing see: http://www.calstatela.edu/ats/desktop/winsupport/dss_stud.htm). Queuing is still quite common in the open access labs (OALs) and a two-hour limit occasionally needs to be enforced in an effort to meet demand. In Fall 1998, a new lab in Student Housing that is open 24 hours a day, 7 days a week and a computerized study area in the University-Student Union opened. A sixth OAL is to be opened in the 1999/00 fiscal year.

Almost all Cal State L.A. students currently have network computing/e-mail accounts. Beginning in the Spring Quarter of 1998 all registered students were issued an account automatically. A new feature of student support is the hiring and deployment of expert consultant staff into the Open Access Computer labs as of Winter 1999, in addition to the student training workshops. The Student Scholar Training Program (SSTP) is a service offered by ATS/IRM that provides free computer workshops in the use of campus-wide network and communication tools, common personal productivity tools, and resources available through the Internet. The SSTP uses a student teaching student model. Qualified candidates from the campus community are recruited and trained to conduct the workshops in two training labs, with enrollment averaging over 900 students per quarter.

The library has moved all of its reference databases (such as Lexis-Nexis) to the web which has also increased the demand for computing resources. These databases are accessible remotely, provided students authenticate through the campus modem pool or via the campus proxy server if using an ISP. Two hundred and forty modem lines are available for students (a ratio of approximately 80 students per line). A remote access

CD, EagleLink, to allow for an easy connection to campus computing resources through the modem pool or an ISP, has been made available to over 3500 students (and 500 faculty). This CD contains Internet tools as well (for a complete listing visit: http://www.calstatela.edu/ats/desktop/winsupport/e_link.htm).

Student access to computing technology and resources has also been enhanced through implementation of the Student Lap Top Loaner Program.. One hundred PC laptops have been made available for weekly loan through a program implemented with ASI.

7. Lessons Learned

An important lesson learned is that cooperation and coordination between the different campus units is essential for a project of this magnitude to be successful. The campus has come to understand the importance of adopting standards that support the necessary diversity, but also allows for user choice. The adoption of new technology requires that training and assistance must be tailored to specific user needs. The support of new technologies must be done in a way that ensures that the diffusion process demystifies the technical process, thereby diminishing intimidation on the part of the user. Technology diffusion relies on both internal and external infrastructure considerations. Finally, it is "easy" to deliver hardware and software to faculty/students, but another matter to get them to use it. A necessary prerequisite is a highly motivated technical staff, with low turnover and a management team to lead with a willingness to innovate practices. Factors for success are also based on internal and external relationships with the technical organization and the campus community it serves. Partnerships with external customers can promote diffusion and adoption.

References

[1] The Campus Computing Project (http://www.campuscomputing.net/)

[2] Higher Education Research Institute at the University of California, Los Angeles. http://www.gseis.ucla.edu/heri/Faculty_Overview.html

[3] P. Pritchett, *New Work Habits for a Radically Changing World*, ISBN: 0-944002-15-3, Dallas, Texas, 1998.

[4] P. Pritchett, et.al. , *High-Velocity Culture Change*, ISBN: 0-944002-13-7, Dallas, Texas, 1998.

Appendix A: Major Technology Milestones

- November 1984-CO executive order 447, which established Information Resources Management (IRM) program within the CSU.
- July 1985 - Cal State L.A. IRM created.
- 1986 - Open Access Lab (OAL) in E&T opened, first on campus.
- 1987 - OAL in Library South opened.
- 1988 - Conversion to Online Administrative Student Information System (OASIS).
- 1988 - New Digital System installed, fiber optic backbone.

- 1989 - Distributed computing network installed.
- 1989 - Student Telephone Access Registration (STAR) system implemented.
- 1990 - First effort to establish network connection to faculty workstations.
- 1990 - Annex Link OAL opened.
- 1991 - Academic Information Resources Committee (AIRC) established.
- 1991 - Online Public Access Catalog system (OPAC) installed replacing library card catalog.
- 1993 - Scholar's Mail, a Unix-based distributed e-mail system, was available to all faculty, staff, and students.
- 1993 - Home drive (H: drive) made available to all students.
- 1996 - Salazar Hall Link OAL opened.
- 1997 - Union Link OAL opened.
- 1997 - IMAP4 e-mail available to faculty.
- 1997 - Major redesign of the campus web site
- 1997 - Baseline planning committee formed for strategic technology planning.
- 1997 - WebCT was implemented on campus
- 1997 - Cal State L.A. participated in Digital Summer School.
- 1997 - Faculty Instructional Technology Support Center (FITSC) established.
- 1998 - Automatic generation of student e-mail accounts and directories upon admission to University.
- 1998 - Web space granted to graduate students and seniors for posting resumes.

The Real Deal: A Clear-Eyed Look at Online Learning

Kathleen Schwarz, M.A.
Computer Research Specialist, School of Education
University of California, Riverside, CA.

Jo Sargent Dutton, Ph.D.
Director of Development, School of Education
University of California, Riverside, CA.

Abstract

As Internet technologies mature and evolve, multiple models of online learning are emerging. Regardless of the online learning model employed, there are hidden costs and unexpected benefits to Internet-based coursework. Internet-based courses and course enhancements have unique advantages and disadvantages. All of the models have common issues in planning, logistics, and student and faculty support. We examine the advantages, pitfalls and successful implementation of online coursework.

"The value of a technology to education is proportional to the need for that technology in achieving an educational objective." [1]

When you ask for reasons to develop and teach online courses, some responses will include: the opportunity to reach a wider student audience; to meet the needs of students who are unable to attend on-campus classes; to involve outside resources, such as speakers or locations, which would otherwise be unavailable; and, to connect students of different backgrounds, abilities and mobilities. Online courses are sometimes believed to be characterized by superficial learning, non-motivating experiences, low retention rate and the lack of interaction. Even so, these issues cannot and should not be the deciding factors about whether to invest in online courses. There is a need to address a large population of adults who are seeking retraining, and re-certification, and through them, opportunity for continuous learning. Applying good course management principles and the "new pedagogies" may mitigate these problems.

Online learning can be divided into three general categories on a continuum from completely sychronous to completely asychnronous. Online *sychnronous* communication takes the form of videoconferencing through computer connections, "whiteboard" conferencing, and various "chat" applications. Streaming video, e-mail, bulletin or message board, listservs and web pages all constitute *asychnronous* interactions. Most online courses or course enhancements combine some features from at least two of the models, and fall between these points:

Table 1. Online Learning Models.

Distributed Classroom	*Technology extends a classroom-based course from one location to students at another location* *Synchronous communication among multiple sites* *Interaction replicates classroom*
Course Enhancements	*Traditional classroom is extended by online activities.* *Communication among instructor and students may be asynchronous (e-mail, bulletin board) and/or synchronous (chat, whiteboard, video conferencing)* *Instructor's classroom role extended to developing, monitoring and moderating online activities* *Interaction occurs during class meetings (which may be less frequent) and by the use of interactive technologies*
Independent Learning	*Learning is place- and time-independent* *Asynchronous communication between instructor and individual students* *Instructor provides guidance and evaluates work* *Interaction takes place at the convenience of the parties, by telephone, e-mail, regular mail, and electronic bulletin board*

Obviously, there are many levels of institutional involvement in distance learning, from a few individual courses developed by faculty working on their own with few outside resources, to organized distance learning units within a traditional school. Entire schools may be devoted to distance learning, or institutions may combine with other groups to form consortia.[2,3] Whatever the size of the enterprise, the major problems confronting those wishing to develop online courses are the lack of technical skill among faculty and the need to support and manage distance education. Marsh, et al., point out that if most instructors were capable of developing their own courses, it would be reasonable to expect that online courses could be handled almost as routinely as traditional courses. Inasmuch as most instructors at both the college level (or K-12, for that matter) lack the skills necessary to produce and manage online coursework, technological solutions to "step over" the lack of skills and the infrastructure problems are in demand.[4]

According to the *Cassady Report* at the Ohio State University, encouraging the use of new technologies for instruction, including online courses, relies on the development of adequate and appropriate resources, developing a "culture of innovation," and the investment in a dynamic and responsive infrastructure.[5] The fundamental challenge facing institutions is to increase the *value* for faculty members to be involved in technology-based projects, including online courses. The report proposes that this can be accomplished through the creative partnership of colleges, central administration, and other units working together to reallocate current resources, locate new resources and funding, and to re-evaluate the contribution of such activities to promotion and tenure.

One example of such development is the Yavapai Community College initiative, "The Innovation College," which was established to support the efforts of faculty and staff efforts in creative activities that support instruction, particularly in technology. Funded at $100,000 a year, full- and part-time faculty may apply for released time or a stipend to work on specific innovative projects related to teaching. Additionally, the College is working with established campus committees on issues, such as faculty load for the development and delivery of online courses, intellectual property rights, copyright issues, and models for long-term profit-sharing between the institution and the faculty.[6]

Other difficult issues are faculty resistance to distance education, training and technical support, and job security. Betts found that deans who support or have experience in distance education will have greater faculty participation in distance education. Importantly, he found faculty who have extensive experience in higher education *and* faculty not involved in the tenure and promotion process are *more* likely to participate in distance education than faculty with less experience in higher education and/or faculty who are competing for tenure. [7]

Asynchronous instruction changes the role and activities of the instructor, and requires an entirely different view of instruction. The instructor and students are not required to have real-time contact on a regular basis: access to any remote resource is at the student's convenience. It most often occurs place- and time-independent. According to Locatis and Weisberg, students are active "apprentices" of an instructor who guides the students in acquiring knowledge with "diverse and rapidly changing content."[8]

A 1999 study examined student demographics, academic background, and experience in two sections of an introductory sociology course, one section taught completely on the Internet, the other in a traditional classroom. The courses were designed to be similar in content and requirements. When the groups of students were compared, the Internet-based students tended to be older, working more hours, and more likely to be married with children. They tended to have achieved higher scores on standardized tests and GPAs than the oncampus group. Student performance on examinations differed significantly between the groups but the author attributed better performance by the Internet-based group to the fact that the open-book exams were available online for a 24-hour testing cycle vs. a regular class session (1.5 hours) for oncampus students. More telling, perhaps, is that performance on papers did *not* vary significantly, which the author interpreted as evidence that Internet-based instruction can deliver a quality course that is comparable in content, expectations and learning standards with face-to-face instruction in a traditional college classroom.[9]

One early adopter, first teaching on the Bitnet about 15 years ago, believes that there are "at least seven good reasons not to teach via Internet. He proposes that "people are taught best by people -- not by computers . . . Because asking and answering questions is slow and clumsy by email, it is impossible to demand the same degree of rigor via Internet." He also notes that there are inevitable technical problems, little demand, and that offering Internet courses co-opts resources for oncampus programs. He states that "Students do not like Internet courses. Most traditional students will not enroll in electronic courses unless there are absolutely no alternatives." Since "about double the time is required" for faculty to teach courses via Internet compared traditional courses, professors "quickly become frustrated, tired, disappointed, and demoralized."[10]

However, another experienced instructor of history enthused " . . . No more waiting for office hours, juggling of schedules, fruitless searching for relevant historical information by the mentor or the student, and the tough decision about what to leave in or exclude in a particular class lecture or set of photocopies. It is the information age and while we cannot communicate all of the information to a class of students we can make all of the information available to each student via the online teaching approach." [11]

Beatty found that participants valued "collegial relationships" in computer mediated courses, and it was very important to their learning. He cited the importance of group work in getting to know each other better, and that too large a group hindered the ability to form these relationships. Most important, the instructor was perceived as setting the tone for interactions forming interpersonal relationships. Paraphrased here are his recommendations:

1. Make it an active goal to humanize the online classroom.
2. Use good course design and maintenance, selecting technology that fits the course, knowing the technology you're using.

3. Adapt your text to the visual constraints of the screen (shorter paragraphs).
4. Online instructors must practice not just active reading, but assertive reading. As Freudian psychotherapists learn to let their attention "hover" above the patient's freely associating stream, so online instructors must learn to hear the unasked question behind the words on the screen.
5. The presence of consistency of standards, expectations, and practices makes students at home and relatively relaxed in one online classroom; the absence makes them progressively more anxious in the others.
6. Draw on the emerging community standards of the Internet—and help establish them.
7. Provide active models of good email conduct, and seek to build good practices of electronic textuality. [12]

Many institutions do not anticipate the commitment to planning and resources that are needed to make this endeavor a true success. It is never assumed that the traditional students do not require the basic presentation, communications and intellectual skills. Assumptions about technical skills of distance education students should likewise never be made. Support must be provided, most effectively in the form of call-in help desks, guides and technical tutors. There is a direct relationship between support and instructional effectiveness [2]

A critical question is the issue of access. Online course developers must account for wide disparity between access to information technology. We currently do not have the bandwidth necessary for streaming all different forms of media to a distant student. Higher speed cable and T1 lines are available on campuses and businesses, but generally not available to important constituencies of distance learners, such as those in rural settings.

And how do these activities fit into the business of the institution? Registration, fee-collection, non-traditional terms and financial aid create special problems of authority and mechanisms. Access to academic libraries is a crucial problem, only part of a sea-change in how libraries function in the Electronic Age.

The quality of the bulletin board experience in both online courses and Internet-based enhancements for traditional courses is frequently mentioned. One instructor writes: "The most common misconception is that online classes will be fairly sterile and impersonal. But once a person starts to interact with other group members, they quickly discover that an online learning environment can be very rich and very personal . . . People typically find that they are drawn into the subject matter of the class much more deeply than in a traditional course because of the discussions they get involved in." [13] Several hypotheses are suggested:

- The medium forces students to take time to think before and during their participation.
- Students recognize the bulletin board as a place where their thoughts and work is "published." The essential difference between writing in "real world" classrooms and cyberspace is that "in cyberspace, everything is written for publication."
- The technical challenges inherent in on-line bulletin boards just a few years ago have been eliminated . . . allowing students to focus on reading, writing, and thinking while at the computer,
- Finally, students can't see each other. They can't get by on good looks (or a sharp wit) alone, and they know it.[14]

The assurance of quality in online instruction is a matter of pivotal importance and one upon which a future of online education will turn. Although distance education may seem to be a cost-saving measure for financially-strapped institutions, issues such as class size and the use of teaching assistants must be carefully evaluated. Internet education poses significantly higher course development costs and greater teaching costs, because individualized interaction of email and bulletin boards are very time consuming. The increase in faculty costs is estimated up to 33% more than traditional courses. Faculty spend as much or more time in course management with an online course as they do with traditional courses. University of Phoenix reports that a site-based course is usually conducted with a 14- to 16- to - 1 ratio. For an online course, UOP's ratio is 8-to-1. In a survey of 17 instructors offering full Internet courses through the Southern Regional Electronic Campus, the top concern of the respondents regarding distance learning was the workload, with faculty reporting a mean internet course development time of 155 hours.[15, 16]

Table 2. Smith's Comparison of Cost Structure for Traditional Courses and Online Courses.[16]

TRADITIONAL COURSE	ONLINE COURSE
Fixed Costs Content Development Instructor Expertise Instructor Design Time Researcher Support Staff Classroom Space Any laboratory equipment Instructor teaching time	Fixed Costs Content Development Instructor Expertise Instructor Design Time Technical Expertise Technical Design time Researcher Support Staff Content Delivery Internet charges Server/network costs Network/computer maintenance and support
Variable Costs Tutor/Assistant's time Classroom space (at levels of enrollment)	Variable Costs Instructor Teaching time Tutor/ Assistant's time
Indirectly Related Costs Student support services Registration Academic Counseling Course catalogue Tutoring Bill payment Library services	Indirectly Related Costs Student support services Registration Academic Counseling Course catalogue Tutoring Bill payment Library services

For online education, fixed technology costs replace fixed facility costs, and faculty costs, formerly fixed, become variable. Institutions may find that fixed costs can be reduced by streamlining and standardizing course development across the institution. Higher fixed costs are defrayed by minimizing variable costs, which is achieved by "re-engineering pedagogy."[16]

An important investment crucial to the success of an online course is the hardware and software which will support the courses. The acquisition, setup, troubleshooting, maintenance and upgrades of hardware and software appropriate to the level of interaction and the number of students is a critical component which is often subsumed into the regular business of an institution. Servers and software for online coursework have particular demands (for example for chat, streaming media, or graphics) which are specific to online course activity and for which existing campus services may not be suitable. Technical considerations are as important as course quality, and may, in fact, determine course quality.

The most important factors for success in online learning are: to identify the constituencies; provide support and training for participants; to understand the applications and limits of internet technologies; and to work within the best practices of the new pedagogies. With careful planning, online learning can be a rich and rewarding experience, one which can change people's lives.

References

[1] Dorbolo, J. Web Course Case Study: Oregon State University Challenging Students' Paradigms. International University Consortium and Institute for Distance Education, College Park, MD. May, 1997. Online: http://nova.umuc.edu/ide/potentialweb97/dorbolo.html

[2] Moore, M. and Kearsley, G.. Distance Education: A Systems View. New York: Wadsworth Publishing, 1996.

[3] Stenerson, J. Systems Analysis and Design for a Successful Distance Education Program Implementation. Online Journal of Distance Learning Administration, (1998) 1(2). Online: http://www.westga.edu/~distance/Stener12.html

[4] Marsh, G., McFadden, A, and Barrie, J. An Overview of Online Educational Delivery Applications Online Journal of Distance Learning Administration, (1999) 2(3). Online: http://www.westga.edu/~distance/marsh23.html

[5] Faculty Instructional Technology Development Committee. Integrating Technology into the Teaching and Learning Process at The Ohio State University. FITD Final Report, Columbus, OH. July, 1999. Online: http://telr.ohio-state.edu/faculty/de/resousrces/fitd.cfm

[6] Sasmor, J. Promoting Innovation in Teaching : An Institutional Value. 1999 Teaching Online in Higher Education. School of Arts and Sciences, Indiana University-Purdue University Fort Wayne, Fort Wayne, IN. Online: http://as1.ipfw.edu/99tohe/presenters.htm.

[7] Betts, K. An Institutional Overview: Factors Influencing Faculty Participation in Distance Education in Postsecondary Education in the United States: an Institutional Study. Online Journal of Distance Learning Administration, (1998) 1(3). Online: http://www.westga.edu/~distance/betts13.html

[8] Locatis, C and Weisberg, M. Distributed Learning and the Internet. Contemporary Education, (1997) 68(2), 100-03. Cited in Stenerson, J., Systems Analysis and Design for a Successful Distance Education. Program Implementation. Online Journal of Distance Learning Administration, (1998) 1(2). Online: http://www.westga.edu/~distance/stener12.html

[9] Trier.,K. Comparison of the Effectiveness of Web-based Instruction to Oncampus Instruction. 1999 Teaching Online in Higher Education. School of Arts and

Sciences, Indiana University-Purdue University Fort Wayne, Fort Wayne, IN. Online: http://as1.ipfw.edu/99tohe/presenters.htm.

[10] Johnson, E. Teaching via Internet: Problems and Questions. 1999 Teaching Online in Higher Education. School of Arts and Sciences, Indiana University-Purdue University Fort Wayne, Fort Wayne, IN. Online: http://as1.ipfw.edu/99tohe/presenters.htm.

[11] Howell, C. Teaching History Online. 1999 Teaching Online in Higher Education. School of Arts and Sciences, Indiana University-Purdue University Fort Wayne, Fort Wayne, Indiana. Online: http://as1.ipfw.edu/99tohe/presenters.htm

[12] Beatty, G. Ethos in the Online Classroom. 1999 Teaching Online in Higher Education. School of Arts and Sciences, Indiana University-Purdue University Fort Wayne, Fort Wayne, IN. Online: http://as1.ipfw.edu/99tohe/presenters.htm

[13] Kearsley, G. The Virtual Professor: A Personal Case Study, 1997. Online: http://www.fcae.nova.edu/~kearsley/virtual.html

[14] Merron, J. Managing a Web-based Literature Course for Undergraduates. Online Journal of Distance Learning Administration, (1998) 1(4). Online: http://www.westga.edu/~distance/merron14.html

[15] Wilson, C. Concerns of Instructors Delivering Distance Learning via the Internet. Online Journal of Distance Learning Administration, (1998) 1(3). Online: http://www.westga.edu/~distance/wilson13.html

[16] Smith, B. Is Online Learning Cost-effective? Converge, (1999) 2 (4), pp. 18-19.

Teaching and Learning in a Network World
P. Hoffman and D. Lemke (Eds.)
IOS Press, 2000

Inquiry-Based Biochemistry: Critical Thinking Skills Taught By Interactive Multimedia

Duane W. Sears
Department of Molecular, Cellular, and Developmental Biology
University of California, Santa Barbara
Santa Barbara, California 93106
sears@lifesci.ucsb.edu

A web-based biochemistry curriculum has been developed with the aim of teaching students fundamental biochemical concepts by integrating the educational process with the scientific method of discovery and hypothesis testing. Through self-paced, interactive multimedia exercises students are guided in the "discovery" of protein structure/function relationships by examining manipulable three-dimensional molecular images of proteins, and by analyzing manipulable "experimental" data graphs. With interactive practice quizzes, students are guided in the process of making conclusions and inferences from their observations, and they are presented hypotheses for "testing." Several multimedia enhancements improve the "hands-on feel" and interactivity of the learning environment. Customized Javascripts enhance the analysis of molecular image analysis with the *Chime* browser plugin. *Visual Basic* buttons add dynamic, interactive capabilities to *Excel* charts used for protein functional data. Self-scoring practice quizzes and computer-graded tests created with *Authorware* modules or *Access*-database-linked active server pages (ASPs), provide students "instantaneous" feedback on critical-thinking activities and provide the instructor with electronic feedback on individual student performance profiles and resource utilization. Preliminary results from a rigorous educational assessment of the computer lab curriculum suggest that students taking the computer lab improve significantly over a ten-week period in terms of their biochemical problem solving skills, basic concept understanding and retention, and resource utilization.

1. Educational Objectives

By definition, scientific knowledge derives from the application of the scientific method, a process that includes making objective observations (experimentation); questioning and evaluating data; making inferences and hypothesis from observations; and testing hypotheses or predicted experiments outcomes against new experimental results. In the most fundamental sense, a scientific "fact" is only as good as the experiments upon which it based. Thus, it seems reasonable -- and even desirable -- to teach science by the same methodology used to establish the scientific knowledge database. With this goal in mind, a web-based biochemistry curriculum has been developed[1] with self-paced, interactive multimedia exercises designed to guide students in the exploration of protein structure/function relationships. By examining and manipulating three-dimensional molecular images of proteins, students "discover" the nature of protein structures. By manipulating and analyzing dynamic "experimental" data graphs students "observe" the

[1] Instructional biochemistry web site at UCSB: http://mentor.lscf.ucsb.edu/mcdb108a/

functions of proteins under different conditions. With interactive practice quizzes, students are guided into drawing conclusions and making inferences from their observations; and students are presented hypotheses for "testing." These pedagogical strategies encourage students to garner a basic understanding of the relationships between protein structure and function in the context of the scientific methodology used to establish such relationships.

2. Multimedia Strategies and Enhancements

Self-pace instructional computer exercises have been designed to be as interactive as possible with easy navigation between topics and quick access to resources on the web site. The instructional environment of the biochemistry web site has been enhanced in the following ways:

1. Web Site Navigation Features

In order to enhance resource utilization by students and streamline navigation between different topics found on the biochemistry web site, the home page is structured with HTML frames so that several navigation features remain visible during the instructional activities and during testing. As illustrated in Figure 1, the navigation features include a topic-specific pull-down menu; topic "tabs," and topic buttons that open "library,"[2] "contents,"[3] "syllabus[4]," and "search"[5] popup windows.

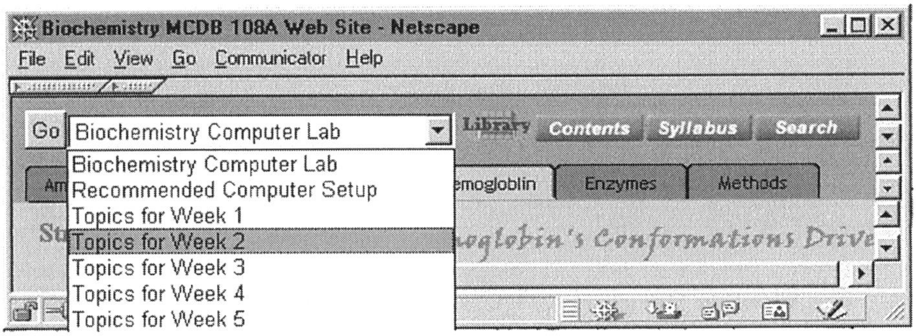

Figure 1 Navigation tools on the Biochemistry Web site home page include a topic-specific pull-down menu; topic tabs; and buttons that launch "library," "contents," "syllabus," and "search" popup windows.

2. Data analysis with dynamic Excel charts featuring interactive Visual Basic buttons

Interactive *Visual Basic* buttons have been added to *Microsoft Excel* spreadsheets in order to enhance the "hands-on" interactivity of exercises designed to explore protein functional data. The buttons allow students to conduct "experiments" in which they

[2] Biochemistry web site "library:" http://mentor.lscf.ucsb.edu/mcdb108a/libraryf.htm
[3] Biochemistry web site "contents:" http://mentor.lscf.ucsb.edu/mcdb108a/toc.htm
[4] Biochemistry web site "contents:" http://mentor.lscf.ucsb.edu/mcdb108a/weeks/syllabus.htm
[5] [5] Biochemistry web site "contents:" http://mentor.lscf.ucsb.edu/mcdb108a/searchinstructions.htm

interactively monitor the effects of altering data parameters on functional readouts. In the example shown in Figure 2, a student can graphically analyze the inhibition properties of three different types of enzyme inhibitors with the up-and-down buttons; these selectively alter various parameters of the enzyme kinetics "experiment."

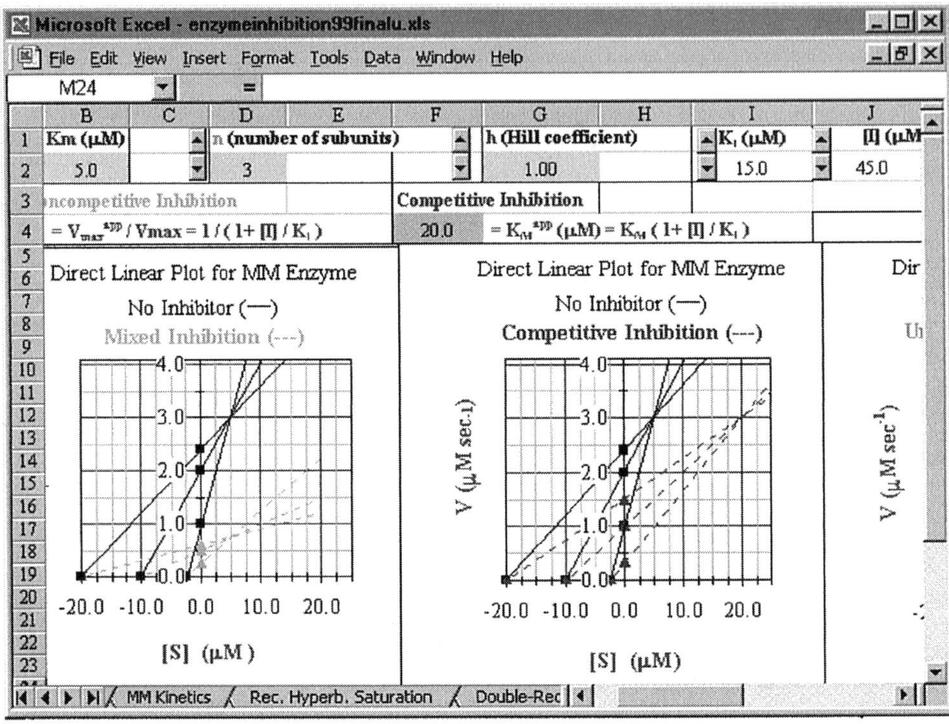

Figure 2 *Excel* data charts[6] showing enzyme kinetic data that can be dynamically manipulated with *Visual Basic* up-and-down arrow buttons. These buttons incrementally increase or decrease constants shown at the top. The constants are linked to the formulas from which the lines shown derive. As the buttons are clicked, all lines change instantaneously and simultaneously.

3. *Integrating the Chime browser plugin with customized Javascripts for enhanced molecular image analysis*

MDL, Information Systems, Inc. has been created the *Chime* browser plugin (v. 2.0) for manipulating three-dimensional molecular images in embedded web pages. While the latest version of this plugin features a robust set of popup menus and mouse drag options for manipulating molecular images, certain tasks are difficult if not impossible to implement with the popup menus. This plugin is based on the *RasMol* molecular imaging program, developed by Roger Sayle, which has much more sophisticated imaging capabilities. While not widely known, almost all of the functionality of *RasMol* can be

---

[6] Enzyme Inhibition spreadsheet: http://mentor.lscf.ucsb.edu/mcdb108a/sprdshts/enzymeinhibition99p.xls

added to the *Chime* plugin using customized Javascript command and message boxes as created by Eric Martz (University of Massachusetts) and Tim Maffett (*MDL, Information Systems, Inc.*). These Javascripts have been added to most of the web pages on the biochemistry web site devoted to interactive molecular imaging activities. The combined functionality of the *Chime* plugin popup menus (see Figure 3) and the Javascript command and message boxes (see Figure 4) are illustrated in the images below.

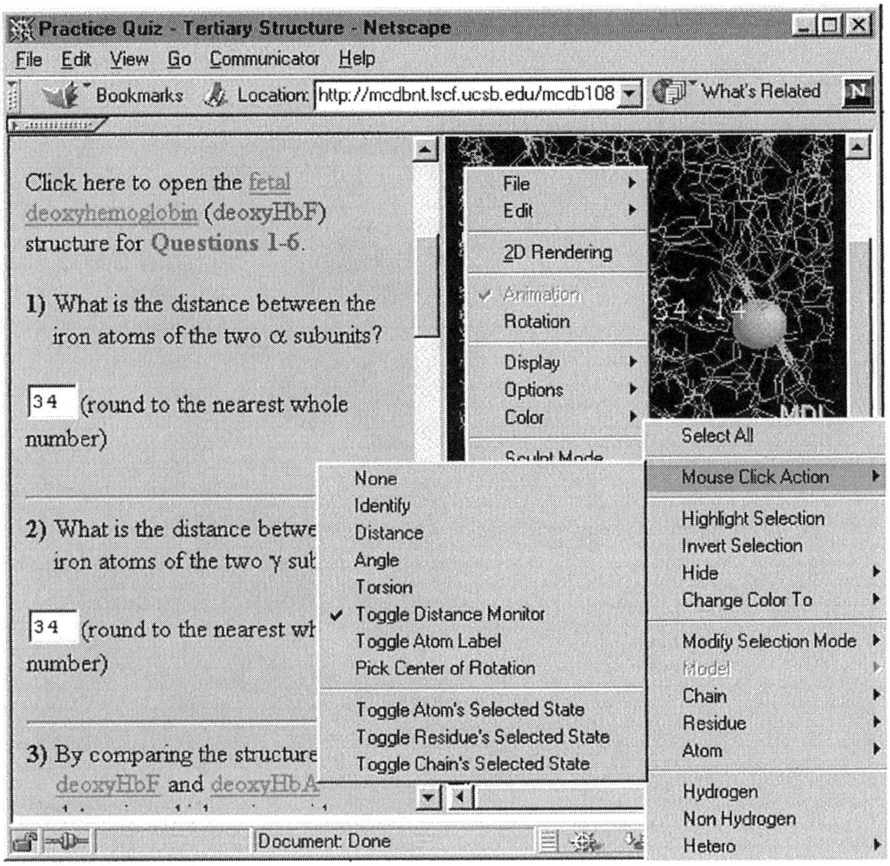

Figure 3 Practice quiz exploring the three-dimensional structure of fetal deoxyhemoglobin[7] (visible above right) with some of the *Chime* plugin image manipulation commands shown in the popup windows.

4. *Self-grading and instructor-graded quizzes created with Access-database-linked active server pages (ASPs) and Authorware.*

Experience has taught that one of the major keys to the overall success of the instructional web site is requiring students each week to complete one or more self-guided

[7] Interactive ASP practice quiz: http://mcdbnt.lscf.ucsb.edu/mcdb108a/quizzes/prqz12/prqz12f.htm

tutorials and practice quizzes, and also take a weekly graded quiz. Only then will students spend ample time systematically and thoroughly exploring the instructional activities of web site. To this end, self-grading practice quizzes have been created with active server pages (ASPs) where answer keys are stored with "cookies." When a student submits his or her answers on the ASP form page for grading, an HTML-embedded *Visual Basic* program returns a table with the student's answers matched against the answer key. As shown in Figure 4, incorrect answers are highlighted in rust color. Students can easily return to the quiz in order to refine their understanding of any desired concept. *Authorware* has also been used to create self-grading practice quizzes and other interactive instructional exercises.

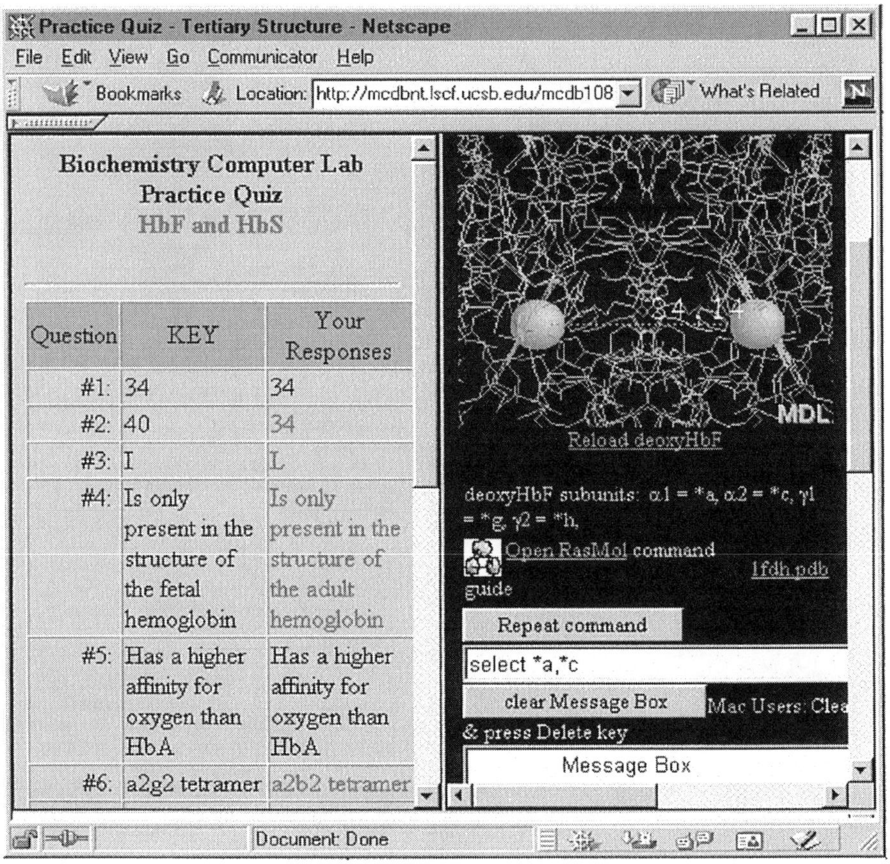

Figure 4 Self-grading practice quiz (URL in footnote 7) using *Visual* Basic and "cookies" created in collaboration with Shalem Shem-Tov. Note the interactive Javascript "Command" and "Message" boxes in the right frame where *RasMol* commands can be entered in order to modify the image of oxyhemoglobin selectively.

3. Educational Assessment

All computer-graded quizzes and examinations are conducted with ASPs, web linked to *Access* databases where student exam responses are stored for grading and eventual analysis. Custom *Visual Basic* modules, created in collaboration with Shalem Shem-Tov, an honors student at UCSB, are linked to an *Access* "Administrator" form that is used to enter exam keys; initiate exam grading; and control access to specific exams when students login for an exam. An *Access* database has also been created in order to record student resource utilization during examinations while they navigator to specific web site resources. This is accomplished with a "library" ASP that returns student URL activity to the database for every "hit" a student makes on the main web site. The time each question is started by a student and a student's response to each question is also returned to the database. As illustrated in Figure 5, considerable information can be retrieved pertained to student performance as well as resource utilization. Information of this kind is extremely valuable because it helps in the assessment of the instructional activities. For example, one can determine which web site resources are used by individual students; how effective those resources are as instructional aids; how easy or difficult certain types of test questions are; etc.

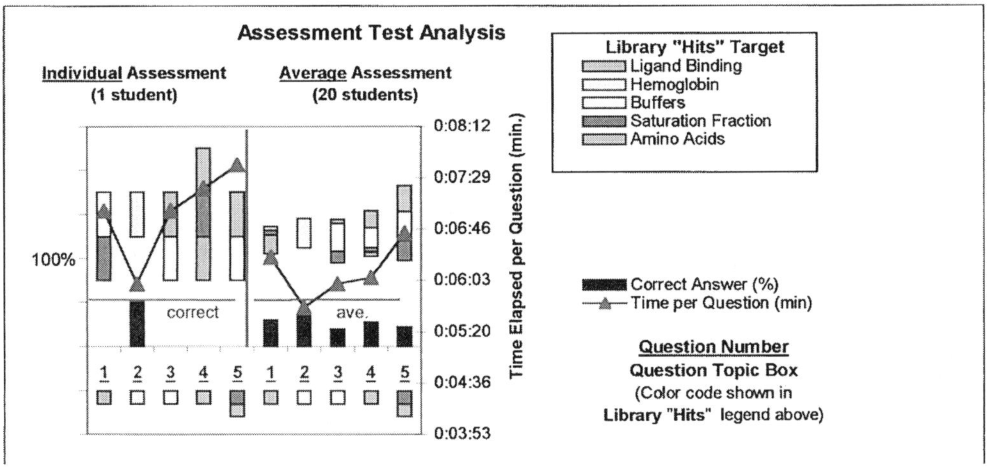

Figure 5 Sample *Excel* chart analysis of student performance and resource utilization during a computer graded examination. Student performance data was retrieved with ASPs linked to an *Access* database as created in collaboration with Shalem Shem-Tov. The examination performance of one student is shown at the left and the average class performance is shown at the right. Colored boxes symbolize the question topic (below the question numbers) or the library resource topics accessed by the student during the exam (histogram in the top of each figure). The time on each question (green triangles) and the student responses to the questions are recorded (block rectangles).

Rigorous educational assessment of the curriculum is currently underway. In one assessment, two student groups have been compared in terms of basic concept understanding, resource utilization, problem solving, and knowledge retention. One student group, designated "CL" students, consists of students who were enrolled in the computer lab as well as the traditional biochemistry lecture course that I teach concurrently. The other group, designated "LO" students, consists of students who were only enrolled in the lecture course. In the two halves of Figure 6, the written Midterm (MT1 and MT2) and Final exam results for ten CL students who were enrolled in the computer lab (horizontal scale) are correlated against the <u>average</u> written exam results (vertical scale) for all LO students who took the same examinations. Most of the questions on these examinations related to material covered in both the lecture and the computer lab courses, but with a different approach. Two CL students consistently performed on par with (Figure 6A, open triangles on diagonal) or below the class average (Figure 6B, open circles off-diagonal to the <u>left</u>). The remaining eight CL students consistently performed above average or well above average the LO student averages (see Figure 6A, closed circles and squares; and Figure 6B, closed circles, squares, and diamonds off-diagonal to the <u>right</u>).

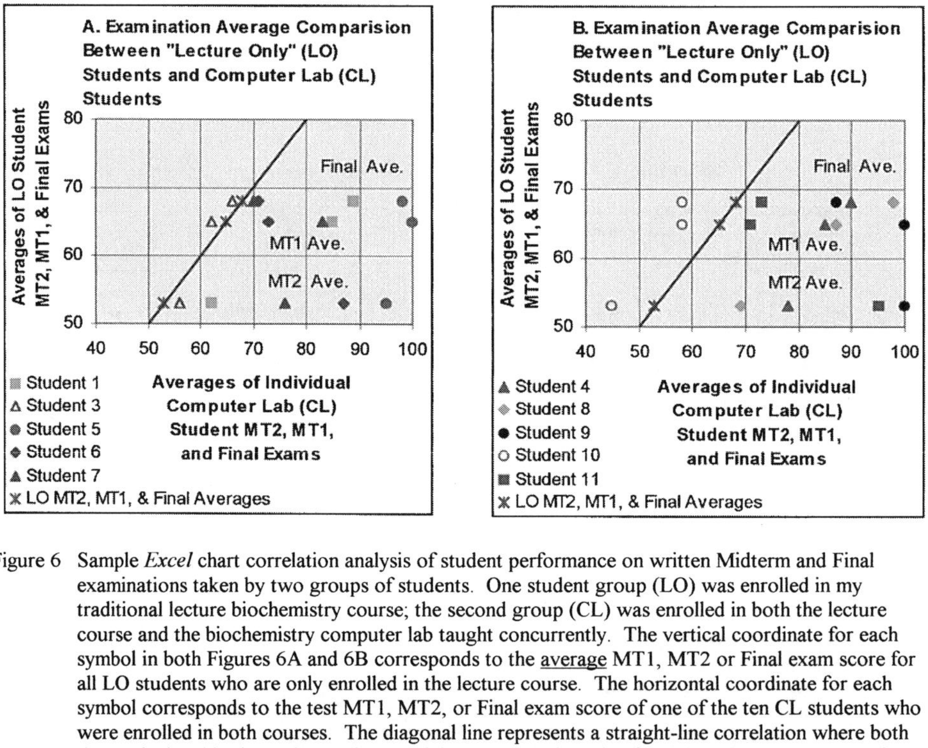

Figure 6 Sample *Excel* chart correlation analysis of student performance on written Midterm and Final examinations taken by two groups of students. One student group (LO) was enrolled in my traditional lecture biochemistry course; the second group (CL) was enrolled in both the lecture course and the biochemistry computer lab taught concurrently. The vertical coordinate for each symbol in both Figures 6A and 6B corresponds to the <u>average</u> MT1, MT2 or Final exam score for all LO students who are only enrolled in the lecture course. The horizontal coordinate for each symbol corresponds to the test MT1, MT2, or Final exam score of one of the ten CL students who were enrolled in both courses. The diagonal line represents a straight-line correlation where both the vertical and horizontal coordinates of the "x" symbols derive from the LO average scores for MT1, MT2 and the Final exam as indicated. Thus, symbols found <u>on the diagonal</u> correspond to CL student performances that are <u>on par with</u> average LO student exam performances. Symbols falling <u>off diagonal to the left</u> correspond to CL student exam performances that are <u>below average</u> compared to average LO student exam performances. Finally, symbols falling <u>off diagonal to the right</u> correspond to CL student exam performances that are <u>above average</u> compared to average LO student exam performances. .

4. Conclusions

An instructional biochemistry web site has been designed with the aim of teaching students fundamental biochemical concepts along the lines of the scientific method of discovery and hypothesis testing. The pedagogical strategy is to encourage students to learn basic information about the relationships between protein structure and function in the context of the scientific methodology used to establish such relationships. Several multimedia enhancements have been built into the instructional biochemistry web site in order to improve the "hands-on feel" and interactivity of the learning environment as well as the ease of navigation between web site resources. In addition to some of the more standard types of enhancements that can be effected with popup windows, pulldown menus, and active buttons, other enhancements include: 1) customized Javascripts to enhance the interactive analysis of molecular images viewed with the *Chime* browser plugin; 2) *Visual Basic* buttons with dynamic, interactive capabilities for manipulating *Excel* charts in protein functional data analysis; and 3) self-scoring practice quizzes and computer-graded tests created with *Authorware* modules or *Access*-database-linked active server pages (ASPs) to promote the critical-thinking activities and provide the instructor with electronic feedback on individual student performance profiles and resource utilization. Finally, rigorous educational assessment of the computer lab curriculum has been initiated and preliminary results from one assessment are presented. By comparing the examination performances of students who are in my traditional biochemistry lecture course (the LO "control" group) with comparable performances of students who are also in the biochemistry computer lab (the CL "test" group), it is found that eight of ten CL students appeared to: 1) demonstrate a better grasp (over a ten-week period) of basic concepts compared to the LO control group, on average; 2) have become familiar with and readily use web site resources; and 3) are better equipped at problem solving. The web site resources described here will permit deeper and more meaningful levels of assessment of this mode of distance learning in the future.

Teaching and Learning in a Network World
P. Hoffman and D. Lemke (Eds.)
IOS Press, 2000

SOLVING STUDENT ADMINISTRATION AND REGISTRATION ISSUES WITH ORACLE STUDENT SYSTEM

Mollie Smilie
Oracle Corporation
500 Oracle Parkway, MS3op12
Redwood Shores, CA 94065, USA

1. INTRODUCTION

No component of the higher education enterprise solution is more crucial than the student system. Yet no system upgrade is more fraught with challenges than replacing the robust functionality of a legacy student system with a commercial application.

Oracle's commitment to a student system sets a new standard for system design and expectation. Increasing competition from all sectors and a changing student population will increase the student service challenge. In order to survive and thrive in this new environment, student systems will need to provide a higher level of functionality. From unlimited scheduling, to online learning management, to user controlled rules-based management, to full Web deployment and student/faculty self service, tomorrow's systems must provide the flexibility and cost effectiveness to support the adaptation and evolution of institutional programs, activities and initiatives.

Oracle provides a student system that provides a solid foundation for addressing the challenges of the new millennium. Beyond providing competitive process management and reporting functionality, the Oracle Student System focuses on five key areas that provide unique value to our clients:

- Lower configuration and modification cost
- True web functionality and student self service design
- Infinitely flexible academic calendars and rules based management
- A single, integrated technology platform providing lower total cost of ownership
- Controlled cost implementations providing immediate and ongoing value to both administrative and process users

2. STUDENT SYSTEMS OF TOMORROW

The notion of effective student information management as a productivity issue is being replaced by the need for effective student management as a competitive advantage. Tomorrow's systems will go far beyond productivity related features (such as web based registration) to development of student information as a strategic advantage. The concept of "student as customer" will become a competitive imperative with profound impact on how colleges and universities attract, retain and serve students of all types. Three key themes encompass Oracle's vision of the role of student systems in tomorrow's competitive college and university.

2.1 'For' vs. 'About' students

While today's student systems support processes and provide information *about* students, tomorrow's systems will expand to provide information *for* students. The notion of student as customer has dramatic implications for the increasing demand institutions will face for a flexible and robust student self service function. The essential foundation of this capability is a true web-enabled applications environment designed specifically for use by students. Vendors offering web modules tacked on to client server architectures will not meet this need. This capability will come alive through a process that includes input from students and student services professionals in the design of the self-service functionality.

2.2 Flexibility to adapt and evolve

The technology foundation upon which applications are built is the core of system flexibility and adaptability. For most vendors, today's applications are delivered as millions of lines of code, requiring modification of code each time you need to make a process, rules or data meaning change. These 'old technology' applications represent only an incremental change in cost effectiveness and productivity, given it is somewhat easier to modify and maintain newer language code than older mainframe code. Tomorrow's applications code will be generated from rules engines, workflow tools, and case tools. You'll be able to configure and modify the applications using these tools without the need to write new code. For student systems, this means institutions can change basic student related processes and rules easily and use functions like flexible scheduling - unlimited start and end dates for student programs - as a competitive advantage.

2.3 Enroll, access and manage online learning activities as effectively as classroom instruction

Today's student systems are designed to support traditional classroom instruction. *Period.* Tomorrow's systems will need to support the full range of learning activities, from traditional classrooms to online distance learning courses and every conceivable combination of online, classroom, virtual and group learning activity including the technology-based communications needed to facilitate these innovative learning models.

3. THE ENTERPRISE WIDE IMPACT OF NEW FUNCTIONALITY

Emerging technologies will drive the growth of new types of resources and services. Within the higher education enterprise, much of this new functionality will be focused in the student area. This exciting new level of student related functionality and performance will impact not only students, but also administrative staff and management, faculty, and the institution as a whole.

3.1 Students

Today's student systems have little if anything to offer students, particularly the new breed of technology savvy students that want to be more in control of their learning environment. They will demand a higher level of access to information about their options, performance, and their future. They will demand that technology resources be an integral part of their learning experience. Even in traditional classes, their instructional program and interaction with instructors and their classmates will have a strong virtual component. The standard for access to faculty and student services will change; traditional faculty office hours will be a thing of the past, as students come to expect virtual access to faculty and student services resources. The old ways of interacting with students will become untenable—expecting them to line up for hours when they can choose an institution that can meet their needs on their own terms, on their schedule, with virtual support systems.

3.2 Administrators

The introduction of true self-service systems will empower the administrative team to rethink the investment of administrative resources in student services. By shifting responsibility for information maintenance to students and faculty, and empowering them to complete relevant processes and securely access vital information, administrative staff can focus on more productive, rewarding and satisfying activities—such as making personal connections with students and helping them plan for the future. In this environment, technology "gets out of the way" of meaningful student contact. In addition, true enrollment management and demand-based scheduling become feasible options in a self-service student systems environment.

3.3 Faculty

Today's systems provide little of value for faculty. Indeed, in many institutions there is a complete disconnect between student services and instructional programs. This disconnect is often mirrored in the rift between administrative and academic computing. In the new learning environment, faculty and student services are closely linked, dynamically sharing resources and strategies to enable student learning. Envision a future where faculty can securely access student learning profiles assembled in the admission process to prepare custom learning options for students who are having difficulty. Imagine a process whereby a faculty member can make immediate student referrals to key support programs on campus—even when working at home. Finally, with a system that is dynamically linked with key learning applications, faculty curriculum planners develop an accurate picture of which technology resources truly make a difference in student learning.

3.4 An Institution-Wide Impact

All constituent groups in the institution will benefit from increased access to information: Because all of the applications are Web-based, students, faculty and staff can access and update information from any Web-enabled device, anywhere in the world. The evolution from point-to-point integration between applications to a single institution-wide database with integrated business rules and a workflow process library will blur the distinction between student, finance and human resource systems.

Users will access information from these applications from their own logical perspective. New levels of functionality will be enabled. The needs of students, faculty and staff become the focus, rather than a focus on the rigid process structure of today's systems. The power for evolving systems will be placed in the hands of the user communities, and will not be reliant on technologists to modify rigid process code.

Administrative systems will be seamlessly integrated with instructional computing and communications systems. This new virtual environment will provide the infrastructure for new levels of flexibility. Your institution will be able to manage and deliver online learning as effectively as you manage traditional classroom programs today.

Most important, however, is the ability of a truly robust 21st century student system to bring the entire institution together around student services and student learning. With this sort of system, the lines between academic and administrative computing disappear. Developed in this way, a student system is so powerful, flexible, and accessible that it simply "goes away"—the work of higher education should be focused on the students, not on a student system. Oracle's vision is to create an integrated, flexible data management system that meets the needs of all constituents and powerfully supports the institutional mission of improving student learning.

4. KEY FEATURES OF THE STUDENT SYSTEM OF THE FUTURE

A student system should provide unique and forward-thinking functionality in every area:

4.1 Recruitment

Growing competition has increased the importance of the recruitment capabilities for most institutions. Key recruitment features include the ability to:

- Track and report prospect status through the recruiting cycle for each academic program
- Create and manage recruiting events and prospect pools
- Coordinate internal and external recruiting ambassadors for each prospect pool

These features will allow institutions to target, attract, and retain students who are most likely to attend as well as those most likely to succeed. Key benefits include:

- Prospect identification and recruiting to meet enrollment plans
- Effective tracking of recruitment activities against the enrollment plan
- Ability to modify recruitment activities based on results

4.2 Admissions/Registration

Making complex processes transparent and quickly adaptive is a key goal for admissions and registration management:

- Create multiple admissions criteria by applicant request and characteristics
- Evaluate applicant qualifications
- Retain transfer credit information and evaluate for program admission
- Accommodate multiple accepts and denials by academic period and institution
- Allow block registration by student
- Allow section changes for a group of students

Through the use of flexible rules-based admissions and registration functions, complex and labor-intensive processes will be simplified and easily maintained and changed.

Key benefits include:

- Distributed responsibility for definition of program requirements to faculty and academic departments
- Ability to change admissions and registration requirements as the academic program requirements change
- Less reliance on the information technology professionals to modify system routines
- True self service functionality for students, faculty and staff

4.3 Student Records

Key student record features include:

- Support for multiple grading schemes
- Defining program and student-specific degree requirements
- Maintaining course inventory file, allow copy feature, and link to program requirements
- Creating and maintaining course schedule for multiple variable length academic periods

Through the use of flexible grading schemes and user-defined academic calendars, non-traditional programs can be brought into the mainstream of activities within the institution. Key benefits include:

- Flexibility to accommodate emerging academic delivery methods
- Student-defined course characteristics particularly relevant to advanced degree programs
- Consolidation of student system administration for credit and non-credit academic programs which may follow non-traditional calendar periods

4.4 Advising

The student advising function supports the ability to:

- Maintain and report academic period degree audit for academic advising and student self-monitoring
- Offer alternative courses when selected class/section is filled
- Monitor course progress and share with student

Through access to this information on the Web, students will gain greater control over their own academic planning and progress. Key benefits include:

- Ability for students to immediately review impact of registration decisions on completion of degree requirements
- Minimize student registration decision errors which extend the student's time in attendance

4.5 Billing/Receivables

The student billing and receivables function provides the ability to:

- Define fees and fee rates based on term, flat rates, student credit hours, break point, and student attributes
- Maintain third party accounts including enrollment and fee limits

- Integrate with accounts payable for payment of credit balances
- Calculate tuition and fees online or in batch
- Consolidate all student receivables
- Apply payments and refunds in hierarchy defined by the institution

Through true integration of these functions with the full administrative applications suite, duplication of effort and inconsistency will be eliminated. Key benefits include:

- Flexible tuition and fee calculations which reflect new academic delivery methods
- Effective management of institution's revenue stream
- Reduced manual effort to calculate student refunds or adjusted tuition and fees based on enrollment status changes.

Teaching and Learning in a Network World
P. Hoffman and D. Lemke (Eds.)
IOS Press, 2000

Don’t Ask, Don’t Sell: Protecting the Data Privacy Rights of Admissions Applicants

Karen Torgersen, Virginia Tech
201 Burruss Hall
Blacksburg, Virginia 24061

Abstract

Just protecting the data privacy of your students isn’t enough any more. You also need to be proactive in safeguarding the data of potential students during the admissions process. In choosing an outsource provider for their online admissions applications, Virginia Tech made sure the data privacy rights of applicants would be honored.

1. Introduction

As they apply to college, young people fill in and submit forms containing highly personal information about themselves and their families. Before the advent of the Internet, they could trust that the application process was secure and private -- that personal data would be kept confidential.

Now, however, heavily financed marketing companies have set out to intervene in the online admissions application process, often succeeding in skimming off sensitive data even before it’s submitted to the school. Under pressure to provide Internet services to an Internet hungry audience and fielding a bombardment of high-pressured sales calls filled with enticing promises, many college and university admissions administrators are becoming unintentional collaborators with these vendors.

As Virginia Tech discovered, however, there are cost-effective alternatives to these data pirates - economical outsource providers who don’t sell or broker applicant data.

2. Students and Their Families Care About Data Privacy

According to a recent report by the Center for Democracy and Technology, there is a growing concern with individual privacy on the Internet. [1] These are some of the studies they cite to prove the point:

- A survey of parents found that their biggest concern overall about their children's use of the Internet is the abuse of personal information - an issue more troubling to them than credit card fraud, unsolicited email, and exposure to pornography and/or strangers. 65% said their children had been solicited to buy goods or services on the Web and more than half said their children had been asked to provide personal information at a site to access content. [2]
- 87% of Internet users are concerned about threats to their personal privacy while online. [3]
- 42% of users cited sale of personal information as the most pressing issue on the Internet. [4]
- 66.7% of respondents cited lack of information about how their personal data would be used as the reason for not filling out registration forms online. [5]
- The most important factor to respondents in deciding whether to provide information is whether or not information will be shared with other companies and organizations. [6]
- 74.3% of Internet users believe that web sites do not have the right to resell their personal information. [7]

3. The Code of Fair Information Practices

The privacy expectations of individuals, identified in these and other survey results, are reflected in the Code of Fair Information Practices -- broadly recognized data privacy principles proposed in 1973 by a US government advisory committee, but never enacted into law. The principles in the code that directly affect data privacy in the online admissions process are these:

- Control -- The individual has the right to control the use of his/her personal information.
- Openness -- Those who collect information must describe the purpose and uses they make of the personal information they collect.
- Limited Collection -- Personal information must be collected by lawful and fair means and, where appropriate, with the knowledge and consent of the individual.
- Limited Use -- The use and disclosure of personal information must be limited to the purpose for which it was collected, unless the individual has granted consent.

Adherence to these principles by web site operators would address many consumer concerns about data privacy, but in the online admissions arena there are additional concerns.

4. FERPA Is Not Enough

Under pressure from industry groups to maintain a hands-off approach to data privacy issues, the Federal government has yet to take any regulatory action that would stipulate how web sites must request permission to use personal data. Further, although the Family Rights and Privacy Act (FERPA) offers data privacy protection for a school's enrolled students, it doesn't expressly protect applicants, nor does it protect students who may provide information about themselves and their families to independent web site operators during, say, a scholarship search.

For the moment, the government seems narrowly focused on whether or not web site operators publish privacy policy statements and whether or not they comply with their own statements. There is no regulatory attention being paid whatsoever to how web sites ask users for permission to use their data - even though there is ample evidence of confusing and misleading questions that can trip users into unwittingly consenting to commercial use of their personal information.

5. Shortcomings of Private Sector Privacy Protectors

A number of online admissions web sites use private sector privacy enforcement programs such as TRUSTe to ensure users of data privacy protection. These programs emphasize providing consumers with (1) notice of company practices, (2) the ability to opt-out of information sharing, and (3) assurance that appropriate security is used to protect their personal information. While this is certainly a step in the right direction, many of these programs don't require companies to comply with the full set of Fair Information Practices and, because some programs have multiple versions, individuals must read the fine print to find out what protections and rights the programs afford them.

In addition, data privacy explanations and opt-out questions can be confusing to users -- especially young users. Young people applying to college may not realize the potentially detrimental effects of sharing their personal data. They may be naive about the potential abuses of such data gathering efforts. Because of their lack of life experience or the confusing nature of the data privacy statements they encounter on the web, they may not choose to opt-out of data sharing, even though it is in their best interest to do so.

6. Virginia Tech's Admissions Data Privacy Decision

Applying for college is faster and easier over the web, and, as Virginia Tech discovered, it can also be done without vendor registration forms and legal "mumbo jumbo." CollegeNET -- the outsource provider Virginia Tech chose to serve and support its online admissions application forms -- has taken a firm stand on the data privacy issue. It has consistently refused to sell or broker applicant data.

CollegeNET has no vendor registration forms, opt-out statements, or small print legalese, because it is committed to data privacy, and its pricing structure doesn't rely on selling or brokering data. The company is able to provide a highly economical online admissions solution for colleges and universities *and* protect data privacy. Prospective students can be assured that when they apply to Virginia Tech using the online admissions form designed and delivered by CollegeNET, that their personal information is kept private.

7. Why Your School Should Care About Data Privacy in the Admissions Process

The admissions process is often people's first experience of your school - their first opportunity to assess your institution's integrity, moral leadership, and commitment to students. If you make decisions aimed at safeguarding personal privacy in the admissions process, you'll demonstrate your respect for students and provide a powerful incentive for them to apply to your school.

The admissions process is one of the first rites of passage through which millions of people form impressions about higher education. As we apply the power of the Internet to this process, let us all make choices that will not only make college admissions more convenient and efficient, but also safe for personal privacy and protective of the image of high integrity traditionally ascribed to higher education.

References

[1] Center for Democracy and Technology, Beyond the Numbers: Privacy Practices on the Web, 1999.

[2] FamilyPC Special Report: Annual FamilyPC Internet Survey Results, 1998.

[3] AT&T survey, Beyond Concern: Understanding Net Users' Attitudes About Online Privacy, 1999.

[4] Center for Democracy and Technology Privacy Survey, 1998.

[5] The 10th semi-annual poll of Graphics, Visualization, and Usability at the Georgia Institute of Technology, 1998.

[6] AT&T survey, Beyond Concern: Understanding Net Users' Attitudes About Online Privacy, 1999.

[7] The 10th semi-annual poll of the Graphics, Visualization, and Usability Center at the Georgia Institute of Technology, 1998.

Teaching and Learning in a Network World
P. Hoffman and D. Lemke (Eds.)
IOS Press, 2000

COPYRIGHT AND FAIR USE ISSUES RELATING TO EDUCATIONAL MULTIMEDIA

Michael H. Trenholm
Knobbe, Martens, Olson & Bear, LLP
3801 University Avenue, Suite 710, Riverside, California 92501

With the explosion of the World Wide Web, students and educators have a much greater opportunity to obtain educational materials from a variety of different sources. Moreover, the preparation of multi-media presentations by educators and students is now an increasingly common occurrence on campuses. However, the use of such material implicates the U.S. copyright laws and educators should be aware of the limits imposed by the copyright laws.

1. What Is A Copyright?

A copyright is a property right in an original work of authorship which is fixed in a tangible medium of expression. Original works of authorship can include articles, books, artistic renderings, such as sculptures, paintings, drawings, public performances, and the like. Basically, copyrights can arise whenever an individual expresses an original idea in some manner so that the expression is "fixed". The work is considered "fixed" when it is in a form that is permanent or stable enough to permit it to be perceived, reproduced or otherwise communicated for a period of more than transitory duration. Storing an article or an image in a website would constitute fixation of the article or image. It is important to note that under current U.S. law, the owner obtains the copyright when the work is fixed and the creation of the copyright does not generally require the owner to file an application or even place a copyright notice on the work.

Copyrights afford the copyright owner several exclusive rights, including the right to reproduce the work, to adapt the work, to publicly distribute the work, to publicly perform the work or to display the work. The owner of the copyright is typically the author, although the author may have assigned the copyright to another entity, or the copyright may be owned by the author's employer under the work for hire doctrine. A copyright generally has a very long duration. For example, works created by individual authors after January 1, 1978 exist from the time of creation of the work to a date 50 years following the death of the author[1].

---

[1] 17 U.S.C. § 302 *et seq.*

2. What Is Fair Use ?

While copyrights afford the owner the above-listed exclusive rights, there are some statutory exceptions which permit some uses of the work by others that would otherwise be a copyright infringement. One very important exception is defined by a doctrine called "fair use". Generally speaking, the fair use doctrine typically applies to reproducing portions of copyrighted works for news reporting purposes, criticism, teaching, scholarship or research. In these circumstances, some appropriation of copyrighted works is permissible. However, one practical difficulty with the fair use doctrine is that there is no clear definition of fair use in the U.S. Copyright laws. Instead of defining what fair use consists of, Congress chose to codify certain factors that are used to determine if a particular use is a fair use.[2]

The first factor is the purpose and character of the use. In other words, for what purpose is the copyrighted work being used. Generally, commercial uses of copyrighted work, e.g., reproducing the work for financial gain, are generally less likely to be considered fair use. For example, the copying and binding of articles for sale to students as course work materials in lieu of a book has been found on several occasions to be a commercial activity that is not protected by the fair use doctrine.[3]

More purely educational uses of the copyrighted work are much more likely to be considered fair use. For example, a professor reproducing a single quotation from a book to stimulate class discussion is an educational use that is not for profit and is more likely to be a fair use. However, it should be clearly noted that the U.S. Supreme Court has stated that "The mere fact that a use is educational and not for profit does not insulate it from a finding of infringement, any more than the commercial character of a use bars a finding of fairness."[4] Hence, the fact that a copyrighted work is being used in a non-profit educational setting does not always mean that it is protected under the fair use doctrine.

The second factor that is evaluated in determining the application of the fair use doctrine is the nature of the copyrighted work. If, for example, the copyrighted work is more factual, e.g., an article reporting a newsworthy story, the reproduction of the article for educational purposes is likely found to be a fair use. The thought is that fair use supports the broad dissemination of facts in an educational setting. On the other hand, if the work is viewed to be more fictional, then the character of the copyrighted work does not always support such wide dissemination of the work without compensation to the original author.

The third factor that is evaluated for fair use determination is the amount and substantiality of the portion used in relation to the copyrighted work as a whole. A complete and wholesale reproduction of an entire book, for example, is more likely not a fair use than the reproduction of isolated passages out of the book. In some circumstances, the courts have evaluated whether the person appropriating the work appropriated only that which was necessary to accomplish the fair use purpose. For example, in a recent case involving the San Diego Chicken performing a routine where the children's television character Barney was parodied, the court evaluated whether the potential copyright and

[2] 17 U.S.C. § 107.

[3] *See, e.g., Princeton Univ. Press, MacMillan, Inc. v. Michigan Document Servs.*, 99 F.3d 1381 (6th Cir. 1996) (en banc), *See, also, Basic Books, Inv. v. Kinko's Graphic Corp.*, 758 F. Supp. 1522 (SDNY 1991).

[4] *Cambell v. Acuff-Rose Music, Inc.*, 510 U.S. 569, 584 (U.S. S.Ct. 1994).

trademark infringer took only so much of the original work to establish to the audience that Barney was the subject of the parody. The fact that the San Diego Chicken only appropriated the likeness of Barney and not the song or other identifying features of Barney was an important consideration for the court in determining that the parody was a fair use.[5]

The last factor that is considered in determining the application of the fair use doctrine is the effect of the use upon the potential market for or value of the copyrighted work. For example, an entire text book being completely reproduced and placed on a webpage for the simultaneous use by the students, such that none of the students have to purchase the book, would be a direct and negative consequence on the market for the copyrighted work. As a consequence, it is less likely that this use of the copyrighted work will be considered a fair use. This factor has been viewed by some courts as perhaps the single most important factor in many circumstances in determining the applicability of the fair use doctrine.[6]

Hence, when evaluating whether a particular use is a fair use or not, it is important to evaluate each of the above listed factors. Only after all of the factors have been weighted and balanced can a use be characterized as fair. The fact that a use is for educational purposes will not alone shield the individual or entity from liability for copyright infringement.

3. Fair Use And Educational Multimedia

With the advent of widespread use of computers by instructors and students and the ready availability of content on the internet, educational multimedia is a valuable instructional tool. Generally multimedia is a method of presenting information by using more than one medium of communication, such as text, graphic images and sound. Multimedia presentations are being prepared both by students and instructors using copyrighted content obtained via the internet or through more traditional sources. As discussed above, however, the mere fact that these multimedia presentations are for educational purposes does not automatically make these presentations fair use. Each project should be evaluated using the fair use factors described above to determine if the use of particular copyrighted subject matter is a fair use.

In order to facilitate an understanding of what is permissible in this context, various guidelines have been developed by a consortium of educators and industry groups. In particular, "Fair Use Guidelines for Educational Multimedia" and "Fair Use Guidelines for Electronic Reserve Systems" have been developed to provide a guide to educators as to what is permissible in educational multimedia and what is permissible in posting instructional materials onto a course web page.[7]

In general, for educational multimedia prepared in connection with courses at non-profit educational institutions, use of copyrighted subject matter may be permitted under certain circumstances. Generally, the students will be able to prepare the project and incorporate copyrighted subject matter and individually perform and display the project.

---

[5] *Lyons Partnership v. Giannoulas*, 51 U.S.P.Q. 1365 (CA 5 1999).

[6] *See, e.g.Cambell,* 510 U.S. at 574.

[7] The Guidelines are reprinted in *Technology and Copyright Law: A Guidebook for the Library Research and Teaching Professions* by Arlene Bielefield and Lawrence Cheeseman.

These projects may also be used in the students' portfolios as examples of their academic work for later personal use such as job and graduate school interviews. However, the use of these projects for non-academic commercial purposes is generally not going to be permitted.

Educators are also able to produce educational multi-media for curriculum based instruction to students in non-profit educational institutions in certain situations. These situations include face-to-face instruction, assignments to students for directed self-study and instruction provided to students over the educational institutions secure electronic network. Generally, however, the guidelines limit the time period for which the educators can use the presentation to two years.

It should be appreciated that these guidelines do not guarantee that an educational multimedia presentation will fall within the parameters of fair use. These guidelines do, however, provide some guidance such that the educational multimedia presentations are more likely to be considered fair use when analyzed using the factors described above.

Teaching and Learning in a Network World
P. Hoffman and D. Lemke (Eds.)
IOS Press, 2000

Girls and the Digital Divide

Lynn Van Gorp

Technology Coordinator, Pegasus School
Web Site: www.pegasus-school.net/girls
Email: lvangorp@pegasus-school.net

Resources - Books and Videos and Extras

1. This book is a must. Wonderful research, teaching ideas and resources "Girls and Technology: An Idea Book for Educators and Parents"
   National Coalition of Girls' Schools
   228 Main Street, Concord MA 01742
   Phone: (978) 287-4485
   www.ncgs.org

2. Email: ncgs@ncgs.org Janese Swanson, Ed. D. has done considerable research on gender preferences of boys and girls and provides detailed findings with recommendation for parents and teachers including a detailed section on "What We Can Do To Get Girls Involved In Technology". This web site www.girltech.com is also the home page for Club Girl Tech who published a book in 1997 called "Tech Girl's Internet Adventures". This book is a must for all teachers and students alike.

3. Explorer Tech Team has published a book called "The Tech Team". This book is a step-by-step manual of worksheets, templates, forms and examples designed to help those interested in training Technology Aides. It also includes strategies and lesson plans. To order "The Tech Team", call 1(800) 786-5017 and mention the Linworth Web Page to receive a 20% reduction in the $34.95 price.
   www.kent.wednet.edu:80/KSD/DE/technology/tech_team/index.htm

4. A video produced by The National Coalition of Girls' Schools "Girls and Technology - Expect the Best"
   www.tiac.net/users/ncgs or www.ncgs.org

5. The American Association of University Women (AAUW) has many excellent resources. Their reports and research are superb. Books for your library: "Shortchanging Girls, Shortchanging America" (1991), "How Schools Shortchange Girls" (1992), "Growing Smart: What's Working for Girls in School" (1995), plus the newest foundation research released in 1998 "Gender Gaps: Where Schools Still Fail Our Children" (1998). Based on the findings of over 1000 research studies, this report reveals where public schools are failing to meet the needs of girls and outlines recommendations to put all children on a path to high academic achievement. The association's web site is www.aauw They also monitor a girls' web site chat room at www.girlzone.com

6. Girls Incorporated is a national organization dedicated to "helping girls become strong, smart, and bold." Offers many programs for girls including Project SMART which is aimed at promoting girls' interest in careers involving technology. www.girlsinc.org

7. GirlTECH web site offers a teacher training and student mentor program with lesson plans and on-line resources to explore gender differences in computer use and access, along with innovative teaching strategies. www.crpc.rice.edu/CRPC/women/GirlTech

8. Review Zone's Web Sites for Girls is an excellent site that reviews web sites for girls. This site is managed by Tina Velgos. Go to www.thereviewzone.com/links.html

9. Girls, Girls, Girls: Sites Encouraging Girls - An informative site hosted by Cathy Fiore providing links to great sites. Discussion, research, programs and internet connections are included. www.edsoasis.org/Treasure/GrlEncour.html

10. School House Software Reviews offers great software reviews. www.worldvillage.com/wv/school/html/scholrev.htm

11. Another great site that reviews CD-ROM titles for girls is www.cdaccess.com/html/pc/58girls.htm

12. Also Girl Games is a wonderful site at www.deakin.edu.au/fac-arts/VPMA/media369/girlgames

13. Hyperspace Cowgirls was founded in 1995 by Dr. Evelyn Shaw and her daughter Susan Shaw. They create CD-Roms and web sites with the primary objective to produce work that empowers girls and women. Some of their programs include the Crayola historical series Magic Wardrobe, Magic Princess and First Ladies Paint and Play Pony. Great role models. www.hygirls.com

Teaching Strategies and School Activities

1. Connect technology to the real world. Students often need a reason to take a class, They need to know how it will help them. Girls often see computers as glorified typewriters and game players.

2. Make sure students know the breadth of careers that use technology. Explore the many occupations that use technology: business people, athletes, medical professionals, fashion designers, teachers, musicians, movie producers...nearly every profession today relies heavily on technology skills. The leaders of tomorrow must be technologically competent.

3. Encourage girls to act as experts. When the teacher doesn't know everything, students are empowered to take charge and display their competencies. They are not afraid to critique their own work and feel more comfortable participating even though they might make mistakes.

4. Experiment with alternatives to note taking. Don't be afraid to let students use

laptops or hand out notes ahead of time and have students highlight relevant headings.

5. Making sure the women on staff, and parents are actively involved using technology and in planning technology programs. They influence students.

6. Offer classes to Moms and get them involved as Technology Assistants.

7. Get the word out. Be a speaker at PTO meetings, write articles in your school newspaper, design a web page, and bring in female speakers and mentors.

8. Have a special club or activities just for the girls. After school or lunch work well.

9. Involve the girls in a Teacher Assistant Program with training and class credit

10. Getting involved with Email projects or a pen pal combines language arts, technology and girls' social needs all at the same time.

11. Create a Girls' Only Web Site. Check out pages already on the internet designed by girls, for girls and maintained by girls.

12. Make sure that girls participate in discussions. Don't let the boys take over.

13. Require homework to be done on the computer.

14. Give extra credit for projects done on the computer.

15. Carefully develop projects, lesson demonstrations and activities so girls' interests are equally represented.

16. Topics should cover a wide range, choices should be available, and creative activities should be included if possible.

Software Examples

1. Madeline's European Adventures; Madeline's Thinking Games and Madeline's Magnificent Puppet Show (ages 4-10) These are wonderful, wonderful, wonderful, adventure based programs that involve critical thinking, problem solving, French and Spanish language experiences and a great deal of fun. Madeline has to think logically, and follow directions carefully to be successful. She provides a superb role model for young girls. Find this company on the web at www.cwonders.com and www.ea.com/crwonders.html

2. Ariel's Story Studio (ages 4-10) This program involves a read along adventure with problem solving fun activities. The player can play many fun little games, do creative scene design, write music and join a singalong, make her own storybook and collect interesting fish fact cards. Ariel's Print Studio is great too. It has print related activities- cards, birthday invitation etc. Information on the web at www.disneyinteractive.com

3. Crayola Magic Princess: Creative Historical Activities and Crayola Magic Wardrobe - Time Travel with Paper Dolls and First Ladies (ages 6-12) Through art and creativity girls can discover history. Twelve historical periods are included - Ancient Egypt, Imperial China, Medieval France, Elizabethan England, Pre Revolutionary France, the American Pilgrim, Southern Belle, Western Pioneer, Native American Navajo, and Hippie, and the cultures of India and Ghana, Africa. Clothing and accessories can be designed and decorated, girls' diaries from each time period can be read, diaries and letters can be written, and profiles of famous women can be studied. Great fun. On the web at www.us.pc.ibm.com/multimedia

4. Fisher Price Time to Play Doll House and Dream Doll House (ages 4-7) Ten glittering games and activities, eight enchanting play areas and a house filled with hidden surprises. Host a summer tea party, pop bubbles in sequence for treats, play dressup, decorate a cake, create your own bedroom, start a bug collection, and decorate your own Jack O Lantern. Fisher Price at www.fisherprice.com

5. Sheila Rae, the Brave (ages: 3-6) Sheila Rae wasn't afraid of anything: not spiders, not the dark, not even monsters in the closet! Then one day she decided to walk home a different way and got hopelessly lost. Like a Broadway show, the story is brought to life with catchy melodies. Children can hum along with Sheila Rae as she faces her fears and gains a new respect for her little sister...and herself! "Sheila Rae, the Brave", is based on the book by Kevin Henkes. Story text and dialogue is in English and Spanish. Features include seven sing-along songs and skills developing: word recognition, phonics skills, vocabulary, use of maps. Created by Broderbund at www.broderbund.com

6. Laura's Happy Adventures (ages 3-6) A Playmobile world created just for girls. Includes creative challenges, problem solving and skill building fun. Guillemot - Scholastic Software Club www.scholastic.com/swclub

7. Girls Only - Secret Diary and More (ages 7+) Keep secrets safe with a password protected journal, create personalized stationery, organize your life with a calendar and address book, write secret messages with a secret message writer to send coded notes to your friends. Encore Software or Scholastic Software Club www.scholastic.com/swclub

8. The American Girls Premiere (ages 7-12) Creators can bring the American Girls to life by creating, directing and performing plays in a multimedia theater. The author can choose characters, scenes and props, direct actions, and add sound effects, music and lighting. When finished, the scripts can be printed. Staging ideas and director's guides for production are also included. There are even many sample plays and great tutorials. The Learning Company at www.learningco.com

9. Diary Maker (ages 7+) This is a wonderfully rich program containing exerts from Anne Frank, Zlata Filipovic and Latoya Hunter. Students can explore their diaries, and learn about their life experiences as well as create their own multimedia diary. The diary has such tools as a highlighter, stamp tool, sticky notes, text to speech and a writer's block too. Available from Scholastic at www.scholastic.com

10. Barbie Fashion Design - New Version - Cool Looks Fashion Design (ages 6-14) Become a fashion designer and create outfits, add accessories, see your designs in a 3-D fashion show, print your outfits on to special fashion designer fabric or print out usable patterns. Also see your creations on a fashion magazine cover. Mattel and Digital Domain. Find at www.mattelmedia.com/barbie/fashiondesigner Also from Barbie: Barbie Magic Fairy Tales: Barbie as Rapunzel; Barbie: Magic Hair Styler; Barbie Print'nPlay; Barbie Storymaker; and Barbie: Talk with Me

11. Secret Paths in the Forest, Rockett's New School, and Rockett's Tricky Decision (ages 8-12) are three adventure experiences designed specifically for girls. The themes relate to friendship and involve problem solving challenging adventure based puzzles. The software is packaged with cool stuff like a backpack, T-shirt, jewelry, and lipgloss. They have a great web site with programs and activities just for girls www.purple-moon.com

12. Carmen San Diego Series Jr. Detective, Where in the World, USA, Time, and Word (ages 6+ depending on the title) Great adventure learning series. Designed by a woman, therefore a woman detective. Bravo Broderbund! www.broderbund.com

13. Pippi Longstocking (ages 4+) An animated storybook with interactive rooms full of surprises, games and puzzles. Translated into 11 languages. It involves decision making, reading comprehension and puzzle solving skills. Publisher - HER Online at www.her-online.com

14. Desktop Tool Kit (ages 9+) Use this easy to use program to make your own home page (My Home Page), a progirl interactive 3D screen saver, and an electronic calendar. Designed for the beginner. GirlTech at www.girltech.com

15. The 3D Adventures of Sailor Moon (ages 10+) Enter the magical and mystical world of Sailor Scouts and explore new places and play challenging games all in the latest 3D technology. The Sailor Scouts are ordinary high school girls who transform into glamorous powerful super heroines who stand for justice and fight against the evil forces of Negaverse. There is a puzzle room, fashion salon and fitting room, fighting arena, and library source for each scout. Produced by 3VR at www.3vr.com/products/sailormoon/sailormoon/htm

16. Chop Suey (ages 7-12) Go on escapades with Lily and June Bug and two young girls who discover the magic in their own hometown. Meet flowers with faces and clouds shaped like teapots and sneakers. Visit Aunt Vera's house, search through Dooner's messy room, find hidden secrets. Use X-ray glasses that let you see through walls. Easy to use has great illustrations, movies on the moon, songs, and more. Magnet Interactive

17. Vampire Diaries (ages: 10+) A vampire? In Fells Church? Can you find out who it is, and save the town, without getting bitten yourself? Why did Caroline suddenly turn into your ex-best friend? Who can you trust? Explore the town, search for clues, and solve some puzzles! Publisher - HER Online at www.her-online.com

18. The Baby-sitters Club Friendship Kit and Clubhouse Activity Center Also separate titles for Grades Level 3 and 4 (ages 8-13) Join the Baby-sitters any time by dropping into Claudia's room to explore; to get messages from the

club; to create great things like calendars, stationary, letters, tickets, posters, secret messages, and many other things; to play games; or to write in your own journal. Very creative and interactive! Individual material stored with passwords so the program supports multiple user files. Creative Wonders at www.cwonders.com and www.ea.com/crwonders.html Also check out World Kids Network - Babysitters Club. www.worldkids.net/clubs and www.philipsmedia.com/bsc

19. Clueless (ages 9 - 16) Using a specialized cell phone you can speed dial your way through Cher's World. There are 10 different phone buttons, each leading to a different activity. Some include fashion design, makeovers, career help, and dating game quizzes. More info on the web at www.mattelmedia.com

20. Snap Shot (ages 9+) Turn photos into postcards, stickers and other crafts. Create personal web pages and slide shows. Sierra On-Line or available from Scholastic Software Club www.scholastic.com/swclub

21. Nancy Drew: Secrets Can Kill (ages 8+) Solve a mystery, over 75 puzzles and clues. Catch the criminal. Her Interactive or Scholastic Software Club www.scholastic.com/swclub

22. Emergency Room 2 (ages9+) Life and death are in your hands as the attending room physician. Over 40 3D tools, do lab work and make diagnosis. Legacy Interactive or Scholastic Software Club www.scholastic.com/swclub

23. Let's Talk about Me and Let's Talk About Me Too (ages 13+ Parents should view before letting their girls play) These are excellent programs for teenage girls. These programs were designed to provide the preteen and teenage girl with the opportunity to explore her relationships, personality and potential within the privacy of her own interactive experience. These programs were developed by Girl Games at www.girlgamesinc.com and Simon & Schuster Interactive www.simonandschuster.com

24. McKenzie & Co. (ages: 10+) McKenzie & Company is an interactive role-playing program set in a high school. Through the extensive use of video clips, the user is presented with the opportunity to choose their characters, situations, locations (home, the mall, school, a friend's house), what to say, and what to do. Each decision leads down a different path. Publisher - HER Online at www.her-online.com

25. You Can Be A Woman Astronomer, You Can Be A Marine Biologist, and Woman Engineer (ages 5-12) Join Astronomer Dr. Andrea Mia Ghez in her fascinating work with the Hubbell Space Telescope or Strap on your air tanks. Books also available "You can be a Woman Architect, Eqyptologist, Engineer or Marine Biologist. All these titles involve female role models with inspirational stories, and include science principles, an animated story, activities and lesson plans for teachers, parent resources and games and puzzles. Cascade Pass at www.cascadepass.com

26. Telling Our Stories: Women in Science (ages: 9-18) Explore the exciting work of inspiring women in science! Highlights science careers. Introduces strong role models and challenges stereotypes. Discover first-hand the compelling stories of eight diverse women scientists and their exciting work through personal photos, interviews, biographies, interactive experiments,

multimedia field trips and more than three hours of audio and video clips. Meet scientists working in a variety of scientific fields: astronomy, biology, chemistry, animal communication, geology and physics. Also included in Women in Science, an extensive database of 130 women scientists, past and present. Publisher Tom Snyder www.tomsnyder.com/products/products.html

27. Women in Literature (ages: 12+)Take your students on an interactive exploration women in literature with this excellent CD-ROM set. It charts the transition of women in literature from object to subject, from biblical and Greek times to the recent past. Numerous excerpts from Homer, Virgil, Ibsen, Woolf, de Beauvoir, and Plath help students understand how changes in the literary and social scenes were reflected in the portrayal of women in literature. Publisher: Clearview

28. Teen Digital Diva, the OFFICIAL Teen Magazine CD-ROM game, lets teens express their style with their own virtual magazine! Mix and match fashions, do on screen make overs, plus personalize quizzes and horoscopes. www.teendigitaldiva.com

Internet Site Links and Activities

1. Club Girl Tech - produces the book and girls' internet adventures. www.girltech.com

2. Girl's World - http://www.agirlsworld.com/clubgirl/membersonly/joinclub.html

3. World Kids Network - Babysitters Club www.worldkids.net/clubs

4. The Super Sitter - A handy guide for future babysitters as well as parents to follow, providing information on what toys children should play with, safety warnings, and when to leave. www.medaccess.com/workbook/supersit/supersit.htm

5. The Girl Scouts - Gives a complete history and mission of Girl Scouts, and contains all sorts of information on scouting. www.girlscouts.org

6. American Girl - "Celebrating Girls Yesterday and Today" This site is run by the American Girl Magazine. It offers a "Things to do Category" and has many different activities for kids to do and participate in. You can also join the American Girls Club. - www.americangirl.com/ag/ag.cgi

7. Beanie Babies Official Web Site - Pictures and information about all of the Beanie Baby Characters. You can also join the Beanie Connection Club. www.ty.com You can get gear for your Beanie Babies at www.bhome.com.gearfor.htm

8. Color-ful-Fun - Get party ideas and more by joining this jazzy girls' net club. www.crayola.com

9. Cookie Recipes - Check the recipe for the cookie of the day. Search for cookie recipes, or play recipe roulette and get a surprise from the cookie jar. www.cookierecipe.com

10. Disney's Web Site - Great activities and projects for students. Promos too, of course. www.disney.com

11. National Geographic - A wonderful site to visit with great graphics and interactive activities. Great place to explore the world or get information for school projects. www.nationalgeographic.com

12. Curiocity's Free Zone Presents Kellogg's Club - Cereal fun! Enjoy Tony Talk, Tremendous Trivia, and an Action Arcade. Go to http://freezone.com/kelloggs

13. Yahooligans - Web guide for kids around the world. Art Soup and Dr. Book are a few of the activities kids will find. www.yahooligans.com

14. Family Education Network - This site has several search engines, lists of sources for learning about everything from English to foreign languages, to art and science. This site is sponsored by Microsoft. www.familyeducation.com

15. Smart Girl Internette - SmartGirl houses a continually updated collection of reviews, surveys, and stories written by and for teenage girls. www.smartgirl.com

16. New Moon - New Moon is a magazine for "girls and their dreams." It publishes stories about girls and women active in sports, the community and other groups and activities. www.newmoon.org

17. Planet Girl - A great range of options with quizzes, games, e-cards, and cool sites that include work ideas, school help and study tips, volunteer projects, relationship info and help, sports and health, entertainment and the arts, travel, fashion and beauty, and a section called Fun Stuff. Many, many different choices. Very comprehensive. www.planetgirl.com

18. Girl Site - Phenomenal Women, Virginia Avenue Writing Project, Follow Your Dreams, New Jokes, Good Books, Jessica Volunteers at the Y, Take Your Daughter to Work, Cool Gigs, and Friend Problems and some of the great options at this informative and creative site. www.girlsite.org

19. A Girl's World Online Clubhouse - A safe place on the Net where girls from all over the world can meet and make friends. www.agirlsworld.com

20. Go, Girl! Magazine - Dedicated to getting girls of all ages and fitness levels involved in sports. Profiles of women athletes, excellent fitness tips, editorial essays and news in health and fitness. www.gogirlmag.com

21. Cyber Sisters - The Club for Wired Net Girlz - Girls between the ages of 6 - 18 can join Cyber Sisters and discover a bunch of new friends from all over the world via the computer. The site sends out a newsletter every month featuring girls in the news and email addresses of new cyber sisters. http://worldkids.net/clubs/CSIS

22. G.I.R.L. - G.I.R.L. stands for "Girls Internationally wRiting Letters" and is an international penpal club for girls ages 8 - 14. There is also a newsletter written and compiled by members. In addition, the activity list has games that

allow winners to receive prizes by postal mail. www.worldkids.net/girl

23. Girls Place - Sections like Our World, Well Being, Favorite Things, Speak Up, Links to Favorite Web Pages, Travel, Contests, and Art make this a well rounded and fun site. www.girlsplace.com

24. Family PC Family PC on the web has a Parental Guidance section and Girls Just Want to Have Fun Go to www.zdnet.com/familypc Associate Editor at Family PC is Valle Dwight. Contact her at valle_dwight@zd.com

25. Planet Girl This site was designed by a company that makes software just for girls. One of the most interesting things on this site is their magazine, Girls Interwire. This magazine has news and reviews by girls, stories of real life heroines (past and present) and a place for you to give your opinions. The creator of this site has worked hard to make this an enriching place for girls! www.girlgamesinc.com

26. Encyclopedia of Woman's History - Kids made this encyclopedia after they realized that there were no women's history sites on the web. The encyclopedia currently has entries from students in grades 3-12 www.teleport.com/~megaines/women.html

27. International Woman's Air and Space Museum - Stop here to learn about the history of women in flight - from balloonists, to jet pilots, to astronauts. Check out t women's biographies and see photos of your favorite flying women. www.infinet.com~iwasm

28. Women of NASA - Live web chats with women from NASA. htttp://quest.arc.nasa.gov/women

29. Women Artists Archive - Changing galleries of artwork and biographies of female artists from all over the world are presented. www.sonoma.edu/library/special/waa

30. FeMiNa Web Search for Women and Girls - Latin for "women" FeMiNa is the first web search engine for women. Geared mostly to girls in their early teens, this search engine has over 30 links to sites like New Moon, Girls Tech, and Her On Line. www.femina.com

31. Cybergrrl - (not a typing error) Informing, inspiring and celebrating women. For older teens and young adults. Great technical information, advice and help, views on issues relevant to young women today, and a great "Fun" area. www.cybergrrl.com

Teaching and Learning in a Network World
P. Hoffman and D. Lemke (Eds.)
IOS Press, 2000

Technology Companies and the Academy: Why Are We So Evil?

Kathryn Winograd, Ph.D.
eCollege.com
10200 A East Girard Ave.
Denver, CO 80231

Faculty resistance to the partnerships between academic institutions and technology companies arises from fears of job loss and the loss of intellectual freedom, and faculty mistrust toward research on technology in the classroom that they see as mostly industry-driven. Administrative moves toward greater faculty accountability and public attacks upon the institution of tenure they see as consequences of these emerging corporate/university partnerships. That technology subverts education into training is another concern for faculty who envision the academic institution as the future breeding ground for corporations. Because technology in the classroom, and as the classroom, is a rapid-rise phenomena, there is little long term research available and what is available is suspect, whether it's quantitative, qualitative or anecdotal. The formation of the Center for Internet Technology in Education is one company's first step toward addressing faculty fears through a symbiotic relationship with the academic institutions it serves.

One of the main strategies in the art of Rhetorical Writing is to not only thoroughly understand the opposition, but to be willing to thoroughly and fairly present their arguments to your own audience even as you are attempting to persuade it to your side. The task of the Rhetorician then is to "answer" these arguments so soundly that they are essentially nullified. This is the cornerstone of academic discourse, the hallmark that distinguishes for most faculty what is academic from what is mere hype. If the education technology company wants to gain credibility in the eyes of the faculty it serves and wants to serve, then it must be willing to engage in this kind of discourse.

In keeping with this truism, eCollege.com proposed to create a tighter symbiotic relationship between interested academic institutions and itself. The formation of CITE, or the Center for Internet Technology in Education, would allow for open dialogue, leading to cooperative research initiatives into the issues of online education, and the creation of effective online teaching tools, as well as, better institutional support. As a past higher-education instructor and present Director of Academic Services for eCollege, I began to understand that in order for this to work, all who were involved in the venture of CITE needed to understand the barriers between us, and how CITE proposed to break down those barriers. And I decided that because administrators often do not have the same perceptions of technology that faculty do, and because faculty often perceive the administrators to be a threat in themselves, I would focus primarily on the concerns of faculty and then discuss how CITE would work with faculty.

The question then is this: Why are we so evil in the eyes of faculty?

Basically, faculty fear the loss of their jobs. Basically, faculty fear the loss of their intellectual freedom. And, basically, faculty profoundly distrust the results of research on technology in the classroom that they see as mostly industry-driven.

For a great number of faculty, the rise of technology means the demise of teachers. David Noble, cofounder of the National Coalition for Universities in the Public Interest, has said this of technology and the academic institute: "As in other industries, the technology is being deployed by management primarily to discipline, de-skill and displace labor" [1]. What are the roots for such a conclusion?

Faculty are watching these two things happen in the academic world-- first, a move by administration toward greater accountability from their faculty, which for faculty represents the standardization and quantification of education and, second, public attacks against the whole institution of tenure, which for the Faculty represents the academic freedom to pursue research and social commentary no matter where either might lead.

They view these trends as direct consequences of an emerging partnership between the academic institution and the corporation, which they see as anti-tenure, devotee of the bottom line, and creator of a technology that allows courses, which were once individualized, original creations resting in the soul of each professor, to easily become standardized shells, passed along the Internet highway from university to university.

Jane David, in an article published from the U.S. Department of Education, suggests that: "The acquisition of technology has been viewed as an end to itself, and the more "teacher-proof" the better" [2]. As administrators look to high tech companies and their offers of equipment and training as a way out of financial burdens, they also look at the attractive prospect of further reducing the budget by reducing full-time, tenured professorships because of complete "classrooms on a disk" educational programs. Feasibly, as they see it, one day, students will be able to take an instructor-less course with just a push of a button. As faculty see it, so much the better for the administrator--gone are not only the fees for the professional development of faculty, but the very faculty itself.

That technology subverts education into training is another concern for faculty. The jargon of the high tech computer industry has filtered into all areas of our lives, education not excluded. Steve Talbott states: "We have slowly been re-conceiving education as the transfer of information from one database or brain to another. . . What we haven't realized is that this fact-shoveling model of education renders both teachers and schools superfluous" [3].

Faculty envision the academic institution as the future breeding ground for corporations eager for high skilled workers and ready to pay for their training at the University level. Companies now supply not only the equipment and the training as incentives, but sometimes the curricula as well. As a consequence, profs see education becoming the business of transmitting efficient "bytes" of information, not of exploring complex issues that require critical thinking and synthesis. Technology is more concerned, they feel, with appearance, formatting and consumer appeal than expanding ways to explore subject matter more deeply.

To make matters worse, recent technology has been embraced by those advocates of learner-centered teaching, rather than teacher-centered, and the ramifications of this paradigm shift have not been fully explored by either the industry or the Academy. All the faculty know is that once more they are being pushed out the classroom door.

Wendy Rickard suggests that "the benefits of IT-infused education . . .typically do not relate to educational quality in its purest sense (improved learning or increased academic productivity)" [4]. Faculty see the corporate world involved in the efficient transmission of information of fact or routine--all in order to achieve that bottom line. This is training, while education is messier, more complex, less quantifiable. It is about a process of learning, of self-discovery, of intuition and ethic. Already there are anecdotal studies out there that claim that computers cause a drop in creativity and innovation, of cognitive skills and higher skilled thinking functions, that it actually creates isolation, not collaboration and community, all of which add fuel to the fires of professorial fear.

A third concern for the professor is the quality of Research done in the area of Technology and education. When they hear that technology improves education, they ask, *where's the proof*?

Edward Miller has said that: "The research is set up in a way to find benefits that aren't really there. Most knowledgeable people agree that most of the research isn't valid. It's so flawed it shouldn't even be called research. Essentially, it's just worthless"[5]. This from a former editor of the Harvard Review.

But why is the research out there so "damned?" One underlying simple reason is this: technology in the classroom, and as the classroom, is a rapid-rise phenomenon. Back in the

'80s the Xerox copier in the back room of the English department was the only reason for celebratory awe. All such short-term research is suspect, whether it's quantitative, qualitative or anecdotal. And there is fear that the biggest effect technology has in the classroom-- fundamental shifts in teaching method-- has never been isolated and eliminated as the cause for improvements in learning when technology is used. And of course there is always the big "damnation"—so many of these studies have been industry-funded, partly because those very senior, tradition-bound faculty members don't consider faculty research into the use of technology tenure-acceptable.

It has been said that "Educational technology is still in its infancy" [6] and this is where CITE can come in--viable, necessary and credible. Over and over again, in even the most hard-core anti-corporation, anti-technology tirades, I found the opposition willing to concede, perhaps half-heartedly, that the real problem with technology in education lies in the lack of faculty skill to effectively incorporate it into their curriculum.

Jane David puts it this way: "The primary reason technology has failed to live up to its promise lies in the fact that it has been viewed as an answer to the wrong question. Decisions about technology purchases and uses are typically driven by the question of how to improve the effectiveness of what schools are already doing--not how to transform what schools do . . Moreover, as has been typical with innovations of the past, scant attention has been paid to preparing teachers and administrators to use technology well. . . "[7].

What is and should be our Mission at the Center?

Only by exploring with teachers and administrators the use of the Internet and other education technologies in the classroom, both the traditional and online, can advancements in the teaching and learning process be both made and adopted on an institutional level. But we must not over-estimate our stature in this enterprise. This push toward the advancement of an educational ideology should come from the very rightful place and people that will be most affected by it—the academy and its own faculty. This is why we see at the heart of our mission the partnerships we will establish with academic institutions over time. It is not our place, even as an education and technology company, to enter their halls preaching a strict pedagogy—to be, in other words, dogmatic in our approach. The academy itself is split on which teaching theorem best serves its student body.

Our mission at CITE is and should be working with teachers to create and use the Internet and educational technologies to improve results in their classrooms, both traditional and online. In doing that let us introduce to them the constructs of as many schools of thought that would most benefit the use of the Internet or the application of a particular technology, venturing, unlike the acolyte, beyond script into the broad spectrum of issues that surround new technologies and their future in education, giving the professional educator the choice to assimilate whatever she or he wants and needs.

By focusing on the teachers, and on that key word, the "use" of the Internet and education technology, we will instigate a three-fold solution to that problematic academic perception of the corporate devil scaling the ivory walls. First and foremost, we will validate the teacher's rightful and necessary position within the classroom, acting as both conduit and source in the process of learning. Second, we will have the opportunity to reassure and illuminate a group of people who chose a profession out of passion, not out of love for money, and who achingly desire not only to touch the minds of their students, but to enflame their hearts.

Third, and last, by focusing on the teachers, by gaining their trust, by showing them the threshold of this new world, we can ignite and support the academic fires that will lead to institutionally-supported research, the validation of which will mean for us validation, and for the professor, who is anxious to pioneer, academy- sanctioned professional development that rightfully contributes to the granting of tenure.

To conclude, I want to tell you about something that just happened recently. It was an early summer night and my kids and I were at an ice cream store. Parked on the curb outside was an enormous telescope pointed at the sky. A small man sat at a card table in front of a laptop that he had connected to the telescope. After deciding he probably wasn't a nut, my kids and I walked up to see what he was doing. And there on that computer screen was the moon in all its craterous beauty.

"Have you ever seen the moon like this?" the man asked my kids, and with that he began to teach them about the moon. As I watched, I was struck by two things: first, by how absolutely exciting all this new technology could be. Now anyone could set up a laptop anywhere and use it to make the world see even the whole universe in an entirely new and wonderful way. But, second, and most importantly, I was struck by the man himself who had harnessed the wonders of technology in such a way that his passions for teaching and astronomy shone through. The computer, the telescope, and what they could do, would have met nothing if not for this man, this teacher, who knew how to engage my children, who knew how to use the Internet and the applications of software so that he could make my children understand the formation of a crater through the computer simulation of a single raindrop striking the surface of water.

"Do you know what gravity is?" he asked my children, and with that, he showed them a video clip of astronauts bouncing on the moon, the earth behind like a new one. He was marvelous. He was awe-inspiring. He erased every argument I could think of against the use of this new technology in Education.

What is and should be our mission at the Center? Let us be lofty. Let us aim for what is marvelous.

And as for CITE and the Academy? As Humphrey Bogart put it in Casablanca: "Louis, this could be the start of a beautiful friendship."

References

[1] D. Noble, Digital Diploma Mills: The Automation of Higher Education. FirstMonday, 3(1), (1998). Available: http://www.firstmonday.org/issues/issue3_1/noble/index.html

[2] J. David, Realizing the Promise of Technology: The Need for Systemic Education Reform. 1994, September. Available: http://www.ed.gov/pubs/EdReformStudies/SysReforms/david1.html.

[3] S. Talbott , Who's Killing Higher Education? Educom Review **34**(2) (1999) 26-33. Available: http://www.educause.edu/ir/library/html/erm99024.html.

[4] W. Rickard, Technology, Education, and the Changing Nature of Resistance: Observations from the Educom Medal Award winners. Educom Review **34**(1) (1999) 42-45. Available:http://www.educause.edu/ir/library/html/erm9915.html.

[5] T. Oppenheimer, The Computer Delusion. The Atlantic Monthly, **280**(1) (1997) 1-32. Available: http://www.theatlantic.com/issues/97jul/computer.htm.

[6] G. Berg, Public Policy on Distance Learning in Higher Education: California State and Western Governors Association Initiatives. Education Policy Analysis Archives, **6**(11), (1998, June) 1-20. Available: http://epaa.asu.edu/epaa/v6n11.html.

[7] J. David, Realizing the Promise of Technology: The Need for Systemic Education Reform, 1994, September. Available: http://www.ed.gov/pubs/EdReformStudies/SysReforms/david1.html.

Teaching and Learning in a Network World
P. Hoffman and D. Lemke (Eds.)
IOS Press, 2000

Perceptual Learning Modules in Mathematics and Science Instruction

Joseph A. Wise, *W. M. Keck Math/Science Institute, Crossroads School*
Tate Kubose, *University of California at Los Angeles*
Norma Chang, *W. M. Keck Math/Science Institute, Crossroads School*
Arlene Russell, *University of California at Los Angeles*
Philip J. Kellman, *University of California at Los Angeles*

Abstract

Research in cognitive science suggests that perceptual learning -- changes in information extraction leading to efficient detection and classification of relevant pattern structure – is a crucial component of expertise in many domains, including mathematics and science. Traditional learning formats do not do much to develop discovery or automaticity in the processing of structure, but appropriate conditions for doing so can be achieved using computer-based educational technology, in the form of Perceptual Learning Modules (PLM's™). Here we report progress in three domains using PLM's: university organic chemistry, multiple representations (graphs, equations, and word problems) of linear functions, and algebraic equivalences. These projects are in different stages of implementation, but objective data collected in two of them strongly support the value of PLM's in secondary school and university mathematics and science instruction.

1. INTRODUCTION

Educators should subject new technologies, along with older instructional practices, to two obvious questions: 1) What are our goals for what students should know and be able to do? and 2) What procedures can accomplish those goals? Especially in mathematics and science, most instructional settings get at least part of the answers to both questions wrong.

One common goal of instruction expects that learning in a given domain consists of stating facts and concepts, what cognitive scientists call *declarative knowledge*. Limitations on this idea are seen in the student who can state the concepts or facts, but fails to correctly apply them to solving a new problem. We encounter the limitation again when experts classify or solve problems, yet cannot convey their insight in how they solved the problem to another person.

Learning and expertise involve other dimensions besides declarative knowledge. Specifically, they involve changes in the ability to detect and classify patterns and structure in a given learning domain [1, 2, 3]. In a classic book, Gibson labeled these abilities *perceptual learning* [1]. The human attentional system seems geared to grow in its ability to isolate relevant detail, suppress irrelevancy and pick up progressively deeper structure, as a result of appropriate kinds of learning experiences. The ability to see patterns can grow to astonishing levels of sophistication, and it is a cornerstone of advanced performance in many domains, such as science and mathematics, chess, aviation, and radiology [2].

As our knowledge of the role of perceptual learning increases, it becomes clearer that classroom procedures must account for and nurture students' natural tendency for perceptual learning. The idea that perceptual learning of complex structure is a natural consequence of certain kinds of learning experiences may come as a shock to teachers.

After all, year after year, many students seem resistant to absorbing even the basics of scientific or mathematical concepts, and even fewer can apply these productively in problem solving. Students continue to struggle with distinguishing relevant and irrelevant information and in mapping appropriately across representational formats. These difficulties are hard to understand from the standpoint of traditional instruction. Teachers often assume that if a lecture has been delivered clearly, or if an example or two has been worked in detail, an attentive, earnest student should absorb the relevant concepts.

From the standpoint of theory and research in perceptual learning, however, the difficulties are not only understandable, they are expected. A given presentation of a concept contains a wealth of information, some relevant and some irrelevant. We may tend to forget that this is true as well of the representations we use. A graph of a function, for example, contains crucial information in terms of the shape of the function, intercepts, scaling, and so on. The student does not intuit immediately what are the relevant and irrelevant features of the representation. The slope and intercept of a linear function, known by the instructor to be crucial, may not "jump out" at the student any more than the color of the chalk.

Basic research carried out over the past few decades suggests that there are classroom procedures that directly address this neglected, but crucial, dimension of learning. Moreover, the requirements for perceptual learning are perfectly suited to being implemented in modern, computer-based instruction. In laboratory experiments, certain learning conditions lead to orders of magnitude improvement in extraction of task-relevant detail [4] and unconscious extraction of complex pattern structure [2, 5, 6, 7]. These conditions also change pattern extraction from an effortful, attention-consuming process to an automatic one [8].

Effective classroom procedures should incorporate *discovery* and *automaticity* [9]. Discovery in the learning of structure is a process of filtering which of the possible details, patterns, and relationships are relevant to a particular goal or task. Although there is some benefit to having relevant features pointed out explicitly, humans possess a basic learning process that progressively isolates the relevant features and directs attention toward them, while suppressing attention to irrelevancies [1]. This learning process advances when the subject makes rapid classifications and receives feedback over many short trials [10]. A large number of trials allows differentiation between relevant and irrelevant information, and leads to discovery of larger patterns and relationships [1, 11].

The same conditions – active classification over many short, rapid trials – allow another change in information processing to occur. This is termed automaticity [12]. Practice in information pick-up allows the same processing to occur with progressively smaller allocation of attention or effort. The student who has mastered a mathematical or scientific concept only at the level of memorized declarative knowledge may need substantial effort to apply it in problem solving. The value of automaticity is that if basic pattern recognition becomes automatic, attention and effort are left for dealing with higher-order aspects of the problem. Perceptual learning modules™ (PLM's) can make such basic concepts and patterns intuitive and therefore less demanding of attention [9].

Moreover, these procedures allow for continuous monitoring of objective performance, e.g., students' accuracy and speed at relevant structure classification tasks. The need for objective data in evaluating instructional methods is crucial, yet often omitted in favor of either subjective student acceptance ratings (or no data at all). PLM's provide online assessment of student progress, allow learning to proceed to set criteria, and readily support objective tests of transfer to other tasks [3].

In what follows, we describe three examples of PLM's in various stages of implementation and data collection. One project addresses students' mapping between multiple representations in the analysis of scientific problems involving linear functions. A second project addresses university-level students' intuiting of molecular structure and patterns in organic chemistry. A third project addresses students' facility with algebraic equivalences. These projects are collaborative efforts of members of the UCLA LIS (Learning and Intelligent Systems) Group, the UCLA Molecular Science Project and the W. M. Keck Math/Science Institute at Crossroads School.

2. THREE PLM EXAMPLES

2.1 Linear Functions PLM

In this study, we applied the ideas to multiple representations of linear functions as they appear in the high school physical science curriculum. Linear functions are a cornerstone of work at this level, appearing in time, distance, and velocity problems in physics, and rate problems in chemistry. Three kinds of representations are important in dealing with these problems: algebraic expressions or equations, graphical representations, and word problems. Each of these representational formats has advantages in making certain kinds of information explicit, but each also carries heavy burdens in terms of students' learning to grasp the important details and structures in each. Moreover, the mapping between these representations is a notoriously difficult hurdle of science and mathematics education. Our goal was to improve students' abilities to perform mappings across the problem representations and to facilitate the use of each and their combined employment in thinking and problem solving.

Method. We developed a PLM involving rapid classification of the sort that has previously proven effective in perceptual learning [3, 10]. We aimed to increase the efficiency and accuracy of mapping across multiple representations (visual, symbolic, linguistic) of the same problem.

Each trial in the module involved the presentation of one representation of the problem and required the learner to choose the correct match of a different representation from among three choices. Note that this PLM did not ask students to solve the problems presented, but rather to match the different representations of problem information. For example, a word problem might be presented, followed by three graphs, from which the subject would choose one. The target was presented by itself for two seconds. Then three choices were presented with the target until a response was entered. Feedback (correct or incorrect) was presented for up to ten seconds. An example of a word problem was:

> An object starts with 1 joule of heat. It gains 4 joules of heat for every 1 degree Celsius change in temperature. How many joules of heat would it contain if the room temperature increased 3 degrees Celsius?

The corresponding equation for this problem would be:

$$y = 4x + 1$$

The graph for this problem would be as shown below:

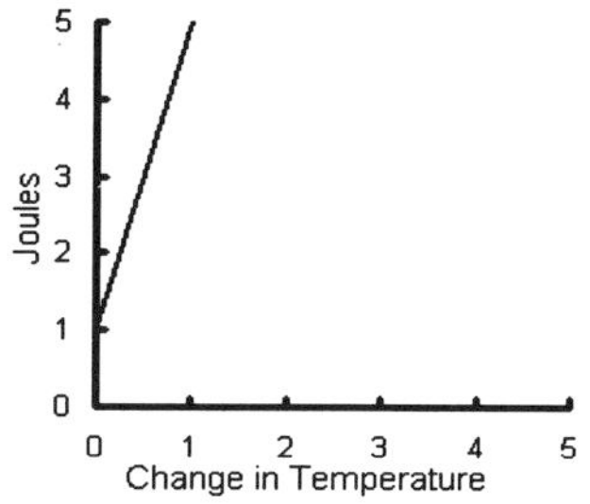

There were six different trial types; subjects received a mixture of all six during the learning phase. The six problem types were:

	Target Representation	Choice Representation
1	Equation	Graph
2	Equation	Word Problem
3	Graph	Equation
4	Graph	Word Problem
5	Word Problem	Equation
6	Word Problem	Graph

Predictions. We predicted that the PLM should: 1) increase performance as measured by increased response accuracy and reduced reaction time, 2) produce accurate near transfer as measured by the high performance on novel problems, and 3) produce remote transfer as measured by the improvement on post-test items designed to assess the learner's understanding of the structure of linear word problems. A more remote transfer test, in which subjects are scored for actually solving these problems, is currently in progress in a separate experiment.

Results and Discussion. The training module was successful in increasing performance and producing accurate near transfer. Figure 1 below shows that accuracy increased reliably during the learning phase and was actually slightly better for novel problems in the transfer test. Meanwhile, response times dropped dramatically, as shown in Figure 2.

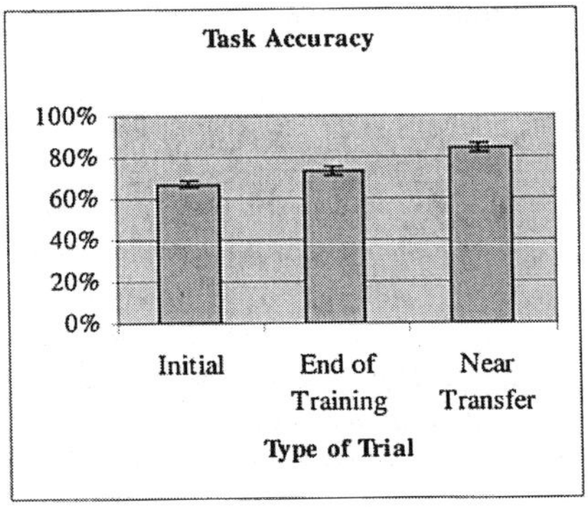

Fig. 1

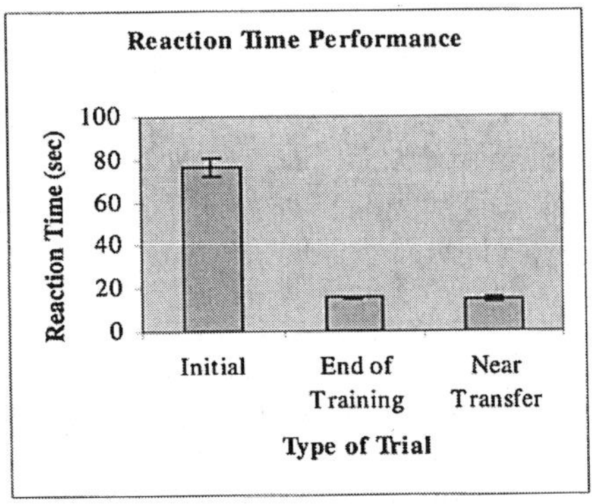

Fig. 2

Whereas in the first trial block (ten problems), students required an average of 80 seconds to do each problem, by the end of training, the relevant mappings were made in about 15 seconds, a decrease of nearly 80% in the time required to grasp the relevant structure. Moreover, this dramatic gain in speed (suggesting more automatic pattern processing) held for novel problems in the transfer test. Although the module did not produce any increase in conceptual knowledge by our measurement, we are currently evaluating a more suitable remote transfer test, which assesses transfer to actual solutions of word problems. The Linear Functions PLM required only one 30-minute period of learning time, yet led to substantial gains in students' abilities to extract the structural similarities between different representations of the same problem and an impressive degree of improvement in the speed of processing.

2.2 Three-Dimensional Angles PLM

A notorious problem in the first term of university-level organic chemistry is that students do not perceive the three-dimensional structure of molecules from two-dimensional representations they are given, despite the careful and extensive coverage of the topic in lecture, in discussion sections, in homework, on exams, and in the use of molecular models. Using research on perceptual learning, we developed PLM's to teach this difficult concept. A controlled study of student understanding of three-dimensional structure was conducted at UCLA during summer 1999.

Method. The control class received traditional instruction. The instruction with the treatment class was followed by practice using the *3-D Angles PLM*. In *3-D Angles*, a rotating, 3-D model of a molecule is presented on a computer monitor on each trial. Subjects are queried about one of three aspects: Either 1) an atom is highlighted and the number of bonds (coordination number) it forms in the molecule must be indicated, or 2) two bonds involving the same atom are highlighted and subjects must indicate (from four choices) the correct geometric angle between the bonds, or 3) students must indicate for a given atom its hybridization from among four choices. All responses are scored for speed and accuracy and feedback is given after each trial, as well as cumulatively after each block of ten trials. The learning phase (ten blocks of ten trials each) took less than half an hour.

Results and Discussion. Students using the PLM improved substantially in making rapid classifications about molecular structure. All reached nearly perfect levels in classifying coordination number, bond angle and hybridization of a large variety of compounds. These abilities transferred readily to new examples (near transfer). Most interesting, this modest amount of training produced significant gains in students' abilities to correctly perceive the structural features of molecules, even when the most impoverished representations were given to them. On the course final exam, students were presented with planar, line-and-letter representations of molecules and asked to indicate bond angles (Table 1) or hybridization (Table 2). Control subjects, who received lecture information only, resembled the experimental treatment group's pretest performance in both cases: Both groups made high percentages of incorrect responses for bond angle and hybridization. After the 3-D Angles PLM, however, accuracies improved reliably for a number of the test molecules. (A full report of this research is in preparation for publication elsewhere [13].)

The results indicate that educational technology using perceptual learning concepts can successfully lead to the learning of molecular structure, and that this learning can transfer to a meaningful task in chemistry, one that is demonstrably resistant to conventional instructional methods.

Table 1 Bond Angle Identification When Presented with Impoverished Representation. (From Russell & Kellman, in preparation)

	% Incorrect		
	Control	Treatment	
	lecture only	after lecture	after *3-D Angles*
	final	pretest	final
H_2O (**O**)	42.3	42.4	11.9 **
CO_2 (**C**)	11.5	5.1	5.1
Cycloalkane(line structure only) (**C**)	42.3	52.5	20.3 **
Carbonyl (**C**)	15.4	20.3	8.5
Alkene (**C**)	7.7 *	22.0	5.1 **
Amine (**N**)	46.2	47.5	20.3 **

* Significant difference between control and pretest of treatment group
** Significant differences before and after treatment

Table 2 Hybridization Identification When Presented with Impoverished Representation. (From Russell & Kellman, in preparation)

	% Incorrect		
	control	treatment	
	lecture only	after lecture	after *3-D-Angles*
	final	pretest	final
Primary alcohol (O)	22.3 *	44.1	35.6
HCN (C)	3.9	18.7	5.1
Benzene (line structure only) (C)	0 *	20.4	5.1 **
Carbonyl (C)	3.9	10.2	1.7
Alkane (C)	7.7	13.6	11.9
Amine (N)	34.6	57.6	39.0

* Significant difference between control and pretest of treatment group
** Significant difference before and after treatment

2.3 Algebraic Equivalences PLM

As in the two domains discussed so far, the importance of conceptual understanding in learning algebra is usually well emphasized. Many problems in learning algebra, however, may relate to the lesser emphasis in instruction on developing pattern recognition and transformation skills. The problems are evident in students' mistakes. Teachers of high school math and science often find students who can explain the meaning communicated by an algebraic statement such as $4x - 3 = 12$ but who will habitually try to solve for x in that statement by subtracting 4 or dividing by 3. Their interpretation of the symbols' meaning is accurate but too slow to engage, allowing competing mental processes to tackle the problem incorrectly. The misapplications that result from these shortcuts suggest that students are relying on half-remembered patterns absorbed during class. To them, the surface similarities between the solutions illustrated below may be more immediately evident than the conceptual conflicts between them:

$$\frac{\cancel{4}x}{\cancel{4}} = \frac{12}{4} \qquad x = 3 \qquad \textit{vs.} \qquad \begin{array}{r} \cancel{4}x = 12 \\ -\cancel{4} \quad -4 \\ \hline x = 8 \end{array}$$

Fig. 3

$$\begin{array}{r} x + \cancel{4} = 8 \\ -\cancel{4} \quad -4 \\ \hline x = 4 \end{array} \qquad \textit{vs.} \qquad x + \frac{\cancel{4}}{\cancel{4}} = \frac{8}{4} \qquad x = 2$$

Fig. 4

$$\begin{array}{r} 2x + 3 + 5x - 4 = 11 \\ -3 \qquad\qquad -3 \\ \hline 2x \quad + 5x - 4 = 8 \end{array} \qquad \textit{vs.} \qquad \begin{array}{r} 2x + 3 + 5x - 4 = 11 \\ -3 \quad -3 \\ \hline 2x \quad + 5x - 7 = 11 \end{array}$$

Fig. 5

These common mistakes illustrate the potency of the perceptual aspects of learning. Not only do students fail to extract the correct structural relations, but they also fall prey to superficial resemblances among expressions that lead to error. Preventing the acquisition of incorrect patterns, increasing students' grasp of relevant structural relations, and improving student facility with algebraic manipulation are all key goals that are not optimally addressed by conventional instruction. To this end, we have designed a PLM for algebraic equivalences. A key assumption of the module is that students will benefit from comparisons of correct and incorrect answers that occur close together [14, 15].

Method. On each trial in the module, an expression (the target) is presented on a computer monitor. Below, several other expressions (the choices) are also presented. The student's task is to select all and only the choices that are equivalent to the target. Unlike the PLM's described earlier, this module allows for multiple correct answers, since solving real algebra problems requires choosing the most useful equivalence from infinite possibilities. (For example, too often, when students solve for x in the example $7(2x-5)=21$, we see rote application of the distributive property, rather than the much simpler division by 7.) Our goal is not to promote default algorithms, but to expand students' library of possible strategies to facilitate adaptable problem solving.

Another important consideration for this module was building in the flexibility of randomly generated problems. Although the specific operations shown in each algebraic representation had to be hard-coded into the program, we wanted to reinforce the concept of variables by literally allowing them to vary. In the future, we may seek to expand this capability by substituting in expressions such as $(x+5)$, rather than just integer values, for each variable in a given template.

Implications. Although we have not begun data collection on this PLM, we present it as an example of the sort of problem in mathematics and science learning that may be perfectly suited to computer-based educational technology combined with perceptual learning concepts. We have high hopes for this module in particular and for this approach in general to improving teaching and learning.

3. CONCLUSIONS

These efforts to apply perceptual learning to mathematics and science education have several features in common. They all address aspects of learning that are considered difficult or resistant to traditional instruction. In each case, they aim to help students discover and fluently process important patterns and structures, and in two cases, to map these structures across very different representational formats.

Our data suggest another commonality. In the two cases for which results are available, and in other research [3], the modules appear to confer substantial benefits, despite being used by students for very modest amounts of time. More research is needed, both to optimize the design and impact of PLM's, as well as to determine how best to integrate this new learning format with existing ones.

A final common theme in our PLM's for science and mathematics learning is that they suggest that perceptual learning principles and computer-based educational technology are easily married. The capabilities for presenting large numbers of displays, collecting rapid responses, and giving quick feedback are important in engaging cognitive processes that discover relevant structure amidst irrelevant detail. Likewise, the capacities to monitor performance objectively, and in the future to adapt the learning to the level and needs of each learner, are relatively new opportunities made possible by digital technology. These opportunities will only increase with the advent of better multimedia and virtual reality technology. The evidence suggests that implementing perceptual learning concepts will be a key means of extracting from this emerging and evolving technology genuine advances in teaching and learning.

Footnotes

Perceptual Learning Modules is a trademark of Kellman A.C.T. Services, Inc.

Acknowledgments

The research reported here was supported by a National Science Foundation grant under the Learning and Intelligent Systems Program, and the W. M. Keck Foundation, the E. E. Ford Foundation, the GTE Foundation, and the Mara Breech Foundation. Development of 3D-Angles was supported, in part, by the National Science Foundation under grant DUE 95-55605. Reprints of this paper may be obtained by contacting Joseph A. Wise, (jwise@kmsi.org). Special thanks to Mark Govatos, Antoinette Parker, and Robert Kuhar for their significant help in this project.

References

1. Gibson, E. J. *Principles of Perceptual Learning and Development.* New York, NY: Appleton-Century-Crofts. 1969.
2. Chase, W. & Simon, W. Perception in chess. *Cognitive Psychology,* 4, 55-81. 1973.
3. Silva, A.B. & Kellman, P.J. Perceptual learning in mathematics: The algebra-geometry connection. In Hahn, M. & Stoness, S.C. (Eds.). *Proceedings of the Twenty-First Annual Conference of the Cognitive Science Society*, Mahwah, NJ: Lawrence Erlbaum Associates, 683-688. 1999.
4. Karni, A. & Sagi, D. The time course of learning a visual skill. *Nature*, 365, 250-252. 1993.
5. Reber, A. S. Implicit learning of synthetic languages: the role of instructional set. *Journal of Experimental Psychology: Human Learning & Memory*, 2, 88-94. 1976.
6. Lewicki, P., Hill, T., & Czyzewska, M. Nonconscious acquisition of information. *American Psychologists*, 47, 796-801. 1992.
7. Goldstone, R. L. Perceptual learning. *Annual Review of Psychology*, 49, 585-612. 1998.
8. Shiffrin, R. M. & Schneider, W. Controlled and automatic human information processing: II. Perceptual learning, automatic attending and a general theory. *Psychological Review*, 84, 127-190. 1977.
9. Silva & Kellman (in preparation).
10. Kellman, P. J. & Kaiser, M. K. Perceptual learning modules in flight training. *Proceedings of the 38th Annual Meeting of the Human Factors and Ergonomics Society*, 1183-1187. 1994.
11. Bryan, W. L. & Harter, N. Studies in the physiology and psychology of the telegraphic language. *Psychological Review*, 4, 27-53. 1897.
12. Norman, D. A. & Bobrow, D. G. On data-limited and resource-limited processes. *Cognitive Psychology*, 7, 44-64. 1975.
13. Russell, A. A. & Kellman, P. J. Perceptual learning in chemistry. Manuscript in preparation.
14. Sweller, John. Cognitive technology: some procedures for facilitating learning and problem solving in mathematics and science. *Journal of Educational Psychology,* 81:4, 457-466. 1989.
15. Cooper, Graham. Cognitive load theory as an aid for instructional design. *Australian Journal of Educational Technology,* 6(2), 108-113. 1990.

Author Index